First printing

Printed in the United States of America

I dedicate this book to my sister Tameka, Daddy, Mama, and Uncle John for helping to shape me into the woman I'm today. I thank Cascade United Methodist Church family and its pastoral team for breathing life into my life when I was broken in spirit. I thank my creative muse for igniting my mind and spirit to allow me to explore the depths of my soul. I thank my Spelman sister, Adriana, for encouraging me to write even when I didn't feel like it. Finally, I also want to dedicate this book to all those who are struggling in this race called life and who need some real inspiration from a contemporary perspective.

Table of Contents

MONTH 1 9

MONTH 2 57

MONTH 3 99

MONTH 4 137

MONTH 5 177

MONTH 6 215

MONTH 7 247

MONTH 8 285

MONTH 9 321

MONTH 10 357

MONTH 11 395

MONTH 12 431

INDEX 467

INTRODUCTION

While I was growing up, I was always given daily inspiration books such as the 'Quarterly Daily Bread' pamphlets. I liked them, but the subject matter didn't really connect with me. This is how this book was born. I wanted to provide a tool for contemporary Christians, a book of inspirational daily passages that was currently applicable to our lives. I have tried to cover things that we all think about but sometimes do not have a proper venue to discuss, things such as toxic friends, hating, celibacy, 'grindin,' and other topics that connect us with others while we are attempting to reach our destinies.

Ambition, for the Christian, is a curious thing. We are conflicted because we have heard the cautionary tales of Christians gone awry with selfish ambition. Yet, we feel the pull of a God-given desire to be productive.

Ambition can be a motivating force for centering your life. There isn't anything wrong with ambition, but you must be able to temper it with your faith. Pursuing ambition as a Christian must involve trust in God. Most contemporary Christians are naturally ambitious people, which is why so many daily messages don't resonate with them.

Having a fulfilling family life is important; during these tough economic times, having a productive professional career is critical for lifestyle and soul.

Dreams and ambitions are gifts for God and are a part of Living the Life God ordained for us. However, how do you step into your destiny and receive the breakthrough you've been praying for?

This book is to be used along with your Bible as a booster shot to your faith and spiritual life. God has a great calling on your life and this will provide you with motivation. Trust. Pray. Believe.

MONTH 1

DAY 1: Unstoppable

Today is about being unstoppable.

I'm a believer in positive thinking. You can manifest anything if you just believe.

We are living in some weird times. There are people who are experiencing the best times in their life and enjoying the fruits of their labor. For them, everything is great. Then there are people like me who are 'grindin.' For us, every day is a different struggle.

Every time you go up one level, the problems become more complex and harder to solve. The hate goes up as well. There are things we cannot discuss with everyone. The risk is greater for all involved.

I'm no longer in the minor leagues; I'm in the major leagues with a lot of danger lurking around every decision. This is when your faith is essential. You must transform yourself into being unstoppable.

An unstoppable person is someone who doesn't falter in the face of adversity, a person who gets knocked down millions of times and continues to fight, a person who can change tactics in order to achieve his or her goals, a person who is willing to make sacrifices in order get to the next level, a person who has an uncompromising spirit and a general hunger to succeed.

The requirements to become unstoppable are faith in yourself and a direct lifeline to God.

The only person you can really depend on to constantly uplift you is God. Everyone else is human and bound to fail you at least once. Know inside, you're larger than the circumstances around you and that God will give you favor to help you reach the next level.

God is such an awesome God that He protects you from enemies you don't even know about. These enemies, a.k.a. haters, are double agents.

They have friend—or family-like characteristics but they don't have your best interest at heart.

Be careful whom you share your goals with; you never know their secret motives.

Some people have just one simple motive: to make sure you never reach your full potential. They can be friends and family. No one is immune.

So on this day, believe in yourself, and become unstoppable. Once you believe and have faith in yourself, you will have the ability to move mountains.

Be the catalyst for change. ☺

DAY 2: Having Direction

Today is about having direction.

Even though I'm girly-girly, I have some masculine tendencies. My dad raised me like the son he never had. LOL ☺

I absolutely hate asking for directions. I have been hours late for events because I was too stubborn to ask for directions. I always believe I'm close to my destination and I can figure it out. I also believe actually asking for directions is giving up in a way.

I think there are many believers who are stubborn with our relationship with God. We believe we are intelligent enough to figure out life all by ourselves and giving our situations to God is giving up in a way.

Faith has nothing to do with intelligence. If you allow your intelligence to get in the way you will never have the close relationship with God we all crave.

God wants all the glory and wants you to be a testimony to others. If He allowed you to believe that you did it, you would take all the credit for yourself and your abilities.

Faith is something that cannot be conceptualized with intelligence alone. Faith works in mysterious ways that cannot always be quantifiable by reason, the main component of intelligence.

Faith does require two items: belief and letting go of your control. You must believe God can do all things, and you must step out of the way so God can do it.

This must be done in order to receive the blessings God has for your life and to step into your destiny.

Allow your faith to be your GPS for God. Allow it to guide your path. It will never fail you. *Not like MapQuest LOL!*

Be the catalyst for change. ☺

DAY 3: Blessings in the Midst of Disappointments

Today is about blessings in the midst of disappointments.

When I was in college, I started at Howard University and then transferred to Spelman due to homesickness. I'm an Atlanta girl at heart. ☺

I had already dreamed of being Alpha Kappa Alpha, despite my father's insistence on me being Delta, but I knew when I transferred that competition was stiff.

I was naturally disappointed when I didn't make line at Spelman. People always ask me now if I would pledge in Graduate Chapter. My answer is no. It's not hate or being salty, that makes me answer so. I think it would change me as a person.

Being a Spelman woman, I'm already part of a rich legacy sustaining me all of these years.

During certain times in life, you will experience disappointment. Sometimes there are things we want that are not aligned with God's will.

I believe I'm a better person without making line. If I had gotten what I wanted, I wouldn't have been strong enough to deal with some of the storms in my life. Not to mention, I would have been completely out of control and drunk with power. I would have been the type who wears some pink and green every day. ☺

I had a lot of maturing to do and I didn't have the right attitude. God kept me from making dumb mistakes by taking my ego down a notch. I needed it. ☺

Despite not making line, I made lifelong friends through the process. As a transfer student, I made a majority of my friends (seven of them) during that process. While none of us made line, the experience still binds us together for a lifetime. ☺

It's not often you get an opportunity to put on an asymmetrical wig and become Salt-N-Pepa for an hour. LOL! We have lifelong memories we still giggle about. ☺

Sometimes there's a blessing in a disappointment. I believed my blessing would be making line, but my blessing was the friendships that were created.

God knows what is best for you. Sometimes God will take away opportunities you can't handle or that may not be in your best interest. While it might be disappointing, after time passes you will realize how much those disappointments shape you into the person you're today.

Thank the Lord that we are all more than what we used to be. ☺

So on this day, stay optimistic, even during your disappointment. You never know what blessing is wrapped into it.

Although the world is full of suffering, it's also full of overcoming suffering.

Be the catalyst for change. ☺

DAY 4: Taking care of yourself

Today is about taking care of yourself.

I was on my way to Miami for my fashion show and it seems like everything kept going wrong. I had to struggle to get an earlier flight. Once I got that under control, I had too many hair products in my carryon bag. They had to be put in storage or thrown away.

So, by the time I went to TSA check out for a second time, I was exhausted.

Many times in life, you won't feel any movement and nothing but struggle.

Everything will go wrong and you'll want to give up. To allow the waves of resentment to wash over and just let life drift you to any shore.

Don't. Do not give up; take a big a vacation from your problems. Take one day and do nothing. Sleep in and just veg out. Watch television, read a book, etcetera. Do whatever's necessary to give your mind a break.

When you've been grindin' too hard for too long you'll lose your sense of perspective. You'll allow disappointment to get the best of you and you won't be thinking creatively. Being creative is an absolute must in order to figure out your situation.

Sometimes Evil will send disappointment and sheer exhaustion to slow you down. You must build not just physical endurance but spiritual endurance as well. God may not come when we want him to but he is always right on time. Progress is always occurring but you may not be able to see it. Trust God that he will handle it all.

So today, don't allow yourself to become emotionally exhausted. Take care of yourself both spiritually and physically. Allow God to seep into your soul so you will have enough spiritual nourishment to make it through the storms of life.

O Lord, thank you for this day. Please forgive me my sins both knowing and unknowing. Allow me to stay focused on You and your will. Help me not become overwhelmed with life and its troubles.

Be the catalyst for change. ☺

DAY 5: Peace

Today is about peace.

Peace is something we all take for granted until we no longer have it. There have been many times in my life when there was so much chaos going on I wanted to scream.

There was nowhere to run to and no one to confide in. I was completely in the wilderness, up a creek without a paddle.

I now know peace is similar to positive thinking: you must manifest it. Peace is a state of mental calm. It's without anger, resentment, chaos, disagreement, or conflict.

Peace is essential for clear and logical thinking. When you're not peaceful, it's difficult to make accurate decisions.

Ask God for peace and mercy when you find yourself in very stressful situations. Peace is the gasoline in your spiritual car. You need it to go just about everywhere.

So on this day, submerge yourself in peace. With peace and serenity, there is no limit to what you can achieve.

O God, thank you for this day. Allow peace to enter my being and strengthen my resolve so I can achieve my goals.

Be the catalyst for change. ☺

DAY 6: Endurance

Today is about endurance.

I recognize the connection between spirituality and long distance running. You see a lot of society when running. However, life is about choices; you must decide whether you're going to see beauty or ugliness in the world. ☺

When I first started long distance running, I thought I was hot because I had been running on the treadmill thirty minutes a day every day for four years. Boy was I wrong. I soon realized I had very little endurance. It was a humbling experience.

When I run the first leg (two miles), I'm good. However, I seem to struggle in the middle of the run until I'm barely hanging on by the time I see my house. I believe running is similar to this great race of life we are in. My daily run is the hills and valleys of life, that is, a trial of life.

My running is similar to my spiritual life. When I enter a trial, I'm good at first and upbeat. When I get into the eye of a storm or when a solution isn't readily available, I get weary. However, I buckle down and finish the trial of life. Even if I'm slowed or beaten down, I always finish.

That's what we all should do in this race of life: finish and remember the trial of life builds endurance. Endurance is necessary to handle all of life's trials. So when you're overwhelmed with life, just know you're in the middle of a little spiritual exercise and it's good for you.

You will never be able to get to the next level in life and business unless you build your endurance. Your endurance is built by trusting in God, not by leaning on your own understanding. ☺

Be the catalyst for change. ☺

DAY 7: Sharing Feelings

Are you really articulating what you need in a relationship? I realize I'm emotionally unavailable, generally. One of my girlfriends told me so, and when I told another girlfriend, she agreed.

I disagreed and was slightly insulted. I've always shared my emotions. However, my Spelman sis broke it down. She said, I'm good at sharing what is going on in my life but not how it makes me *feel*.

I realized she was right. What is this, Epiphany Day? $%$%! Sometimes we think we're communicating our needs well when, in fact, we aren't. All my joking about guys being emotional showed my lack of emotional availability.

Maybe my previous relationships failed because I wasn't clear about what I needed emotionally. I admit I could live a shallow lifestyle with weak connections probably for life. However, I will now work at doing better.

I have always been an optimist. I believe concentrating on emotions takes away from the goals in mind. I guess it's the man in me. ☺

So are you emotionally available in your relationships? We must work hard to improve all of our connections. Feedback sucks, but it's necessary because it tells you what you need to work on. ☺

I believe for me it denotes a need for clarity. Clarity is essential in all aspects of life. We're seeking clarity but we don't provide it.

Work on providing clarity. Living without clarity is like walking around without light. God can help provide clarity. Sometimes He provides you with feedback so you can work on getting the emotional connections you crave. So work on spending some extra time with God to get the clarity you need and then spread the love.

Be the catalyst for change. ☺

DAY 8: Motivation

Today is about motivation.

I have always been ambitious but not always motivated. I had big dreams and aspirations but didn't want to put in the work necessary to get to the next level.

When I was in the fourth grade, I went through a spelling bee stage. I wanted to become a spelling bee champion but didn't have a natural spelling ability. I was a good student but not a good speller. I would enter spelling bee after spelling bee only to lose every time. I became very discouraged. It wasn't an easy task for me, and I never trained for it.

I just kept entering spelling bees and hoping divine intervention would occur. ☺   I was ambitious but definitely not motivated to win.

Motivation is the most difficult condition to maintain and the most important. Motivation is the key to success in every aspect of life.

During this economic downturn, it's easy to become discouraged and unmotivated. Lack of motivation isn't God's response to a possible goal but rather the manifestation of fear. Sometimes it's easier to do nothing than it is to take a leap of faith. Push through the fear and get on track.

God can provide all we need to become successful, so pray for motivation. While it seems to be slightly mundane to pray for something such as this, I believe it's critical for reaching your potential. Rely on God to help you focus on what is important for reaching your goals.

Sometimes prayer doesn't change the situation, but it does change how we respond. A problem or setback is sometimes designed by God to make you stronger.

God has your best interest at heart. The only way your dream will come true is if YOU make it happen. Step past the fear; it's amazing to see what might be waiting on the other side.

Be the catalyst for change. ☺

DAY 9: Answering the Call

This is about answering the call.

For many of us, we have struggled for so long we have dreamed about the way we would act when the breakthrough came. We imagined the way it would happen, even down to what we would be wearing. ☺ I always dream of myself wearing amazing outfits and handbags. ☺

The breakthrough comes in a way or at a time, you don't expect, and often it comes at a cost. Sometimes the Lord will bless you in the midst of chaos and take you places you're not prepared for. You don't know how to walk, talk, or act. You're at a loss.

He can also bless you with all you need except one crucial factor. You must take a leap of faith without that factor. It's often scary and has the potential to be amazingly bad. This is when you know God is truly in the midst. You're now at the end of the journey and on the cusp of your breakthrough.

You can feel it. It feels like something is going to happen but you just don't know for sure. You're excited and scared at the same time.

The fear is normal. Sometimes, when you've been down for so long, you're afraid of happiness, or even the possibility of it, for fear of disappointment. Everything that happens is the divine will of God, even bad works. God places us in situations so we become completely dependent on Him.

Then He blesses us for our faithfulness. Your faithfulness is to shoulder the burden continually, even when you begin to doubt the realization of a dream.

So for those who've become weary in the face of such insurmountable circumstances, keep going. God will bless you; however, you will not know the time or the circumstances. It's right there. Get ready for it.

For those of you who've been working crazy hours, working every day, who've been unemployed for an extended length of time with no end in sight, who've been taking care of others who are suffering or those who are plain exhausted—it's coming. Take the blessing regardless of its shape. It's been waiting on you for quite some time.

Be the catalyst for change. ☺

DAY 10: Motivators

Today is about the motivators.

Growing up in church, I figured out what my role would be there. At the age of five, I joined the children's choir. I was always ambitious, so I requested to do a solo.

My debut came on *This Little Light of Mine*. It became clear to everyone, including my parents, I couldn't sing at all. That was my first and last solo. My dad quietly pushed me toward ushering, which, at the time seemed very dull. Oh, how my church friends teased me about being an usher.

It wasn't until I got older that I understood the power of being an usher. Ushering is one of the most important ministries you can become a member of at church. This can literally make or break a person's religious experience.

A smile from an usher can leave you feeling open to hearing God and aligning yourself with His will. A frown from a "mean usher" can cause discord between you and God. It can even cause you to leave the service early or even decide never to attend that church again. Although my friends laughed and teased me, I'm proud of my ushering history. I truly enjoyed it.

Regardless of what kind of day I was having, I always put my personal feelings aside to ensure worshippers greeted with the spirit of the Lord. I wouldn't be the person I am today if my dad hadn't noticed that although I couldn't sing I was very sociable and could be channeled into being an usher.

My dad has been my motivator, which has been a good and bad thing. While he is always supportive, he will call me out when I'm not going to the next level. He knows all my little tricks and when I'm BS-ing him. We talk about everything, including relationships. He'll tell me when I'm being extra and when I need to be understanding. He is definitely my biggest supporter with celibacy.

When life gets tough, he politely informs me I'm not spending enough time studying the Bible. He gives me some scriptures and gets off the phone. LOL ☺

There have been many times when he's made me so mad by bringing things to my attention, but in the end, he was always right. I've never lied to him (I'll avoid him to keep from lying) and always tell him what is really going on. My dad is my motivator.

There are people in your life right now who are your motivators. It can be anyone. They are constantly supportive but constantly pushing you to the next level, whether you like it or not. They'll call you on your behavior because they have the gift of prophecy and can tell where you're going. These are people you respect; but at times, you feel almost as if you dislike them because they'll not allow you to settle, to stop moving forward.

Embrace these angels. They only want you to live the best possible life. They're the enforcers of God's Will.

Sometimes, God has already spoken a word into our spirit but due to the lifestyle changes needed, we kind of drag our feet. A motivator lights a little fire underneath your butt to get you moving.

God can have you do something mundane at times, which can be frustrating, but fear not: this is all part of God's plan. Sometimes that boring job or task or that trying relationship has the potential to be something instrumental in your life. You cannot see it, only God can. Your motivator can sense it.

So today, thank God for your motivators and become a motivating force for someone else. Help someone move along the path to greatness. Speak God's power into someone else. They need it.

Be the catalyst for change. ☺

DAY 11: Unique Blessings

Today is about unique blessings.

When I was in high school, I went through a major pageant stage. I did okay in them, but considering I'm only 5'0" tall, I wasn't going to go really far, but it did teach me poise and discipline. ☺

Around that time, I really wished I were taller. I didn't want to be greedy; I just wanted to be about 5'4" so I could be 5'8" in heels. What gave me more of a complex was I had a pageant girlfriend who grew like three inches over one summer. She had been my height. ☺ So, I prayed all the time to grow taller.

God blesses each one of us uniquely for a reason. If I were taller, I might not look the same. We all want to be blessed. We want blessings like friends and family. We want to be blessed with a new job, more business, a spouse, children, et cetera.

God will bless you, just not in the same way as He will bless friends and family. He wants us all to feel special. There is a process for blessings. The process is different for everyone and depends on your relationship with God. Every process has two core items that are essential to receiving a blessing: faith and prayer.

Prayer is the medium used to ask for a blessing and faith is the belief that it will occur.

Believe God will provide you with blessings in a unique way. That way, you will know the blessing is for you only.

Be the catalyst for change. ☺

DAY 12: Pushing Through

Today is about pushing through.

Over the last couple of years, I have experienced incredible highs and dizzying lows. The reason I write is because I have been at both spectrums. I want to motivate everyone to fight and persevere through the dark times.

The best thing to happen to me was contact lenses; otherwise, I would be really unlucky in relationships. ;) Prior to my transition to contacts in the summer before seventh grade, I met a new guy through a friend. He had just moved into our school district.

We talked on the phone the entire summer and were in a relationship, but we had never seen each other face-to-face. During this time, wearing glasses was *so* not cool. My secret of having glasses was safe. I figured if I worked hard enough for him to like me, my glasses wouldn't matter—or so I thought.

On the first day of school, I was ready to show off my new boyfriend, until he found out I had really, really bad vision. We broke up immediately. I know that sounds like a horrible story but it really isn't. The silver lining was that I was so upset by the situation my mother finally allowed me to get contacts, which forever changed my life.

Later, that guy got a really bad case of acne that scarred his face. Karma is a powerful thing. God will sometimes put you in a gut-wrenching situation that ultimately has a good outcome in the end. God will place you into the fire, not to damage you, but rather to make you a better person.

Don't resist the process. Allow yourself to be shaped by God. He knows what's best. ☺ So if the heat is getting to you today, push through. This refining process is ordained by God and sets you on the path of your destiny.

Trust. Believe. Achieve. All things are possible. Be kind whenever possible. It's always possible.

Be the catalyst for change. ☺

DAY 13: The End is near

Today is about, the end is near.

I'm now at the home stretch in my training for the Peachtree Road Race and I know the end is near. All my training since January is now paying off and I have much more stamina than I ever had before. However, we are not so lucky in life. When you're in a trial or testing period, sometimes, you don't know the end of near. Endings can be abrupt or extensive.

When God is taking you somewhere, he'll ask you to trust Him and go along for the ride. Imagine you going somewhere and you don't know where you're going. That is what some of us are experiencing. God has a great calling on your life and has removed everything from around you in order to get your attention. Stop and pay attention. Something can be learned in the process.

Endings are not ending; they are putting a stop to life you no longer enjoy. It's really a new beginning of a phase in your life. So an ending may be the beginning of a productive life but you must go through a period of silence before it begins.

Today, embrace the endings in your life that are already here or on the way. Trust God and know there is an purpose to everything. Wait on the Lord and all will be revealed.

Lord, thank you for this day. Please forgive me for my sins. Thank you for allowing certain things in my life to end. I know you have a purpose and allow me to have the stamina to endure this difficult period. Amen

Be the catalyst for change. ☺

DAY 14: Temptation

Today is about temptation.

Since my grandmother's death, and turning 31, I have begun to come around to the fact that I need some changes in my personal life so I can get married and start a family.

One thing about me in relationships is guys either really, really love me, or really, really hate me. There is no in-between.

I spoke with a guy recently who I dated briefly back when we were neighbors in 2006 and 2007. I know, I know—it was a bad idea. :(Of course, the relationship was filled with drama, and I always felt he really didn't care for me but was physically attracted to me. We argued all of the time, and it was a mess—and we still dated other people.

So imagine my surprise when he actually admitted he really did care for me but didn't want to show it because he was angry that I wouldn't break my celibacy.

That had my ears ringing. He actually withheld love because I wouldn't express my love physically. I had made a covenant with God. No man is worth evoking God's Wrath. It did make me wonder how many other guys felt the same way but lacked the nerve to tell me.

Has our society become so jaded and messed up that we have to test-drive everything before we purchase it? The conversation made me wonder about my current friend/relationship drama. I began to doubt the decision I had made so long ago.

As more of my friends get engaged, I began to wonder if I should drop the celibacy just to see what would happen.

Temptation always plays on some element of doubt you've been quietly dealing with. Of course, I've wondered if my celibacy doomed my relationships.

Temptation comes in many forms and in ways that you can't easily resist. It also comes in the areas where your faith is a little low. I've seen God make miracles in my professional life but not in my personal life. For other people, it's vice versa.

Trust God and believe in his word. God will never ask you to go against Him or to covenant with Him. This type of temptation usually happens when you're close to a breakthrough, so hold on, even when you're fed up and frustrated.

Resist the temptation and God will provide more than you ever imagined. God can restore you and give you back the time you thought you had lost. ☺

Be the catalyst for change. ☺

DAY 15: Too Busy

Today is about being too busy.

I'm very a busy person. I schedule everything, even personal time. I'm constantly on the run, going from one meeting to the next. When the meetings are done, it's usually time for sleep. I actually check how long I sleep to ensure I'm sleeping enough. I know, I know—I'm anal-retentive, but for Christians, being busy is sometimes how Evil enters your life.

I schedule time for prayer. You have to be a little flexible to spend some extra time with God. When you're too busy with life, you lose the ability to spend time in God's presence and to hear Him.

I call it spiritual white noise. Spiritual white noise is that feeling you get when you have so many distractions you can't think or pray.

When you feel the pull of God, pay attention. There usually is a reason for you to pay attention. God has our best interest at heart. Be careful not to assume you know the outcome, good and bad.

You never know what is going on behind the scenes. Every frustration, every delay, is ordained by God. Sometimes that frustrating delay, such as when you can't find your keys, can save you—perhaps, in this case from a car accident. Don't try to understand the purpose of God. Just trust.

So if you're like me, busy every second of the day, spend a little extra time with God. You never know how it can really influence your life. Today, continue to fight on the journey of life but allow a little extra time with God. Your soul needs it. ☺

Allow God to change your life. He is truly the solution to all of life's problems.

Be the catalyst for change. ☺

DAY 16: Letting go

Today is about letting go.

Since I have been running so much for training, I have been listening to a lot of new rapper Drake. I can completely relate to his perspective.

I have tried to turn over a new leaf and do more partnerships with other entrepreneurs only to realize why I didn't do that in the past.

I'm a maverick, an innovative thinker. I move fast and it's hard for some to keep up with my pace. I'm not for the weak at heart. I'm also relentless, and I can tell from the first business meeting if things are going to work. I can usually spot laziness, instability, and overall unprofessionalism a mile away. Then I believe I'm being too hard on people and continue to move forward.

I'm disappointed each time. Some people are not ready for the major leagues for a variety of reasons.

I can honestly say I've met more people who are unprofessional recently than I've met in the last five years. I can deal with a lot of things but two things you cannot mess with are my money and my time.

While I try to be inspirational and motivational, I have to keep one hundred percent.

There are some places God is taking you that aren't meant for everyone. God blesses within measure and whether you can handle it. People say they want to be blessed but don't want to do the work it takes to get there. Ambition and success are not for the weak at heart.

Business is really just a game. Everyone has a position to play; pay attention when people can't play their position. If you don't, in the end it will cost you.

Personal feelings, whether good or bad, are out the window. Sooner or later, you'll see the situation for what it is and the people for what they really are: people who are not ready.

Egos should be checked at the door. The best businessperson is the one who is the most humble, the person who will talk to anyone at any level, the person who is focused on the tasks at hand instead of on looking important.

Most people want success handed to them and to be mentored. NEWSFLASH! Mentorship is dead; you better get out here and fight for what you want in life.

God will show you who is ready to ride and who isn't. Allow the situation to play itself out without emotion. It's difficult to let go of the people in your life who are hindering your journey but sometimes it must be done.

You have to choose whether to go toward the happiness you've prayed for or to continue struggling to make it happen so you won't be seen as disloyal. Usually, the most loyal person in the group is the person who eventually gets left out in the cold.

Be careful about being a team player; play your position, but don't ever allow your position to affect your overall happiness. In business, you have to take chances and move on instinct. You can't make major moves in a group.

When God is preparing you for a blessing, He shakes everything in your life. Some of the shaking doesn't feel good but it's essential to your blessing.

So today, stop and pay attention. Get aligned with God so He can speak to which path you should follow. Place your faith in God and everything else will fall into place.

Be the catalyst for change. ☺

DAY 17: Passed Over for a Blessing

Today is about being passed over for a blessing.

In graduate school, I interviewed for an internship I was sure would take me to the next level.

I was sure I had it and then I received news they had decided to go in a different direction, that is, they didn't want to hire me. I was devastated. This was different from the experience I had while in law school. I know, I know, I've been in school forever. ☺

I had prayed for this position and God had spoken that I would be fine. I assumed God meant the job was mine. ☺ It's hard to put a positive spin on things when you've prayed so hard for something that didn't come to pass.

So I watched in horror, as I became the only one without an internship, despite being the top female in my class. I became bitter and frustrated. People told me I was being impatient. How could I tell them I was frustrated with God since I felt like He had told me He would give me that internship?

I gave up, and then an opportunity presented itself. It was bigger than I could have dreamed and eventually became my first job out of school.

I was paid triple what I would have been at the internship I had prayed for and spent the last year of graduate school with the knowledge that I had a job waiting after graduation. The organization with the blessed internship did massive layoffs and didn't hire any students after graduation. Without God's will, I would have been in a dead-end situation.

There are times in life when it feels like God didn't fulfill your requests for a blessing. Hold on. God told me I would be fine and I assumed it to be what I wanted. Not always. God told me I would be fine because He knew I had something coming my way. I didn't know about this opportunity and assumed incorrectly. ☺

Stay in the race even when you don't understand it. God has big plans for you. Always remember, God will never leave you.

Sometimes, there is a lapse of time between a disappointment and a blessing. Trust in God. Reflect on all the times He showed up before in order to get through the waiting ahead.

The bigger the disappointment, the bigger the payday in the end. Allow God to work His magic even when you don't understand the process. Trust Him. He's like a parent. He knows what's around the corner and wants to protect you.

Today, pray for His mercy so you can weather the storm and receive the blessing He worked so hard to bestow.

Be the catalyst for change. ☺

DAY 18: Fight for Your Success

Today is about whether you're willing to fight for your success.

A successful person is someone who embodies the following. The person who is willing to come in early and stay late. While all the others are hanging out and kicking it in the clubs, you're grindin' in the office. The person who is willing to sacrifice a huge amount of personal time and life for their craft.

A person with a huge amount of discipline and inner resolve. Resolve that they are more than the circumstances and that they will win. A person who takes failure as feedback and refuses to back down.

The person who keeps the center aligned; mind, body and spirit. If these spheres are not aligned, you will never be able to achieve success. The person who allows their innovation to shape the world instead of the world shaping their innovation.

The person who knows she or he has the ability to completely succeed in their goals while keeping integrity during the process. A person who isn't afraid of being transparent with their life regardless of public perception.

This will make the general public invest in you and your success. The person who has one sole focus, expanding their brand. What's your brand: yourself. Always respect the most importance brand in your life: yourself. ☺

My goal is to motivate and inspire others. I want to change how the general public sees contemporary Christians. I want to represent the people who are out here grindin' with our minds. There are some of us out here.

I send so much positive energy out to people because I want everyone to live up to their potential.

Today, instead of taking the weekend off, make this weekend one to grind. Create your own destiny; no one is coming to save you. The only way to make your dreams a reality is to invest in yourself.

Remember: The most intelligence doesn't win the race; it's who is the most driven. There are no shortcuts for hard work. So get focused and...

Be the catalyst for change. ☺

DAY 19: Waiting for a Sign From God

Today is about waiting for a sign from God.

Since the beginning of my Christian walk, I have always been a believer in signs.

Lord, if You think I should do this, please knock three times (i.e. send me a sign).…. I'm sure God was laughing at me with the silliness of requesting signs for things.

As you grow in your faith, God will lessen the instant blessings. Instant Blessings are when you pray or think about praying for something it happens. Instant Blessings are commonplace with new Christians.

However, once you grow in your faith, the time between your prayers and blessings increases to the dismay of some.

You've become a master with prayer when you can continue to believe despite evidence of the contrary. Don't stop believing God will bless you just because you haven't gotten an answer or sign.

For those like that who are waiting on signs: Stop waiting. Your Faith is the only sign you need. Keep going in the race of life. God sometimes wants to see your endurance and your faith will illustrate that.

When faith is a little low; go to God in prayer and He will speak to you. You have to be open to hear his words. Sometimes, no answer from God isn't "no" but rather "not yet." Be willing to wait for the Lord.

Prayer is the nourishment that quenches our spiritual thirst. Try it and your life will be forever changed.

Be the Catalyst for Change. ☺

DAY 20: You're Covered

Today is about you're covered.

When I got up the morning of the Peachtree Road Race, I was nervous about the race.

It seems that everyone had a horrible story that they had heard or seen. And they had to tell me about it.

So I knew I had trained for 6 months and I had hydrated the last couple of days and made sure I had eaten the right foods.

In the back of my mind, I was a little afraid. By chance, I ran into this guy who was in wave D, which means he was extremely fast.

He gave the best running advice: always strategize in everything you do. He told me to run the first three miles, walk the fourth (a.k.a. cardiac hill) and then run the rest.

I took his advice and finished faster than I had when training on my own. God will send Angels along your path to greatness to give you the tools for success.

Now, it would have been great if I trained like that but I got information when I needed it the most. God gives you exactly what you need at the precise time you need it the most.

He will never allow you to go into battle without having some tools to get through. So today: remember, God's got you covered. You may not get the details needed until the last moment but it will always be right on time.

Be the catalyst for change. ☺

DAY 21: Giving it all to God

Today is about giving it all to God.

When life throws you the first major curve ball and takes you completely off track, it's customary to feel a bit depressed and resentful. However, this is a pivotal moment in one's life when give up control and give everything to God.

My moment came during my last year in college. My father was sick and I was flipping out. I was hanging out a lot and I was angry with God because my father was sick. My boyfriend and I had broken up. I was feeling really alone.

I got home one night from the club and I became so overwhelmed with everything I dropped to my knees and gave everything to God. I prayed to God to alleviate the pain. I asked for His grace and mercy because I could no longer handle life on my own. I requested help.

Life got much better immediately. My dad got better and I was able to cope with life a little better. Almost 10 years ago, there are many times since then I had to rededicate myself and give everything to God. Even the most well intentioned Christians can begin to care too much and try too hard to solve life's problems until they have taken on too much of life's burdens.

Today, this daily inspiration is for those who are barely hanging on, who feel hopeless and overwhelmed. Give everything to God. Once you relinquish control; watch God resolve everything in the way it should be.

He will create opportunities out of thin air or even revive opportunities that were previously lost. Only God can say when something is over. ☺ You don't need to be perfect to enter God's sanctuary. All you have to be is you. God loves you exactly the way you are.

A joyful heart is good medicine. Allow God's peace to enter your heart and change your life forever.

Be the catalyst for change. ☺

DAY 22: Navigating the waters

Today is about navigating the waters.

Being single in your 30s is quite different than in your 20s. You've become a bit jaded but a little more clear about what you're looking for in a mate.

You know what you can take and can't stand. You have a better idea of what is really important to you.

Things I thought were important to me really have no consequence now. It's amazing what life experiences can do for someone's perspective.

You finally understand how to navigate the water. This is similar to your Christian walk. You now clearly understand you won't have all the answers but you're comfortable in your ability to find the answers. Or in some cases just live without them.

You truly understand God is in control and you learn how to be comfortable within His will in certain areas in your life. Does that mean this extends into all areas? No, but there are always some area where we need improvement. However, the difference is, you know where to go for answers in your improvement areas instead of searching.

So today, be comfortable with navigating the water. While you may be caught in the twists and turns of life, you will always have God close by your side. Use God as your compass and you will never be lost. Just pray, trust and believe. Be more of a conqueror and more than what is around you.

O Lord, thank you for this day. Please forgive me for my sins. Keep me posted on Your will and Your ways. Help me to navigate the waters of life so I may stay focused on you.

Be the catalyst for change. ☺

DAY 23: Refusing to Settle

Today is about refusing to settle.

Jesus died for us to live a better life. Yet, due to all challenges and tribulations we have experienced, we are starting to back down a bit and settle.

Don't. God wants to have the best life and settling isn't an option.

Now, He didn't say you wouldn't have challenges, you wouldn't be lonely; you wouldn't cry or buckle underneath all the pressure.

You will have these things but you'll only endure them for short periods.

In our present time, a minute can seem like an eternity but in God's time, a year could be like a minute. Wait on the Lord.

In the book of Job, it never really details how long he was in his turmoil. Sometimes, turmoil is brought on by God to see how really tough you are.

Job didn't do anything wrong but his peers swore he must have "separated" himself from God ahem… "sin."

No one knows your walk. So don't allow others to determine your perception and relationship with God.

Stay in the Race of Life and refuse to settle.

If you want that job, keep plugging away. Create a matrix (table) of job descriptions and describe some of your practical experience to show how you're perfect for the job. Do not settle.

If you want a house and you don't have the credit, go online and read every credit forum out there. Check the statute of limitations on all debts (seven years) and dispute everything on the credit report. Don't pay someone else to do it. You do it and do not settle.

If you want to be married to that special man or woman, invest in the relationship. That means instead of telling someone you love them, show them. Words mean nothing without action. Allow the Love of God to permeate through to them. Work on becoming spiritually in sync. Build a legacy together. A legacy can be more than children; it can be a financial empire for all generations. Do not settle.

If you've been dreaming of starting that business, write a business plan and get a microloan. Get your credit on track. Get advice from score.org. These are retired business executives who understand where you are and can provide encouragement. Do not settle.

Most importantly, protect your dreams and inspiration. People can be jealous of your dreams and will speak a spirit of doubt into your situation. Do not settle.

Believe in yourself and your decisions. Don't worry if you don't have experience in that area or feel uncertain, or you have had trouble in the past in that relationship. Believe in new beginnings and trust Him. God will give you favor when you are aligned in what He ordained for you.

Evil will try to tell you you're not experienced or allow you to be frustrated in your situation and give up. Do not settle.

Celebrate this day; live up to God's expectations for all of us and do not settle for second best.

Be the catalyst for change. ☺

DAY 24: Constructive Criticism

Today is about the difference between constructive criticism and hating.

During this economic downturn, we rarely hear good news. So when we hear good news, we should rejoice. Wrong! Only if the good news is for you. When the good news is for someone else, we all can come down with an old-fashioned case of jealousy. Jealousy is fine; it motivates you to strive for more. It's not for you to resort to hating.

Constructive criticism is providing feedback on unanticipated aspects of the project/ventures or just being a pragmatic thinker. Pragmatic thinkers like to see all perspectives of a situation. They just want to make sure you're prepared.

I'm a creative type—not pragmatic at all. However, it's imperative in business to have a pragmatic thinker around. A Good business operation has enthusiastic creative thinkers and pragmatic thinkers. Both are equally important.

However, someone who is just picking out flaws in a project, a relationship, or endeavor without possible recommendations or solutions is a hater. Haters are just jealous and are motivated to bring you down. Pray for them to take the energy of hating and allow it to motivate them to pursue their OWN dreams.

Allow your frustration and jealousy to help you think as innovatively as possible. Celebrate others good news; that means you're next in line for a miracle you have been waiting for. Prayer is the answer to all of life's problems.

Be the catalyst for change. ☺

DAY 25: New Beginnings

Today is about new beginnings.

A couple of days ago, I had a really spectacular fall while running. It was spectacular because I didn't see it coming. I was running and must have tripped on something. Next thing, I was on the ground with my legs in front of me. I had fallen into the free newspaper container.

My first thought was "Who saw me" ☺ Then I scrambled to get up and kept going. I was really surprised I wasn't hurt or scratched. Just totally embarrassed ☺

My experience was similar to what we all experience on the journey of life. We take a spectacular fall (e.g., failure or setback). You weren't hurt but something you didn't see coming. You can continue on but you're more embarrassed than anything else.

You must get up and keep going. We are in the time of new beginnings.

Do you believe in them? Do you truly think you can start over and begin again? This is critically important to your Faith. God is a forgiving spirit and we should be as well.

Despite all misgivings, we must learn to let go of the past and keep moving. Stay on the path of Faith. There are many reasons why there is conflict with others. It could be conflicting ideologies, personalities, sensitivity, or just bad timing.

Life is just too short to hold grudges or wonder why things happen to you. Even when you don't understand the lesson God is attempting to teach you, keep going. Sometimes God reveals the truth and lesson in a situation in pieces. Allow time to pass so you understand the breadth of a situation. Allow your disappointment and hurt to fly into the winds of yesterday and begin anew.

Be the catalyst for change. ☺

DAY 26: Establishing a Covenant with God

Today is about establishing a covenant with God.

When people hear the term, "covenant" they quietly think religious fanatic. However, that's really not it at all. A covenant with God is just a promise. A promise that you will do something that illustrates your faith in God. It's faith in action. It's one thing to believe, but quite another to stand on it. ☺ Have you ever done something or had something happen and say, "Lord if you get me out of this situation…" or "If you do this, then I will…"?

In today's society, you don't hear a lot about covenants. Probably in regular society, it's just hard for people to keep their word. Today, make a covenant with God. Establishing accountability helps keep you on the path of faith.

I remember when I was having a hard time closing on my home, I made a covenant with God that if I closed on my home, then I would always attend Wednesday services and not tell anyone until after I closed. I made that covenant on a Sunday. On the next day, Monday, I got word that closing would be the following Friday. It killed me not to tell anyone, not even my parents but cemented the special bond I have with God. I have been attending Wednesday services regularly for almost three years. ☺

God became an actual person and my savior. Not my parents. Up until that point, I had been coasting on the faith of my parents.

I now have lots of covenants now with God. I cannot discuss them until the blessings have come to pass. Today, take your relationship with God a step further; make a covenant with God.

You will be amazed what God can do when you show Him how you're willing to stand on faith. Sometimes, God is waiting for you to take one big step toward Him. Discipline is the bridge between goals and accomplishment. Show discipline in the Doctrine of Faith and see your life expand.

Be the catalyst for change. ☺

DAY 27: Staying Focused and Being Positive

Today is about staying focused and being positive.

Being focused on your goals isn't the only part of your life journey; you must be positive as well. I'm a little more positive than most people are but it's not my nature. I have to work at it. We all do. ☺

We all make a choice whether to see the beauty of the world or the ugliness. Choose the beauty: there is so much of it. A sunrise, a sunset, a rainbow, sunny blue days—these are God's reminders of beauty and bits of optimism. ☺

There are times when you don't feel positive but push through. When you look back over your life and the times when God showed up just in the nick of time; focus on those times. God showed up before and will continue to do so. Trust and lean on your faith. Don't allow your own frustration to get the best of you. Stay busy and focused.

Plan, Pray, Plan, Pray. If you're always implementing what God has spoken to you, you will always stay positive and know the breakthrough is coming. ☺

Spending time listening to God will allow you to be aligned with his Will. Visualize and Believe it. All that I have accomplished because I worked to visualize it. Positive things create positive results.

If you want be a homeowner, start looking for your dream home. If you want to start a business, research, and create your business plan.

If you want to get married, start changing your life so your life can open for that huge collaboration. Make room in your life for your blessing you have been praying for. ☺

Open yourself to the possibility of happiness. It can and will happen, but only if you believe. ☺ Allow God to be the pilot of your life. He will always guide you to what is best for you.

Be the catalyst for change. ☺

DAY 28: Why Believe

There are so many unbelievers or those with lukewarm belief based upon their actions. They ask the question: why believe?

Today is a busy day, so I decided to run at 6 am in the morning instead of the evening today. I usually don't like running in the morning because it's scary downtown and you never know what's lurking behind each corner. I have a belief that I will finish my run in one piece and go out on faith regardless. Life is very similar. Life can become a very scary and overwhelming place. Particularly when problems can come one after another.

It's easy to see how you can allow life's problems to wash over you and overwhelm you. You must believe there is a higher being beyond yourself and life will get better.

If you don't believe life will get better, it's easier to go into your own devices. Your devices can never compare to what God can do. God can be a jealous God. He wants you only to trust Him.

There are some problems in life only God can handle. Leave them with Him. I believe we become so invested in our problems we cause ourselves increased anxiety. For me, the moment I let go of a problem, it's always solved. Usually, in the way I wanted. However, if you keep struggling, you will only tire yourself out.

Jump into the pool of God's love and submerge yourself in it. He will never disappoint, mislead, or deceive you. He's truly the one person who always has your best interest as heart. Those who try to hurt you with incur God's wrath. Pray for your enemies. Let God handle them and trust that He will. ☺

God is the storyteller of life; and holds the book. He is the only one who knows our complete story. Trust the man who holds your life story in his hand.

Be the catalyst for change. ☺

DAY 29: Having a Revelation

Today is about having a revelation.

When having a revelation, it comes in flashes—Pieces at a time.

Revelation shows despite all blunders and moves; we will believe in happiness because we will be aligned with God's will. Revelation is what God has ordained for you to be... not what you want to be.

Revelation to the ending of the movie—God will show what you become but not how to get there. Living in today's times, it can be difficult to understand. We all live with quiet hope that there is more to life than what we see. That our suffering has a purpose.

Trust God that it does. Sometimes, God will give a revelation so that you keep going in this race of life. To keep you focused even when daily life is a struggle and confusing.

He gives revelation without direction because He wants you to trust Him and not lean on your own understanding. Don't ask why; how it can come; when it will come. Trust God. Continue to prepare and a place for your revelation will come to pass.

That is the point of revelation. It helps to drift into the right direction and Prayer is the compass keeping you steady. Prayer won't clear directions but will guide you to where you need to go. Prayer is essential to live in the bounty of the Lord. Daily Prayer is like the MapQuest of Life. It's essential to get your desired location.

Remember: having flashes of revelation without any explanation means you're closer to having and living your breakthrough.

Don't allow impatience to separate you from the will of God. Stay in His will, even when it seems nothing is happening. Things are happening; you just can't see it.

Today, continue to prepare for your revelation to come to fruition.

Be the catalyst for change. ☺

DAY 30: Encouraging Yourself

Today is about encouraging yourself.

While we're all excited about the spring weather, it does give you the sense that days are a lot longer. I believe many are becoming weary of attempting to thrive in less than ideal circumstances. People are preoccupied with their own lives more than ever. A lot is due to economic downturn.

It's easier to become less encouraging and more focused on self during these times. Fear not, this is the time to encourage yourself. No one is more talented, funny, and innovative than you. So don't worry if others have advantages and resources.

You must believe all things are possible. The worst thing you can do yourself is to be afraid to try something new. People might say you can't do it. Don't believe them. Believe Yourself. You can't allow yourself to be bogged down with the idea of failure.

Failing something can be helpful and ultimately make you a better person. Failure isn't anything more than feedback. Embrace it; it can be more valuable to you than success. You'll know exactly where you need to focus your energy. Some of the best ideas come after failure. Always focus on moving forward and instead of looking back.

So continue to stay in the race of life. There are good and bad days but ultimately the good will always outweigh the bad.

When God says it's to be your time; then it's your time. If you continue to work and stay positive, you'll obtain optimal results.

Be the catalyst for change. ☺

DAY 31: Waiting on God

Today is about Waiting on God.

I'm very impatient. I do a lot of things myself because I can't stand waiting on people. Waiting on God is a different experience. That is one person who you cannot hurry along ☺

Waiting on God is similar to trying to sleep on Christmas Eve as a child. I can remember how excited I was as a child for Christmas Day. I couldn't wait to tear into my gifts. It seemed Christmas eve went on and on. I tossed and turned in bed and swore I heard Santa on my roof.

Waiting on God can be a tiresome experience. We often have sleepless nights trying to figure out situations and waiting on God to show up. So while waiting, you get angry and frustrated. You feel like your breakthrough will never come.

Evil uses negative thoughts to throw you off track. He also can use good people and have them do evil things. Forgive. We all have fallen short at time. We are human. Bounce back. Get back on track and stay positive. Positive thinking creates positive results. It's important to stay positive in the darkest times.

God will show up. Sometimes He does build a bit of suspense. Sometimes things have to get a little rough to get your full attention and for you to be fully dependent on Him. Think about it: If it didn't get so bad to make you dependent on Him, you clearly would try to solve the problem yourself. ☺ God wants the Glory in all situations. ☺

God has a special place for us all. While not all of your experiences now may be positive, they will make a stronger and more grounded person. While your place might not be realized yet, continue to fight the good fight. Your time will come.

Remember, God loves you in spite of all of your mistakes in life. Whenever you feel no one truly loves you: God loves more than you can ever know.

Be Catalyst for change ☺

MONTH 2

DAY 32: Keep the Faith

When things are becoming difficult, I always remind myself when I closed on my home. It wasn't easy.

I closed on my home while the mortgage industry bubble was bursting in 2007. I was supposed to close in April and actually didn't close until August. I lived in boxes for five months and was very frustrated.

However, in the end, it worked out for the best. I got a great deal and I had saved enough money I was able to do all the painting for my place and purchase new furniture all it once.

I wouldn't have been able to do that if I had not had those five hellish months to plan and save.

So during those 5 months, I planned for the future and kept busy knowing I wanted everything in place when my time came. My time did come. When life becomes a blur and you're attempting to make magic happen, it's easy to become overzealous. There is such a thing as having tunnel vision. ☺

The problem is, when you have tunnel vision, it's difficult for you to allow God to work. God has no parameters, timeframes, or any additional structure. God comes when He believes its time. He only wants what is best for you.

So don't dismay when things don't work out as you would like. It can seem what God is saying is No. However, sometimes God is really saying "Not Yet"

So on this day: Keep the faith. Every delay and disappointment works for the greatness of God.

Be the catalyst for change. ☺

DAY 33: Panic

Today is about panic.

It's hard to be optimistic when it seems storms are coming from every direction. Sometimes, you have to run for the hills and break. You cannot do anything; I'm the queen of strategizing, however Sometimes, it's difficult to hear from God when you're panicking.

Panic comes in different forms. Panic can come in the form of no action or too much action. When the going gets tough or too emotional, I flee. I like to be alone to think my way out of things but the last couple of days I have been with at least eight other people at any given time.

Evil has a way of scrambling your mind and keeping you off balance. That is when you have to learn to adapt all situations and make it work. I believe panic is an airborne disease and can be spread like wildfire.

You must then pray for the peace of God and always remember: This is always a reasonable solution to every problem. ☺ Then reflect on all of the situations in the past when you were stressed and thought this is a disaster but God came and fixed everything.

Take a break and spend some time with God. Then wait and give God an opportunity to work his magic.

That's the part I have the most trouble with at times. I'm sometimes working so hard to resolve things I don't give God enough time to get into the midst. I had to learn to slow down.

I've learned that while you might be a powerhouse, you must have a good team in place to lean on when the unanticipated happens. I have also learned you have got to ask for help if you're at the end of your rope. It doesn't make you a sucker, it means you're human. ☺

So today on this today: Don't give up. Take a pause and allow God to work. He may not come when you want Him but He's always right on time.

Be the catalyst for change ☺

DAY 34: Drive and an Ambitious Spirit

There have been a lot of questions sent to me about my driven and ambitious spirit.

My driven and ambitious spirit is related somewhat to me wanting to be successful. However, most of my drive and ambition is my caring spirit. I want to help life be better for everyone. Ambition is the force inside looking beyond the circumstances around you. The force believing you can change the circumstances around you to better society as a whole.

That's why it was such a difficult time for me after the campaign because I believed I had let my supporters and staff down. I realize now, you help people and your community in various ways, not just politically. Sometimes, providing individuals with spiritual nourishment, positive thinking, comedy relief, or even taking the time to listen and pray for someone is just as important.

Changing a community and the nation isn't just about the economic downturn. It's about a change of perspective and thinking. It will take innovation and also practical thinking to get us back on track. We're all definitely getting a sense of perspective and clear understanding of what is really important in life. ☺

I want to make sure every person lives the best life possible. I want people to live up to their potential. I feel myself transcending beyond the day-to-day improvements, wanting to ensure all people are healthy spiritually and emotional.

Spiritual health is the single most important thing to me. If you're not spiritually healthy, it can lead to chaos. Spiritual health is largely determined by your communication with God. Learn how to talk to God. Talk to God like a homie. Talk to Him when you're mad, talk to Him when you're happy, talk to Him when you're frustrated. Talk to Him.

That's the purpose of prayer. Prayer is your direct communication with God. Learn how to use and rely on it. It's easy to get frustrated during a storm. What magnifies the strength of a storm is when you stop talking to God. It might take Him some time to answer but He is always right on time. Talk with Him and He will give you peace even when you don't understand the purpose.

Always remember no matter what life hands you; it can change in an instant. If you stay positive and lean on God, the possibilities are endless.

Be the catalyst for change. ☺

DAY 35: Going to Battle

Today is about going to battle.

While I love being inspirational and motivating, there are times, I have to keep it 100%. This is a time in my life where I'm going up for battle. My book was that process for me. The book is a collection of some of my best tweets along with motivational thoughts for Contemporary Christians.

This has been an amazing opportunity. However, Evil has been quite busy during this time. Every time something is irritating, frustrating, stressful or disappointment, it inhibits my ability to write. This writing is from my soul. This isn't like putting a proposal together.

When you're attempting to get a closer relationship with God, Evil will give you crushing body slam to slow your progress. You can cry, moan, and sing Negro spirituals, "Walk with me Lord… Walk with me" Or you can get up and go to battle.

You must fight Evil to get to the next level God has aligned for you. Evil usually picks an important time in your life to distract you. At the brink of your breakthrough. Just before the dawn.

God has a calling for all of us, if you allow Him to lead you. Don't miss out on an extraordinary life you were supposed to lead, out of frustration and anger.

Pray for his mercy and get to work. You know how this story ends: you win regardless of the circumstances right now. You didn't come this far and gone through Hades to get to where you are now.

You MUST NOT faint. You MUST NOT falter. You MUST NOT stop. Failure isn't an option. Turning back isn't possible. You must move forward. The worst thing Evil can do is attempt to confuse you mentally. Then you will be unable to focus and your anxiety will increase.

Allow the serenity to wash over you like a soothing stream. Show your toughness and fight for your blessing. Do not allow anyone or anything to make you feel unworthy of God's Blessing.

O Lord, thank you for this day. Please forgive me for known and unknowing sins. Help me to be strengthened by listening, hearing, and living your Word. Grant me mercy and grace to live the extraordinary life that You ordained. There isn't anything I can't do without your help. Continue to fight the good fight.

Be that Catalyst for Change. ☺

DAY 36: Prayers of Progress

Today is prayers of progress.

Lord, I am so tired of trying to make moves on my own. It seems like nothing is happening. But I know You're working to behind the scenes to help me to achieve my goals. Allow me to become secure in being dependent on You.

You've been walking with me before I even knew You were there. You hugged me when I needed it. You wiped away my tears of frustrations when I was emotionally exhausted. You gave me hope when I needed it. You pushed me far beyond my limits in order to get the best out of me.

You allow me to step forward and back without interference. That's essential to move the evolution of my soul. You allowed me to become a stronger person by weathering the storms of life.

You calmed me when I began to spaz. When I became unfocused, you gently got me back in line. You kept me when I began to go in the wrong direction. You helped me to improve mind, body and spirit.

Lord, you are the only One I trust. You know me in a way no one does. Yet You still love me. You saw only the good in me when I was at my worst. You whispered the future in my ear when the present was dismal. You kept me focused even when I fought you.

Help me to stay focused on my dreams occurring. Allow me to create a plan allowing me to get to the next level. Remove all the fears and anxiety from my heart and mind. Let me become unshakeable.

Allow me to aggressively pursue what I want without any hesitation. Help me to continue to believe I was able to achieve my dream and step into my destiny.

Be the catalyst for change. ☺

DAY 37: The Behind the Scenes Story

Today is about the behind the scenes story.

In today's society, we're totally obsessed with the life of celebrities: their professional and personal lives.

We love all the gossip and firsthand accounts of the behind the scenes story. Sex, Lies, Betrayal, Triumph. Twenty years ago, we had no idea about the personal lives of celebrities. Back then, celebrities felt they needed a bit of mystery to stay successful.

I believe knowing the behind the scenes story is good because it gives a sense of perspective in our lives. It's easy to see all of the problems in your life rather than see the good.

Millions of people are at the top of their game professionally but are struggling in other areas. No one is immune from life's struggles. They are used by God as character building.

So when you're bogged down, when it seems to be problems of life, remember you're building your behind the scenes story. All of the greats have to encounter difficulties to triumph.

Belief in yourself is all you need in life to survive. God will take care of the rest. ☺

Live your life like you're on stage. You never know who's watching Be the Catalyst for Change. ☺

DAY 38: Having Your Guard Up

Today is about having your guard up.

I remember while on the dance team in high school. I began wrestling with another member of the team after practice. We were the same height but she outweighed me by 20 pounds. We were horsing around in the gym and it was all fun until she body slammed on the gym floor.

I chipped my tailbone and couldn't walk properly for two days and had to sit out one game. I was definitely angry and completely caught off guard. Life happens like that.

A lot of times, when disappointment occurs, we're not angry and frustrated because of the situation but rather because we didn't see it coming. Having your guard up is essential. When dealing with life's journey there are unexpected situations we're not always prepared for.

There are situations in life that you can't prepare for but you have to experience. Having your guard up is staying focused on God and keeping an active prayer life. Your prayer life is your direct contact with God.

If you continue to talk to Him, He would provide you with insight and wisdom. When you get caught off guard, you can't weather the storms of life.

So today, keep your guard up. Stay focused on God and trust that He will take care of the rest.

O Lord, Thank you for this day. Help me to stay focus on You and Your Will. Allow me to continue to improve on prayer life, which is essential to daily living. Amen

Be the catalyst for change. ☺

DAY 39: It's all Just an Illusion

Today is about, it's all just an illusion.

I have been working on my clothing line for quite some time. It's definitely been a growing process. At one point, I had a sample maker creating the technical sheet for each piece in the swimwear collection. After I received all of the technical sheets, I received an email from the sample maker entitled "bill." Being that compensation had already been taken care of; this wasn't a good sign.

I immediately became annoyed without even opening the email. I became increasing frustrated because I was already not having a good day. I took an hour to finally calm down and then opened the email. The email was technical sheets with details describing the pricing to create each sample look. It wasn't a bill at all.

It was just an illusion. Many times in life, things can seem worse than they really are. We get ourselves all worked up over things, only to realize they're not really as bad as they seem.

God will always attempt to bless us in all areas of life. However, Sometimes, we can allow Evil to get into our mind and skew our perspective. Sometimes, what looks like "no," is really "not yet." Don't allow yourself to become frustrated over dismal circumstances. You never know what's on the other side of the perceived problem.

So today, remember sometimes trouble isn't anything more than illusion. It's up to you to stay focused on God and know when to believe your instinct instead of what is in front of you.

O Lord, thank you for this day. Please give me wisdom in order to determine what is an illusion and what is real. Help me to stay positive and not give in to negative thinking.

Be the catalyst for change. ☺

DAY 40: God's Promise

Today is about God's promise.

When I was waiting to close my home years ago, I waited in limbo for about four months. My first mortgage lender went out of business and I had to start over again. I lived in boxes and frustration. I felt like my relief would never come.

Then when my breakthrough came, there wasn't anything dramatic. I called my mortgage lender on a Monday morning and she casually said, "you close on this Friday." I was in complete shock. I was so afraid it wasn't going to occur that I didn't tell anyone I was finally a homeowner until it was done and I had the keys.

There were many times I thought I was going to close and I told everyone. I had become sick of looking like a fool. A lot of family and friends had told me to give up and start looking for another apartment. There were many days of frustration but I would stay focused and keep plugging away.

Many of us feel that way right now. God has spoken a destiny; a dream; an innovation. It's so amazing that you're afraid to share it with others. You're getting closer to the dream realized. Instead of becoming more excited, it's increasing your anxiety.

You have a couple of false starts, delayed opportunities, and overall general disappointments. Don't forget God's promise. When God promises something, it's for you and only you. Your enemies cannot harm it.

God will never speak a promise into your spirit that He won't give you the tools to help you achieve. God will even use your enemies; so they will be the ones to give it to you. ☺

Now that doesn't mean the promise won't go through challenges. It doesn't mean the challenges won't occur. Your promise may not come as soon as planned or not under the best circumstances.

So don't fret and agonize. Even if it looks like everything isn't going well. It is. God is giving you a bit of suspense.

So today: Trust God's promise. He will allow it to come to pass but you must continue to believe and have faith. Allow God to bless you and watch your life be forever changed.

Be the catalyst for change. ☺

DAY 41: Looking Around

Today is about looking around.

This weekend gave me a great perspective. It was the first weekend I had more than two or three hours off since November. It's given me the ability to think more succinctly than before. When I first became an entrepreneur back in 2007, I worked every day—all day. I was working toward that pivotal moment to get my first client. It seemed like I was getting close but I could never close the deal.

I decided to add another business—vending—to gain a sense of perspective and more money. The moment I started vending; both businesses exploded. I was focusing too much energy on consulting and was trying too hard. Separating my energy allowed me not to be so impatient and things moved faster.

It gave me a sense of perspective about my personal impatience level being extremely high. Life is similar to that. When you're waiting for a breakthrough in one particular area, it's hard to see the blessings in other areas of your life. You can become impatient and resentful while waiting for the blessing. Don't. Allow the evidence of God in other areas of your life to help you wait on the Lord.

So today: Look around. God blesses us in a lot of ways. Concentrate on those blessings while waiting on your breakthrough.

O Lord, thank you for this day. Forgive me for not seeing various daily blessings You provide. Increase my faith so I can withstand impatience and resentment. Help me to hold on.

Be the catalyst for change. ☺

DAY 42: Don't let Anyone Steal Your Joy

Today is about not letting someone steal your joy.

A tremendous number of people are really stressed out. We all deal with stress in various ways. Some people go toward light and others descend into darkness.

When I was the ninth grade, I joined the dance team. A good friend and I had planned to try out together but her father at the last minute wouldn't allow her to do it. So when I made the squad, she was super jealous but was happy for me—or so I thought.

Then she began to act in various ways: saying little snide comments and just saying I had changed. The fact was SHE has changed because she couldn't deal with my success. We eventually drifted apart. God will speak something into your spirit and then begin moving you into your destiny. Not everyone will be happy for this movement. God anoints us with special gifts not everyone can handle.

The place where God has you going, all of your friends and family may not be along for the ride. Don't get angry and frustrated with those who don't celebrate your success. Pray for them.

So today: Don't allow anyone to steal your joy. Stay focused on the tasks at hand. Pray for them.

If you're jealous of someone else's success, ask God for mercy and peace. Understand God will bless us all in our own due season. Their season is just before yours. Rejoice in others' success; it means you're next in line for a blessing. ☺

O Lord, thank you for this day. Help me to forgive those who hurt me and forgive me for hurting others. Allow me to pray for others so they may obtain their own breakthrough.

Be the catalyst for change. ☺

DAY 43: How to Pray

As Christians, we make a lot of assumptions. I was pondering this statement while running this morning. We assume most people know how to pray but may not. So today is about how to pray.

My dad taught me to pray I guess when I was five or six but I don't believe I fully understood and had an active prayer life until maybe high school. Praying is as essential to your life as intake of water. You can live seven days with no food but only three days with no water. ☺

To pray, there are no general instructions but there are general rules:

Get into the mood—I usually read my bible prior to praying. Some people have songs they listen to. It doesn't matter what you do but you must into get into the spirit

You must remove yourself from the world around you—You cannot pray and watch television, exercise, talk on phone, sleep. You must be willing and ready to talk to Him. Treat your time with God similar that relationship with that special someone.

Praise Him—Thank the Lord for all He is done for you. Don't go into prayer always asking for something. Remember when you were a teenager and wanted to go to a party? You would compliment your parents prior to asking. Same thing. Make sure to articulate how much you appreciate all the blessings He has bestowed before you ask for another.

Talk—Prayer is essentially just talking to God. Tell Him about your life and what you need from Him. Talk to Him in a similar way you would talk to a parent.

Don't limit your time—Make sure you don't pray under time constraints. There is no set time minimum in prayer but pray until you feel you spoken directly to God. Prayer doesn't change God but rather it changes how we respond to situations during this race of life.

Do it daily—I believe it's important to stay in constant communication with God. It doesn't really matter when but I believe that you make sure that your daily activities involved a little talk with God.

One Caveat: I believe you can pray silently but I do feel you get into the prayer better if you do it aloud.

So today: Reignite your prayer life. It doesn't matter when, how, where. However, as long as you use God as the starter to your spiritual battery, there isn't anything in life you can't handle.

O Lord, thank you for this day and forgive me for my sins. Help me to develop a stronger prayer life with you. Help me to continue to pray even when I don't feel like it. Allow my increased prayer life to increase my faith in you.

Be the catalyst for change. ☺

DAY 44: Mercy

Today is about mercy.

Growing up, I was a bit of an overzealous child and didn't like authority. In my case, authority was my mother and she wasn't taking any disrespect. I learned to request her mercy when I was out of order. Sometimes it worked; sometimes it didn't. LOL!!

God's mercy works in a similar way except it works every time. God's Mercy is more than just forgiveness; it's an act of compassion among other things. It's also God's protection against we DESERVE. We all, including myself, fall short of God's expectations. As Christians, we always say, "Ask for God's Mercy" but don't explain how to get it.

The main way to receive God's Mercy is the demonstrate mercy in our lives. We can demonstrate mercy in the following ways:

Compassion—Allow yourself to care and show kindness for others despite their behaviors. We all have moments when we act out based upon the stress in our lives. Allow yourself to be understanding of the struggles in others' lives. Compassion can be as simple as when giving directions to someone who is lost or even holding the elevator for someone behind you.

Forgiveness—Allow yourself not to be affected by others' behavior. While initially there might be anger or disappointment, it's important for YOU to forgive. Forgiveness has nothing to do with another person; it frees you from damaging emotions that can hold your progress.

Peace—Allow yourself to stay in a calm and tranquil state. When life's triggers threaten to invade your mind; allow yourself to retreat in harmonic environment. Allow yourself not to get into unnecessary disagreements and bring all disagreements to an end.

Showing compassion, forgiveness, and peace can demonstrate mercy. Demonstrating mercy to others can allow God to have mercy on you.

So today: Have mercy on others. Allow your mercy to melt your heart and open you up to amazing opportunities.

O Lord, thank you for this day. Help me to demonstrate your mercy by showing compassion, forgiveness, and peace. While I'm showing mercy to others, please have mercy on me. Thank you for allowing me to be more than I used to be.

Be the catalyst for change. ☺

DAY 45: Change

Today is about Change.

Today I officially ran in the rain. It's one thing to run in drizzle and another to run in RAIN like Rainforest RAIN. It was incredible. ☺ It was incredible because it showed how far I have come with my distance running commitment.

Running on the journey of life is similar. The most profound changes occur for you without even realizing it. Sometimes, all it takes is one small step to change your life forever. We are always being told in church to change but not exactly how to do it.

There are various ways to change your life path but here are some items that will help get there:

Make a list—While we say we need to change our lives, exactly what does take mean? Does that mean no drinking, cussing, attending church more often, et cetera? Make a list of changes you would like to implement in your life. Not a mental list but written or typed list that you can refer to when necessary. Place it in your bible so you continually focus on it. FYI…. For some: Purchase a bible as well. ☺

Cement your belief in God—We all believe there is a higher being but actually cementing your belief is different. Do an act that cements your belief in God and His will. You can say it in prayer aloud; you can write it down or join a church. All of these actions illustrate your commitment to God in your life.

Start a prayer life—Prayer is essential in the journey of life. Living life without prayer is like trying to order takeout from home without a phone. Commit yourself to pray once a day. Not only will you feel better; people around you will notice the change as well.

Fellowship with others on a similar path—I believe fellowship with others on a similar path is important. That's why attending a church is important. Not for people to judge you; but help each other to stay on the right path. We are all struggling with the same things and it's good to find a support system.

One Caveat: While you're trying to change something, your biggest critics are family and friends. They may like the status quo, the you who is agreeable and fun loving. Only you really know what makes you happy. Focus on long-term happiness. Change is a part of that. We all have to evolve as people. Dismiss anyone from your life who cannot respect the evolution of your soul. Don't be surprised if you lose family and friends in the process.

Stay committed—When you're trying to change your life, it's difficult to get past temptations. Temptations will come out of the woodwork. Make your change manageable. Tell yourself you're going to make the necessary changes for thirty days, then sixty days, etcetera, until your life has changed forever.

So today: commit yourself to changing your life. Don't try to change all at once. Take it one day at a time. Allow the changes to be gradual and natural. Do this and watch the Lord change your life forever. He will begin to drizzle your life with tiny wonderful blessings.

O Lord, thank you for this day. Forgive me for my sins. Help me make positive changes in my life to align myself closer to Your Will.

Be the Catalyst Change. ☺

DAY 46: Confirmation

Today is about Confirmation.

On importance items, confirmation is necessary. I always make sure I have confirmation for meetings, hair appointments even dates. Webster's Dictionary defines confirmation is something that supports, validates, or verifies something else. Confirmation is particularly important in the Christian world.

God will send a dream, a word that is so radical you're afraid to share it with others. It's so amazing, you wonder if God spoke to you or did you dream it? That's when attending Church is key. Sometimes it's your minister who can give the confirmation and sometimes others in the church.

God will provide you with the confirmation you need in a way you would understand. I can remember when I was making the decision to become an entrepreneur; I needed confirmation.

I was sick of working for other people and not having control over my life. God had spoken to me but I was afraid to jump out on faith.

So I remember God spoke to me in two ways: the pastor gave a Word spoken directly to me. Then, when I was leaving the church, in the parking lot, I dropped my bible and was picking it up; an older woman was standing in front of me. Then she said to me, "I know you're afraid but trust Him. No matter what, God will always protect you." She gave me a hug, which is common at church. I looked with so much wonder; I couldn't believe it.

So today: Spend a little time with God in prayer and then seek confirmation. He will provide the confirmation needed in the most amazing ways. Hey, this could be the confirmation for you.

What God has for you is for you. Never stop believing.

Be the catalyst for change. ☺

DAY 47: Judgment

Today is about judgment.

So it's coming up on crunch time for those training for Peachtree Road Race and there are runners everywhere in downtown Atlanta training.

I'm a new runner, so I still remember when I saw people running down the street panting looking like they were on death's door thinking, "I don't get it."

When I see a runner like that, my first thought now is wow; I wonder where they're running from. Now as I am a runner, I clearly understand running is about your endurance and perseverance. It throws all vanity out of the runner and gives you a tremendous amount of discipline.

Show me a runner and I will show you someone who has great discipline and ability to focus. It also has a calming effect and helps you think clearly.

Clarity is essential to hear from God.

Being a runner is similar to being a Christian. We are all out here running this race of life. We are not always racing against each other but rather toward a higher calling.

So when you see a pessimistic, hateful, backsliding mean spirited Christian, don't judge. You've no idea where they are running from. You may have caught them in low endurance or a weak moment.

Even the best runners catch a cramp at some point. ☺

So today, don't be so quick to judge. You don't know the level of endurance it's taking on someone's Christian walk. Pray for their strength and move on.

When you judge others, the same harshness you bestow can be turned onto you.

Be the catalyst for change. ☺

DAY 48: In our own Little World

Today is about being in our own little world.

With economic downturn, it seems there are two types of people in the world: (1) people maintaining their success; and (2) those struggling to get by. Times like this often bring out the worst in people. We've seen more random acts of hatefulness increasing each day.

I believe the biggest one is neglect. Everyone is struggling with something right now. So it's easy to become consumed with your own life. However, this is where your breakthrough occurs. God wants us to manifest his love on an everyday level.

If you want God to bless you, be a blessing to someone else.

You can bless people in various ways. It's not about money. It's about providing the support needed. Your blessing can be a phone call, kind words, or a listening ear.

When you can think about others while in the midst of your own struggles, your blessings can be doubled or even tripled.

So today, consider everyone's feelings and attempt a blessing for at least one person per day. It can enrich your life in ways you never thought possible.

Be the catalyst for change. ☺

DAY 49: Making it Through Difficult Times

Today is about making it through difficult times.

Congratulations on making it through these trying days. I know I'm not the only one that has struggled. I don't think I have ever been so overwhelmed and at a loss of how manage it all. This is for the people who seem to be disappointed by everyone right now: God has a great plan.

I believe Faith is like swimming in a pool. There are times when you can drown in the waves in a turbulent life. Faith sustains you from sinking. It's difficult to stay positive when it seems like nothing's going right. It's being in front on a box with a lock that you can't seem to unlock.

Isn't strange; the moment when you really, really need someone, they bounce. "Why me?" You ask. I say to you, "Why not you?"

Sometimes, God will isolate you from those you need for support to make you stronger. This will make you focus solely on Him. So when people are disappearing, do not despair. God is attempting to get your attention; it's not them. They are merely playing their part in God's plan.

Also, a reminder to the ladies: There are many men struggling just like us in this economic downturn but too proud to say anything. Women are blessed in one thing: At least we can cry out in despair. Men suffer in stony silence. Sometimes, when a man becomes unavailable, it's not about you. It's about his shame of not wanting to show the weight of the world he is carrying. ☺

It literally kills a man's spirit not to be able to provide for himself and the woman he loves.

So when you're stumbling under the weight of disappointment and loneliness, remind yourself other times you have been in over your head, God kept you. God will keep you now.

This will also give you a great testimony. I remember every trial and tribulation I have ever had because it made me a more compassionate person. It keeps you from holding grudges because you know you have been saved by God's mercy. When God forgives you, how can you not forgive?

Pray for others. Praying for others can be key to your breakthrough because it takes the focus off of your situation.

Be the catalyst for change. ☺

DAY 50: Maintaining Hope

Today is about maintaining hope

Don't give up hope. It just means it isn't your season yet but it will be your season soon. ☺

Sometimes, God goes silent on certain situations in order to get things and/or people ready.

The season you're in might not be about you but rather getting things ready for you. Love cannot exist if one party isn't willing to be transparent and open.

Love has nothing to do with pride, ego, arrogance, losing your edge, and manipulation. Love is able putting it all on the line for the person. Love is looking like a fool, a loss of perceived dignity in certain situations.

Love is willingness to sacrifice for that other person. However, this must be done by both parties not one. So if you're waiting on someone else, be patient.

You never know how people will surprise you… wait on God.

Be the catalyst for change. ☺

DAY 51: Learning to Love

Today is about learning to love

Loving is very similar to learning to walk. It's a scary but empowering experience.

Everyone learns to walk at their own pace. Some go from crawling to walking in a flash. Some stand for months before taking a step. I believe that the way you learned to walk is the way you choose to love. Some are timid and others throw caution to the wind. ☺

We have to learn to be patient with those learning to love. Love is often confused with sex that it can be difficult to decipher. It can be easier for some to share their bodies than to share their hearts.

There are many people who are very experienced sexually but virgins of love. ☺ Everyone develops at their own pace. Allow that special person to develop their love without being rushed. ☺

Now I don't mean enable that person. When you learned to walk there was a point when your parents allowed you to figure it out without their input. They were usually watching but there was no helping either. You had to learn to how balance and walk on your own.

The same is for love. Sometimes you have to step back allow people to figure out their feelings. Love has its good and bad days, its hills and valleys. If this is a bad day, just know good days are coming.

So remember: be patient. Be with the one you love and if they are "learning to walk," love them from afar.

The great thing is just like with walking: everyone does learn how to love.

It takes some a little longer than others. However, when they do, they will love for a lifetime. ☺

Be the catalyst for change. ☺

DAY 52: Fighting for Happiness

Today Is about Fighting for Happiness

Today has been such a long day but wanted to give encouragement to those fighting for happiness.

Happiness is something that all strive for but rarely experience. It's hard to be happy or even content when it feels like all of the decks are stacked against you.

Happiness has become a dream we are fighting to obtain with uncertainty (or faith) if it will ever occur. I believe happiness is a state of mind, not an effect from your present environment and circumstances.

We must learn to be happy regardless of our stage of life. There is always something to be thankful for. ☺ Never allow society's perceptions of you and your life to steal the joy out of life. If you can hold onto the shred of hope and faith that things will get better; they will. I'm a true believer you can positively think yourself out of a storm.

Even when it looks like the chips are down and you're going to lose; push through. This is a critical moment when positive thinking is absolutely necessary to get to the next level.

If you can learn to prosper and flourish in less than ideal circumstances, then imagine the possibilities of the future. ☺

Be the catalyst for change. ☺

DAY 53: Love and Being Single

Today is about love and being single

Congratulations to all singles who may it through another Valentine's Day. It was like pulling an old band-aid off—a necessary evil. ☺

Remember: Be patient with those who are learning to walk (i.e. love). There might be some resentment in the process.

Some kids enjoy being independent and go from crawling to walking in a flash. However, some kids cry every time their parents try to put them down. There are some similar issues in love. ☺

Most people don't like change; they would prefer things to remain the same. I'm sure there were some kids who would have preferred to be carried for life. Alas, change is necessary.

It's easier to wait for someone else to make the move toward reconciliation. However, that isn't going to happen.

If you believe you should, but you're afraid, then you must pull yourself out of your 'playa' comfort zone. Take a chance on love. ☺

We must all grow up. Being loved and loving others comes with responsibility. Only when you accept the responsibility is when you can accept the purest form of love.

Be the catalyst for change. ☺

DAY 54: Dream Killers

Today is about Dream Killers

Let's talk about dream killers. Dream killers are people who, for whatever reason, have allowed failure to define them.

Failure and problems are a part of life; no one is immune. How you rebound from failure and trials is what defines you. Learn from every hard lesson in your life. Otherwise, you're bound to repeat them.

Be careful who you share your dreams with. Jealousy is a powerful thing. Guard your dreams in their inception stage. Don't allow yourself to be discouraged. Keep going. ☺

Encourage dream killers to dream again; they will thank you for it. It's a blessing for all. ☺

Commit yourself to do one kind action each day. It's amazing how it can impact others who will be inspired to do the same. ☺

Positive energy helps promote positive actions. ☺

Be a catalyst for change. ☺

DAY 55: Finding the Perfect Mate

Today is about finding the perfect mate.

This is rare so here is my take. Finding a man is similar to getting the exclusive Birkin Bag regardless of race. The 'Birkin' bag is a hand-built purse from Hermes that starts at $6,500. They are distributed to Hermes boutiques on unpredictable schedules and limited quantities.

A Whole Sex in the City Episode was dedicated to it. I will always covet a Birkin Bag the way I covet someday getting married. Most women would love a Birkin Bag. They would go about getting one in two different ways:

Some women will get an imitation Birkin Bag and rock it like it's the real thing. It doesn't have special amenities that a Birkin Bag does. It also doesn't last as long. You know you're frontin' and pretending it's real. ☺

Then there are the women who will save their money for years until they afford one. Then they will treat themselves to one. The way you go about obtaining a Birkin Bag is the way you date.

Now, I have tried a couple of imitations but they only made me want a real one more. The imitation have been so good that I didn't even really if it wasn't real or not. However, they never lasted, which illustrates they weren't real.

I'm willing to wait for a real Birkin Bag and treat myself. Now I have no judgment on whether you want entertainment instead of true love (imitation bag versus real bag). However, I do have one request: Just pick something. ☺

I believe at times women are so picky, we make no choice at all and waste a lot of time. Enjoy life; don't limit the possibilities in your life right now. Have fun during the process.

#NEWSFLASH# Every man isn't marriage material and shouldn't be treated as such.

When a man is ready to settle down; he should be convincing you. Not the other way around. When he is ready, he will contact you. We don't give men enough credit. When they want something, they know how to go after it. Make him get aligned with God and chase YOU.

We, as women, make situations complicated when they're not. They are either being serious or entertaining themselves. Pure and Simple. It took me a long time personally to get this. Now, instead of showing my interest and coming at dudes hard, I now wait to see what they are going to do. Life has been SO much better once I changed my perspective.

I'm not that romantic but I'm passionate about what I care about. Guys must now show me their passionate side. It's show time. ☺

If a man really wants me; he must be willing to show me AND BE WILLING TO COURT ME. I'm done proving myself. My reputation speaks for itself. Either you want me or you don't. Instead of acting like a man, I'm now the true lady God and Spelman College wanted me to be. A lady allows a man to lead the relationship. This cuts out the posers, imitators of love and serial dates.

If he doesn't want to put in the work to keep and maintain you. It's on to the next one. ☺ Men are like buses; another one will come along. Now the bus might break down or be hours off schedule; but it will come along. Just be patient.

Be the catalyst for change. ☺

DAY 56: Toxic Friends and Stress

Today is about toxic friends and stress.

We're all under a great deal of stress. We deal with it differently. Sometimes we go directly into light… some descend into the darkness. Those who descend into darkness eventually will gravitate toward light. However, the darkness drains the light. So on this today, be careful with whom you surround yourself.

When you're close to your breakthrough, Evil will send trouble in the form of emotionally draining friends. It's funny; in a relationship, we'll cut someone fast if they are emotionally draining. However, we will keep friends around who drain our light (positive) energy.

You keep them around because you're treating them the way you want to be treated. However, they keep you around because of something to gain. Or because they feel like they are better than you and it makes them feel good to discuss your problems. You don't notice their toxic nature because it takes time for people to reveal their motives. Until your life is getting better and they are descending into darkness. Then they reveal their toxic nature.

These toxic friends can dream and relationship killers as well. I believe toxic friends are worse than bad relationships because you're more open and transparent with friends than with relationships. They can ruin potential happiness and success.

Have you ever stopped dating someone because your friends didn't like them? Have you dropped a business venture because your friends thought it was stupid? I'm sure the people who invented the Pet Rock and Snuggle had friends who discouraged them. However, they didn't listen. Who's laughing now?

Take care of yourself. Allow God to speak to you. Sometimes you can be friendly but from a distance. God is taking it to the next level. You're going from the minor leagues to the majors. However, sometimes not everyone can go along on the ride. Trust God; He knows what's best.

Be the Catalyst for Change. ☺

DAY 57: Relying on God

Today is about Relying on God.

With problems associated with the economic downturn, people are acting out. Everyone deals with stress in various ways. Some retreat into their own world and others attempt to wreak havoc everywhere they go.

It's easy to be disappointed and angry in people. However, remember sometimes people allow themselves to be used by Evil without realizing it.

These people are working outside the will of God. Pray for them.

It's easy to scream, cuss, yell, and attempt to bring them down just as they did to you. Don't. Share your disappointment in their actions. They want the anger; they feed off the drama.

Sometimes the disappointment is so great you're at a loss for what to do. Allow yourself to be enveloped in God's love.

I know you might not understand the purpose, but there is purpose to all that happens in life.

Pray for God's mercy, and grace to guide your path. Lean on God when you don't understand the storms raging in your life.

When you're being spiritually attacked, trouble will come in every aspect of your life. When this happens, rejoice. This means you're close to your breakthrough.

Whatever God has for you; is yours. No one can take away an opportunity God has ordained. So step back and allow God to work. He is truly amazing and can bless beyond the highest expectations.

Be the catalyst for change. ☺

DAY 58: Repeating our Parents' Mistakes in Relationships

Today is about repeating the mistakes of our parents in relationships.

So this weekend was filled with unnecessary drama. While being sick yesterday, I began to wonder, are we repeating the mistakes of our parents in relationships?

No one is perfect. While growing up in certain environments, you become accustomed to certain behaviors that may not be normal. You take those behaviors with you as you grow up and then exhibit them in your own relationships. For example, if you grew up in a house where your parents argued all the time, then, as an adult, you end up in a relationship where you argue all of the time in relationships.

Maybe that person treats you like dirt because they saw their parents interact that same way growing up. They think it's normal.

Women do this a lot but what's interesting, I see it a lot more in men. Just because your parents did it, doesn't mean it's normal and healthy. Some men and women think it's ok to banter and antagonize each other. It really isn't. That can easily cross the line into verbal abuse and build resentments.

God knows I picked up some habits from my parents. ☺ I'll hold resentment in until I explode. Especially if someone is deliberately annoying me on purpose. We must learn to fight certain urges because they may be unhealthy.

We all pick up on people's weakness fairly quickly. Some people deliberately touch people's weaknesses for their own amusement or jest. When others do, it's because of retaliation. That's me. ☺

However, both are wrong. We must ask God to give us a pure heart, forgive ourselves for our actions, and move on. I want a better relationship that was more than what my parents had; I don't want to be with someone who likes drama and argue all the time. I do not want to be with someone where we are constantly hurting each other because we can't communicate our needs. It's not healthy and not normal.

We must find significant others who are willing to discuss inclinations and triggers so we can have drama-free relationships. Make an effort to stay healthy emotionally and physically.

Sometimes, God will take a bad situation or not intervene to show you what you need to change about yourself. God has to send trouble so you can fix the way you deal with trouble in your life. God will however continue to send you the same problem until you resolve it. ☺

Break the cycle of destructive habits and treat people better regardless of your own inclinations toward drama—or in my case, putting an end to it.

Be the catalyst for change. ☺

DAY 59: Becoming a Visionary

Today is about becoming a visionary.

Being a visionary is wholly a mental thing. I remember when I first began to get a sense that I'm in control of my destiny; I became somewhat of a recluse. I needed to process all the events taking place.

There have been many moments when I felt so burdened that I wasn't sure I would be able to get through the storms. However, I have vision for myself and while I may have felt overwhelmed, I would pick myself and continue on the path of life.

When you have a vision for your life; you know where you're going. Vision is a map to the destiny of your life. You can lose hope for a time; however, never lose your ability to create vision and to dream. During the time when creating your vision, it doesn't mean you're immune to delays, disappointments and even despair.

Keep yourself focused on your vision and continue to fight the good fight of life.

Be the catalyst for change. ☺

DAY 60: Knowing where you stand

Today is about knowing where you stand.

Being an entrepreneur at times is like being a bill collector. There are times when everyone pays on time and then there are times when payments don't come at all.

Imagine working hard only to find your paycheck bounced. That has happened to me before but this is the life of the entrepreneur. It's hard to be positive when you thought you were working toward something only to realize you were working for free.

It's frustrating and anger begins to build inside of you with no real outlet. You can become hateful and cynical with life when it feels like nothing is going your way.

There are times in your life when you'll not know where you stand. There will be a lack of clarity and consistency. These can be the darkest moments.

It's easy to want to take situations in your hands. To try to may it happen. That's exactly when trouble can enter your life.

God wants us to have a grindin' spirit combined with a focus on His will. Allow God to be the captain of your tugboat of life. He knows our heart and desires. I know it's difficult to trust during a time when everyone is out for themselves, but trust God. He will never mislead, deceive or cheat you out of the best life possible.

So today, embrace the fact God has your back despite it all. Allow yourself to be submerged in God's sea of love and blessings. While there may be some bad days; stay focused on the memories of the good days and know they are coming soon.

O Lord, thank you for this day. Please forgive me for my sins. Help me to stay focused on you when I don't know where I stand in my life. Help me to trust you to navigate the waters of the unknown.

Be the catalyst for change. ☺

DAY 61: Maintenance

Today is about Maintenance

When I first got my hair cut, I had no idea about the maintenance of short hair. It has to be constantly monitored to determine when you need a trim. Short hair has a lot of maintenance both long-term and daily. Add the pressure of running and figuring how to manage my hair can be a little overwhelming.

But I got into the swing of it. I got into a routine going on hair maintenance and I haven't looked back since.

Being in this race called life as an Christian is similar. You must be aware of your spiritual nourishment at all times. There are times you can become spiritually dehydrated. When life troubles threaten to overwhelm you, you must take precautions to keep yourself aligned with God's will.

Prayer is essential for spiritual maintenance. It keeps you focused on living a good and just life. Running this race called life can be difficult at times. It can be lonely; distressing and just plain overwhelming.

Prayer helps to give you nourishment needed to stay the course. While everything may be positive; the belief that life will get better in due time is powerful knowledge during your darkness hours.

So today, create a maintenance plan. Allow yourself to get a regime so you can stay focused on him. Allow God to take the lead in your life path and watch your mind expand in the most amazing ways.

O Lord, thank you for this day. Please forgive me for my sins. Please help me to develop a spiritual maintenance to keep me focused on the race called life. Help me not become disheartened in the face of adversity.

Be the Catalyst for Change. ☺

MONTH 3

DAY 62: Protection

Today is about Protection

After I finished my training for the Peachtree Road Race, I felt resilient and unstoppable. I believed I could do anything. I felt like an Olympic Athlete. Add to the fact that I finished the race in 69 minutes and I was really feeling myself until I passed out from heat exhaustion two weeks after.

No matter what stage of your life, you still need protection. Protection is defense, guard or a form of security. In my case, I need protection from heat aka water despite my speed and mental toughness.

Life will send you trials that will be so powerful they will knock the wind out of your sails. That's when you need to reach for your protection; God. God will protect you from all the trials of life when you call on his help. God will never fail you; disappoint or deceive you. He only has your best interests at heart.

God uses trials to strengthen you; not to diminish you. Remember there's a purpose in all of God's actions. While all may not be revealed to us; it's all used to increase our faith.

So today: Dare to look to God as your protector. He knows what's best for us. Trust him and believe the Lord can work it out.

O Lord, thank you for this day. Please forgive me for my sins. Please protect me from hurt, harm and danger. Allow me to believe all things are possible.

Be the Catalyst for Change ☺

DAY 63: How to Handle the Journey

Today is prayers about how to handle the journey.

O Lord, I am here on this journey. I'm not sure where I'm going. I'm not sure how to get out. Forgive me for all of my knowing and unknowing sins that placed my in this unfortunate place.

Allow me to patiently walk with you even when I'm uncertain of our final destination. Help me relinquish all control and allow you to lead my path.

When I stumble, you catch me. When I fall, you pick me up. When I am exhausted and cannot walk, you carry me. You provide me with all of the support I need.

Help me to believe in myself so I can stay on my race called life. Help me to believe. Help me to trust. Help me not to doubt myself.

I can make it. I will not falter in the face of overwhelming circumstances. I will trust you despite the chaos around me. I will believe I am more than problems I encounter.

My breakthrough is coming; I can taste it. I can see just around the bend. Help to order my steps so I can make it. Increase my stamina so I won't break down at the critical stage. Allow me to endure this journey in order to reach my dreams.

Be the Catalyst for Change ☺

Day 64: Soul Connection with God

Today is about establishing a soul connection with God.

I meet a lot of guys but one guy who has had my heart consistently for the past three years. I have some great loves in my life but this person ranks number one because of our soul connection. I have never had that with anyone.

We are not without problems. We have huge arguments. We love to make each other jealous. We date other people. We can go months without speaking. We've been doing the nonrelationship/relationship dance for years.

One look or text and all is forgotten.

He has taught me a lot about myself and helped me become a better person. He has shown me I'm jealous and I'm not an effective communicator. Through him, I have learned to slow down and explain my actions instead of just explaining my feelings. There is such a big difference.

Just because you become upset with someone, doesn't mean they understand why you are screaming at them weeks later.

He knows my heart and intentions. He understand the importance of being pure at heart even better than I do. We share the same value system and experiences without realizing it at times.

The biggest thing I love about him is he has a warrior spirit like myself. We both are very career motivated and we are struggling with our carbon footprint in society. We want to make an impact and help those around us.

We also know God is essential to success. All things are possible if you believe.

He's the only person who still gives me butterflies when I talk or see him. He makes me go from a cool and collected sophisticated woman to an awkward middle school geek. We have a soul connection. ☺ Today I encourage you to develop a soul connection with God.

It's essential to develop a relationship/friendship with God to increase communication and transparency. God can see you through everything but he's a little busy. ☺

God wants you to talk to him the way you talk to others in a relationship/friendship. He wants you to give him all the details and even admit when you're angry. When you're able to open yourself to this level of intimacy with God, he can truly bless you beyond measure.

Sometimes, God has a blessing lined up for you but you need to open yourself emotionally to receive it.

It might be that instead of you waiting on a blessing; God has been waiting for you to pick up your blessing. The only way to pick up your blessing is by going to the throne of grace through prayer.

Many pastors I have met told me you can walk in your blessing and you just need to step out.

For a while, I didn't know what that mean. I do now. Instead of waiting for your blessing to occur; begin acting like a blessing has already manifest and it will. ☺

While you're waiting on a new job, begin making a life plan of what you're going to do once you get the job. Create a budget, how much you want to save, etcetera and watch that blessing manifest.

While you're waiting on a house, begin picking the type of colors you will paint your house, the type of furniture. Walk into your blessing and watch it manifest.

While you're waiting to get married, anticipate all of the lifestyle changes necessary. Begin to cook and clean more on a schedule. Begin to shut down single ways of doing things; Hang out with more married people to get a sense of the change.

Most importantly, stop trying to change men and take them as they are. Learn how to pray for your man. That is, be a person who manifests change. Walk into your blessing and watch it manifest.

While it seems a little crazy, every blessing I have received when I begin to attempt to walk the blessing. When I could not visualize and walk into a blessing, it usually didn't occur.

So on this today: develop a soul connection with God.

Once you have a soul connection with God, walk into your blessing and watch your life begin to change.

Be the Catalyst for Change ☺

DAY 65: Getting the Basics

Today is about getting the basics.

During this training for the Peachtree Road Race, it's become clear getting the basics is necessary. All vanity is out the window.

At first, it was a little difficult when you're a cutesy girl like myself. I don't the wind messing up my hair; being sweaty outside, etcetera.

Now three months into training, vanity is gone. I will usually run in my lucky Spelman College hat and I've gotten used to running in all conditions even in snow.

Training for the Peachtree Road race has been humbling because it allows me to adjust my behavior and also the vain parts of myself I didn't know existed.

God gives feedback in various ways. He will take you through situations so you can learn about yourself and adjust your behavior.

Don't get upset. Accept the feedback and use it as an opportunity to grow. Sometimes life has a way of veering us off track to the point but we must start over and get the basics.

Remember: Getting the basics can be as simple as starting the day with prayer so we allow God to guide our steps.

You may not be what you want to be; you're better than what you were yesterday. Keep going in the race of life. ☺

Be the catalyst for change. ☺

DAY 66: How to Deal With Silence From God

Today is about how to deal with silence from God.

One of my pet peeves in relationships is the silent treatment; I cannot stand it. It's very passive aggressive.

Unfortunately, every guy I date has innately picked up on that I hated this and used it constantly. I prefer to talk out problems rather wishing them to go away. However, silence can be necessary at times, particularly when negotiating in business. I've learned to grin and bear it. ☺

Silence can be a blissful experience… Except when it comes from God. Then it can be terrifying.

Even the most diligent Christian can become overwhelmed by the deafening sound of nothing. God will provide silence for various reasons: for testing; for suspense; or due to Him working to get things in order. The longer the silence; the bigger the blessing.

So today: Trust the Silence. God is working to get your blessings in order whether it's through testing or putting things in place.

Have Faith in the process and know it will all work out for greater good of God.

O Lord, Thank you for this day. Help me to deal with Silence from You. Help me believe you hear my cries and You're working it all out because You want the best for me.

Be the catalyst for change. ☺

DAY 67: Call Me When You're Ready

Today is call me when you're ready

There were many times in my life when I believed I was ready for something that I wasn't. When I graduated from high school, I couldn't wait to go out into the world—to leave Morrow, Georgia in the dust. Aggressively and full of gusto, I left Georgia to the bright opportunities of Washington DC via Howard University.

Then I realized I wasn't ready for life outside Georgia.

I got a huge case of homesickness and wanted to come back home. I set my sights on transferring to Spelman College, which didn't make it easy. After all, it's unheard of to transfer in the middle of your freshman year. However, I had ambition, grades and faith to make it happen. Never looked back since.

There were other times in my life when I believed I was ready for something that I wasn't. We all have an idea of what we believe our lives should be and God may have different ideas.

We have an idea and God has a destiny. God has a great calling on all of our lives. God has our best interests at heart and sometimes won't allow you to move until He is sure you're ready.

Until you're ready to give complete control of life over to God; you're not ready to step into your destiny. We all say we are ready but still try to make things happen on our own. That cannot occur when you're ready.

So today: don't call until ready. God will provide all of our wants and needs but you must be willing to fulfill your portion of the bargain: be willing to believe and step back. Allow God to make your dreams happen.

If you're ready: Hold on. God is taking through such sorrow and pain so you will stay humble when you reach your destiny.

All greats have a background story. The background stories help you have compassion for other because you'll be able to relate.

O Lord, thank you for this day. Forgive me my sins and unbelief. Empower me to give You complete control over my life without interference. Allow me to continue to believe despite the circumstances around me.

Be the catalyst for change

DAY 68: Knowing it All

Today is about knowing it all

When I was nine years old, I was an avid reader. I loved the Babysitters Club and those books with alternative endings. You're supposed to make decisions as you read to create a specialized ending of the book. Except, I would read all of the endings and then pick. I wanted to know all of the possible consequences before making a decision.

Many of us are like that in life. We want to know all of the possible outcomes before making life decisions: a career change; marriage, children.

It's easy to become so jaded and beaten down in life that you're hesitant to make any real changes in your life. There will never be a right time to make life changes. You have to jump and take a leap of faith.

Never allow past negative experience to impact your future. If you do, you will never reach your destiny. Your destiny is tied to making life decisions. There is a point in life that you have to allow God to lead your path.

While all experiences may not be good, they were mandatory to molding you as person.

At some point, we are all placed in the fiery furnace but we will not be burned. We may be a little warm but not harmed.

So today: stop attempting to know it all. Trust God. He is the only One who knows all of the pieces of the puzzle. Put on your seatbelt of Faith and jump on the rollercoaster of life. With God as your operator, you will always be safe.

O Lord, thank you for this day. Help to decrease my anxiety and attempts to know everything. Increase my faith in your abilities so I can relax in this race of life.

Be the catalyst for change. ☺

DAY 69: Getting Salvation

Today is about getting salvation.

My sister and I are very close. She was always saving me from trouble when we were younger. She would cover for me when I would get into trouble. I was a watered down girl version of Bart Simpson. ☺

Since I was a little rambunctious; I was constantly on punishment at home never at school. My sister was always my savior and was always attempting to save me from harm.

Today, Christian society always states you should ask for God's salvation but doesn't explain the process or why you even want it. God's Salvation is the deliverance from sin or consequences of sin. God's salvation will save you from harm, destruction, difficulty, or failure. You might feel a little heat but you will not be burned. It doesn't mean you would encounter difficulty however; it will not be as difficult as it could be.

Particularly, when it's due to our inconsistent behaviors. Salvation and mercy works hand in hand. Kinda like Soap and Water. ☺ You need both to get clean.

We will all sin in our lives whether it's knowing or unknowing. However, knowing how to bounce back from sin and mistakes is where salvation comes in.

There are various ways to get God's salvation but there are three core elements:

Faith—In order to obtain God's salvation, you must believe in God's protection. Faith is needed in every aspect of life. You must believe in God's ability without proof. Focus on God's previous work in your life in order to keep your faith constant.

Request Forgiveness—None of us are perfect. Ask for forgiveness for all knowing and unknowing sins. Work hard not to keep creating the same mistakes. God will always continually forgive us; God never runs out of compassion and understanding. However, admission of guilt is important for spiritual development.

Renew of your commitment—Commit yourself to God. Give God your heart, mind, and soul. Take the pressure off of yourself and give to God. The troubles of this world can be too much to handle at times. Allow God to shoulder the burdens.

"That if thou shalt confess with thy mouth the Lord Jesus, and shalt believe in thine heart that God hath raised him from the dead, thou shalt be saved. For with the heart man believeth unto righteousness; and with the mouth confession is made unto salvation." Romans 10:9-10.

Today: Allow yourself to be enveloped in God's Salvation. While all in life may not be perfect; it can always be much worse. Give your life to Christ and His will. Trust in God will protect you from serious harm and stay focused on being aligned with God's will.

O Lord, thank you for this day. Help me to get your salvation by demonstrating faith, requesting forgiveness for sins and renewing my commitment to you. Continue to direct my path so I will stay on the path of righteous and serenity.

Be the catalyst for change. ☺

DAY 70: How to Forgive

Today is about how to forgive.

I have a really, really bad temper, but it takes a lot to get me angry. However, when you do watch out. ☺ On the other hand, I was born with the amazing trait of not holding grudges. I usually don't hold any grudges, but I may decide not to interact with you at all.

I'm lucky. I know many people who are still holding grudges about things that happened to them when they were five. Forgiveness next to prayer is one of the most important elements in your Spiritual Life. However, it can be tough and you will continually be a work in progress.

Forgiveness is more than no longer being angry about something or excusing a mistake. Forgiveness is about being compassionate and understanding.

There are three steps on how you can forgive:

Allow yourself to experience the emotions. A lot of times when we're upset with someone, anger is the emotion that comes to the surface but there is a tremendous amount of hurt and disappointment behind it. Don't allow yourself to stay angry so you won't feel the true emotions. Kick, Scream, Cry but don't run away from your emotions.

Prayer. Talk to God about the situation and your emotions. Ask God to give mercy and peace to get through this trying time. Prayer will settle your spirit and allow you to process the situation.

Let it go. Make an effort to forgive that person. Whether you need to write a statement saying you forgive the person or even telling them; begin the process. Sometimes you have to speak it into being. Speak forgiveness into the atmosphere and it will occur.

One Caveat: Forgiveness doesn't mean you have to interact with the person. It means you have let go of the malice in your heart. Forgiveness is freeing to you because it helps you not to waste energy focused on anger.

So today: Learn to Forgive. None of us are perfect. The forgiveness you bestow on someone is the same forgiveness God will bestow on you.

O Lord, Thank you for this Day. Thank you for forgiving me for all missteps in life. Help me to become more forgiving. Allow me to give everyone a clean slate just as you have done for us.

Be the catalyst for change. ☺

DAY 71: Inspiration

Today is about inspiration.

Inspiration is stimulation of creativeness or creative thought; divine influence; motivation.

Inspiration is important to daily living. However, how do you become inspired? Inspiration can come from anything. I'm easily inspired by the smallest things.

Here are three ways to become inspired:

Dream. It's really easy to become pessimistic with life after disappointment. Allow yourself to dream again. Go to basics: What was your childhood dream? What is your passion? Create a vision for yourself.

Find a muse. Everyone needs a muse. A muse is a thing or person that inspires you. A muse doesn't do anything but exist. I have a muse who inspires me. He evokes me into my most creative state of being. Find your muse so your creativity can flow.

Push through. There are a lot of reasons to become despondent with life. However, don't allow yourself. Push through the pain, resentment, and frustration. Once you push through the negative thoughts, inspiration can come.

So on this today: become inspired. Allow yourself to dream; find a muse and push through to reach your inspiration. God wants you to live up to your potential. Be inspired and watch your life soar.

O Lord, thank you for this day. Allow me not to be dismayed with the circumstances around me. Inspire me; help me to reach my dream. Allow me to stay focused on Your will.

Be a catalyst for change. ☺

DAY 72: Learn to Discern

Today is about Learning to Discern

There are so many risks and dangers lurking behind every corner; having the ability to discern is essential.

Discerning is God's understanding; being able to see; distinguish or perceive. It can also allow you to do and create amazing things based upon God's guidance. The ability to discern is a spiritual gift that has to be cultivated. The ability to discern takes time and even best the Christians can fall victim to their own desires and wants.

How do you know if God's giving you a discerning spirit? There are four ways:

It goes against your wants and desires. God's motives are pure and wholly separate from our earthy desires. Sometimes our wants can align with God's but most of the time they won't. So if you want to call in to work; God's ability to discern will not come over to say that it's God's will. Negative. God's discernment might get you to ask someone if they need a ride home even when you don't want to give it to them.

It aligns with God's Will and people. God's discerning ability will never allow you to hurt and mistreat any of God's people. If your 'discerning' is telling you to do that, go into prayer and listen again.

It creates or protects you from something you will have been unable to do yourself. God's discerning ability will create a chance encounter; opportunities or He will protect you from potentially devastating events. These encounters cannot be predicted; anticipated or sometimes imagined.

God's instruction is very clear. When God speaks and gives you an ability it's discernment; his voice is very clear. He will tell you, don't turn down this street. Walk this way; Leave; Move. It will definitely be hard to ignore and an urgency in your spirit will grow.

So today: Learn how to discern. Emerge yourself in prayer so God can speak directly into your spirit. Allow yourself to grow your spiritual gifts and change your life in an amazing way.

O Lord, Thank you for this day. Help me learn how to discern. Help me to have the ability to distinguish between my own ways and your ways. Allow your love to constantly stream into my heart and soul.

Be the catalyst for change.

DAY 73: Don't Worry

Today is: don't worry

As I've noticed, as I've gotten older, I struggle more with worry.

I have always been a risk taker; I used to be able to jump without looking down. However, now I see how far I am in front of the ground due to all of the responsibilities of being an adult. ☺

Worry is being concerned, anxiety, troubled and a general uneasiness. As a Christian, worrying is definitely looked down upon. It's seen as a lack of faith.

However, I believe now it's the results of the tough economic times we are living in. I believe we all have worried about something at the some point.

God places a burning desire for more than what's around you. You will reach your goals but you must learn to deal with the uneasiness that occurs when taking a risk. Risk taking isn't for the faint of heart. It's character building and strength building.

Evil can creep into your mind when you take a risk and step out of your comfort zone. It comes in the front of worrying.

None of us are perfect. Ask God for strength to place your mind into a positive place. What if it's not you worrying but your friends and family suffering from constant worrying? Pray for them when they start experiencing anxiety and start to worry.

Remind them God has rescued them before and will continue to do so. You must believe and speak it into the atmosphere.

O Lord, thank you for this day. Help release me from fear and worry. Renew my faith in knowing there isn't anything you cannot handle.

Be the catalyst for change ☺

DAY 74: The Last One Standing

Today is about the last woman or man standing.

As you make your way into your late 20s and 30s, it becomes difficult to be alone and single.

There are fewer people to hang out with and fewer quality people to date. For women, it becomes a test against time. When you don't have children by a certain age; you're being looked at a little strangely.

When you were younger, you were praised for being childless but now you get the question like "Do you want children?" Of course we want children. However, under the right circumstances. Trust, I would be the worst baby mama ever. ☺

For women, we sometimes treat a single life like jail and we are waiting to be paroled (i.e. married).

I have seen God work in other aspect of my life except this one. Evil tends to get into areas where your faith is most shaky. Trust in God. You will get married and have kids; you will settle down. You will find that special person.

God blesses in our unique time and space. While your blessing may have taken a little longer, there's a reason that hasn't been revealed.

Pray for patience while you wait. Patience is an important skill to have as a Christian. If don't obtain enough patience you can make silly mistakes that can take your life in different direction than what God has for you.

So today: don't worry if you're the last man or woman standing in your group of friends. God has a special place for life and He will bless beyond your wildest expectations if you can trust and believe.

That special someone is worth the wait; be patient, trust and believe.

O Lord, thank you for this day. Help me not become pessimistic in my personal life. Allow my faith to grow so I'm able to sense when my blessing is here. There isn't anything God cannot handle.

Be the catalyst for change.☺

DAY 75: Confusion

Today is about Confusion

Many of us are living in confusion. Confusion is uncertainty, chaos, turmoil and without understanding. There isn't anything more difficult to live than in confusion. While in my mayoral campaign and afterward, I lived in totally utter confusion.

So many people had disappointed me, and more importantly, I had disappointed myself

I wasn't sure exactly what I wanted to do with my life and the calling God had on my life. I was angry, frustrated, and disgusted with humanity. Sometimes, when you're living in confusion, it has nothing to do with sin or some action on your part. Sometimes, it's merely a living experience and upheaval.

When you say you want to be successful; remember, it comes with a price. However, the question is, "Are you willing to pay the price?" Some of the most successful people who ever lived have gone through some hard times. This is part of the grooming process. There are no shortcuts during this grooming process.

The longer the period of confusion; the bigger the blessing and breakthrough in the end. When you feel like you cannot live through it; rejoice. You're in the eye of the storm and close to the end of this trying journey.

So today, understand there is a purpose in the confusion. Understand that God is grooming you for something big.

O Lord, thank you for this day. Please forgive me for knowing and unknowing sins. Give me peace and serenity in order to overcome the confusion in my life.

Be the catalyst for change.☺

DAY 76: Enabling

Today is about being an enabler.

While my family is an extremely talented group of people, we sure do have our problems. My father has struggled with substance abuse and bipolar disorder for most of my life. However, I do believe my father has also struggled against the hits from the world.

While in my last year of college, my father really struggled. I was at a loss. I couldn't figure out how to fix him and was really upset that I couldn't. Then I met a guy when I was 28 who was one of the great loves of my life. He is still my creative muse but unfortunately has drinking demons to overcome. We cannot be together until he works on this damaging issue.

I also become increasing upset that I couldn't fix him either. I've realized I'm enabler. An enabler is someone who allows people they love to act in destructive ways. With my dad, I would act like everything was ok even when it wasn't. I would try to confront him but would eventually back down of out of fear. Fear that he would stop loving me.

Have you become your own enabler? Have you allowed yourself to act out in destructive ways and are afraid to stop?

It's easy to act out with all the pressure we are all feeling and everyone being preoccupied with their own lives.

Remember, you're always worthy of God despite your actions and misgivings.

So today: Stand up to yourself. Push yourself to stop destructive patterns and focus on getting yourself closer to God.

God will never give you disappointment or hurt you. Allow yourself to be enveloped in God's love.

Be a catalyst for change. ☺

DAY 77: Creating Your Destiny

Today is creating your destiny.

Most of my biggest triumphs have been things no one believed in but God and me.

Destiny is always anointed by God and filled with the Holy Spirit. Destiny has nothing to do with luck or chance. It was sent by God.

These are the most satisfying experiences because I know the only One who helped me achieve it was God.

There are some dreams no one will believe in. No one wants to help you. Don't become resentful. Just know you're next in line for testimony. When God doesn't send you the tools you need; expect and believe in a miracle. When you break through, you will become so humble under the will of God that you will never question His action again.

You can create your destiny in the following ways:

Faith—How can you ask God to do something you don't believe in? You must believe God can do it. Focus on the many times God has provided miracles in the past in order to push your faith to the next level.

Prayer-The lifeline to God. It's essential when creating your destiny that you keep in constant communication with Him

So today: don't be afraid to create your destiny. God has your back; take a big step toward the life you have dreamed of.

Be the catalyst for change. ☺

DAY 78: Feeling Whole

Today is about feeling whole.

I think we all struggle with feeling whole. We always feel like we need a little extra something to better ourselves.

Although I've had short hair before; I was a bit hesitant to go back due to my own personal preoccupation with hair. I have always felt pretty with more hair since I have such a wide Kool-Aid smile.

However, this time, I was determined to own it and take a stronger persona with it. It worked. People tell me how beautiful I look now with short hair and how they didn't like me with long hair. $%&*!!!

Sometimes in life you have to make yourself feel whole.

We all have insecurities about ourselves to overcome. However, we must allow ourselves to morph into what God has for us to be.

Feeling whole means where you are right now in your life is enough. You can make yourself happy at any stage in your life. You can't constantly live your life in pause.

So today: make yourself feel whole. Dare to be a more confident self. Remember your strangeness makes you unique and makes you stand out from the crowds.

Be the catalyst for change. ☺

DAY 79: Getting Caught Up

Today is about getting caught up

During Memorial Day holiday, I was at a party when I wasn't interested in a guy who approached me. He was extremely persistent. I told him I was dating someone and it still didn't help. I finally decided to give him a fake number to get him off my back.

I thought he would take it and walk it off. However, low and behold, he called me and my phone didn't ring. He immediately said, you gave me a fake number and began to beg for the real number. It was so sad; I eventually relented.

I got caught up.

There are many times in life we have had the best intentions. However, somehow we get caught up. God gives us a roadmap to life but unfortunately for various reasons we go down a different path.

God loves us despite all of our mistakes. Pray for forgiveness and get back on track.

No one is immune from trouble and issues. While you may stumble, or even fall, it's important to get back up and continue in this race of life.

Losing with grace is an important win.

Be the catalyst for change. ☺

DAY 80: Courageous

Today is about being Courageous.

Being courageous is being bold, daring, and gutsy in the face of shaky circumstances. I've had many friends who eventually had to be removed from my life. Various reasons but usually because of my personal growth.

However, it was always the same: suffocating friendship. Becoming their friend became overwhelming and their actions selfish. I want friends where we can lean on each other. It can't become one-sided; while I do have some wisdom. I do have my problems as well. I need light in my life, not judgment.

Moving on doesn't have to be bad; it can be positive. Everyone can't come along on your ride of life. God sends us specific help on certain assignments. However, once the assignment is over, the help may need to leave your life.

Any additional time can become toxic to your life and soul. However, we as Christians have a problem letting it go. How do you know when it's time to let go? When this friend brings chaos, confusion, and encourages you to go against God's path.

Be careful of the wolves in sheep's clothing. Trust your discerning spirit; it will never fail you. Remember: Satan was a choir director and knew all the scriptures by heart. He knew God but still denied Him.

Allow God to speak to your heart. Dare to be courageous and remove friends who have expired in your life. Trust God's urging in your spirit and allow room for angels to enter your life.

O Lord, thank you for this day. Help me find the strength to remove friends who are no longer a positive influence in my life. Please allow new energy to enter my life to allow a new lease on life.

Be the catalyst for change. ☺

DAY 81: Quiet

Today is about being quiet.

When I get angry, I have no problem telling anyone how I feel. However, if I'm so angry that I can't talk to you, you've sent me to another world. Watch out. ☺

During these times, I believe being quiet is absolutely necessary. Being quiet is about being restrained and displaying calmness. Evil knows the areas we need to work on and will send trouble our way to test us.

So if you're like me and have a loose tongue, you must learn how to be quiet. There's a tremendous amount of peace in silence. While it's difficult, you may have fake calmness and restraint by being quiet.

This allows God to speak with you so you can attempt to get a sense of the situation. It also keeps you from saying things that you may regret.

None of us are perfect. It's normal to get angry. However, it will become extraordinary to resist the urge to become mean spirited and just plain ugly when provoked.

O Lord, thank you for this day. Help me control my tongue when angry. Allow Your Love to permeate into my spirit.

Be the catalyst for change.☺

DAY 82: Deciding to Wait

Today is about deciding to wait.

When I made the decision to be celibate, I put a lot of thought into it.

I had just experienced a pretty bad breakup with a college boyfriend (i.e. the great love of my life). He had said some pretty awful things. I prayed that I wouldn't have another sexual relationship until I was sure that person and I would marry.

That was over nine years ago. I don't regret my decision. Now that doesn't mean I haven't been uncertain. God leaves some things to be shared within the confines of marriage. One of those items is sex. When you have sex with someone you can take on their spirit, for better or worse.

Sex is something ordained by God and meant to encourage closeness in relationships and procreation. When you use it outside those confines you're playing with fire. Allow yourself to get to know someone emotionally without the sex and see how positive the relationship can be.

Does that mean you won't have problems? No. Does that mean you won't be tempted? No. Celibacy is a sunscreen of God's will. You may feel the heat but you won't be burned.

So today, allow yourself to be worthy of the wait. Anyone who truly wants to be with you should be willing to get to know your emotionally not physically.

O Lord, thank you for this day. Help me to control my sexual urges. Allow me to become more focused on Your will and getting to know someone on a emotional level. Forgive me for my sins and help me to forgive myself when I get off track.

DAY 83: Transformation

Today is about being transformed.

During this journey called life, I have gone through an amazing transformation.

From the ending of the mayoral campaign onward, I have lived through things I didn't believe I could. I have allowed myself to rely on God in a way I have never done before.

I have been humbled and truly realize all my blessings come directly from God. I can truly do nothing without Him. Transformation is the process of being changed, a revolution or in this case a spiritual makeover.

Sometimes we have a yearning in our spirit for change but don't exactly know how to initiate it. Do you want to be transformed? The key is active prayer life.

An active prayer life is something crucial to success. You must be willing to talk to and hear from God. The direct communication from God is prayer.

God can change you by changing your heart. Once He melts away all the resentment, frustration and overall impatience, you will see and feel a change.

One Caveat: Be aware of setbacks. The moment you decide to give God your heart and become transformed, evil will come after you. The evil can come in your most vulnerable area: your heart and your mind. If either place isn't in order, it can become difficult to make good decisions.

So today: allow yourself to be transformed by God. Ignite your spirit with active prayer life and become forever changed.

O Lord, thank you for this day. Help to transform me. Allow my ways to become your ways. Help to have active prayer life so I can follow your instructions and will.

Be the catalyst for change.☺

DAY 84: Letting go of Pride

Today is about letting go of pride.

Pride is your sense of value or satisfaction of yourself. I have always had a problem with pride. I always want to see that I have things under control even when I don't. I also don't like to admit when I'm having a problem.

Part of the reason is because I'm an optimistic person and part is because of pride.

For me, it got to a point when so many problems were coming at me all at once I didn't care anymore. I just wanted God to work it out.

Pride can be a damaging force in your life, Not only will it inhibit your ability to ask for help and it can hurt your spiritual release abilities because you won't want to admit any issues in your life.

Humble yourself before God. God has power to solve any problem in your life. However, you must be able to ask God for help. God is all knowing but you must actually request God's help in your life.

Evil will tell you God already knows and God is deliberately not answering you. Don't allow those negative thoughts to enter your mind.

So today: attempt to let go of your pride. We all have problems and it doesn't make a failure. It makes you human. Allow yourself to be humbled by your experiences and let God handle it all.

O Lord, thank you for this day. Lord, I'm so tired to trying to handle everything myself. I cannot do this alone. I now humble myself to you. Help me let go of my pride and submit to Your will.

Be the catalyst for change. ☺

DAY 85: The Importance of Worship

Today is about the importance of worship.

Growing up as a Preacher's Kid, I always was an avid churchgoer, but not necessary a worshipper.

I would actively listen to the Word but was really not into the music ministry (due to my lack of singing ability). I would just focus on the Word and nothing else.

My sister is the one who caught me by the leg. Worship is really when you can feel your breakthrough. Worship is when you give reverence to God and respect.

Worship is also an expression of love for God. Would you like someone to tell you constantly how they love you so much but yet never show you?

That is exactly what you're doing when you don't participate in worship. When you allow yourself to participate in worship, you can get so caught up into the spirit that is when you can really hear from God.

Allow yourself to become immersed in worship. Show God how much you love Him and watch Him allow blessings to rain down on you.

So today: try something different; allow yourself to be an active participant in worship instead of an observer. Once you become a participant, watch your communication with God increase and become clearer.

O Lord, thank you for this day. Help me to worship You more. Allow me to give You just some of the love that You give to me. While my expression may never equal Yours, allow me to express myself with more ease over time.

Be the catalyst for change. ☺

DAY 86: Obedience

Today is about obedience.

Growing up, I was always a little extra...extra unbehaved. I never liked authority and always pushed the limits.

My mother was always the disciplinarian and authority figure. She made me obey despite all of my antics. Many of us are like me with God.

We know all of God's rules but we consistently break them. We rebel against authority because we believe we are in still in control.

God is like the Strict Mother or Father here on earth. God will not indulge us but rather give us structure on how we must live a righteous life. This is non-negotiable.

Watch how difficult life can become if you knowingly and consistently break God's rules. God doesn't give us rules to punish Him but rather to discipline us so we can handle the blessings when they come.

Nothing would be worse than praying for years for a particular breakthrough only not to be able to handle it because you were unprepared.

So today: work on your obedience. While it might be slightly boring and less exciting than blowing off the rules, it's better for you in the long in run.

O Lord, thank you for this day. Help me to become more obedient. Allow me not to struggle against your will and trust it. Help me to stay on the path of righteous.

Be the catalyst for change. ☺

DAY 87: How to Listen to God

Today is how to listen to God.

When I first began my adult spiritual journey, I had to learn how to listen to God. People always say just listen to God but I always wondered how do you know if it's Him or your own wishful thinking?

There are various ways to listen to God but there are three core elements:

Remove all distractions. It's difficult to listen to God when you're watching television, sleeping, talking, texting, et cetera. You must remove all distraction when attempting to hear from God. Otherwise, all you will receive is white noise.

Be in a calm mental place. It's extremely difficult to hear from God when you're experiencing anxiety or really stressed out. The best time to listen to God is in the morning when life's problems haven't been able to touch you yet.

Be in some stage of Praise or Prayer. Whether you're praising Him or in prayer, the communication line must be open to hear from God. If you're not in either one of the stages it will be difficult to determine what He is really saying.

So today, work on your ability to listen to God. God can provide amazing wisdom and insights in your life if you can settle your spirit to listen. God has power to speak directly to you at any time and not just on Sundays.) Allow yourself to be open to hearing from God and He will speak with you.

O Lord, thank you for this day. Forgive me for knowing and unknowing sins. Help me work on creating an environment to hear from You.

Be the catalyst for change. ☺

DAY 88: Powerful

Today is about being powerful.

I believe being powerful can be an aphrodisiac. It's also addictive. I have always wanted to be powerful. Not to just make myself feel good. However, rather to be a voice for those without a voice.

To impact change in our community, our minds and most importantly our souls. Do you want to have power? Are you willing to pay the price?

There's a price to be paid for the power bestowed. Much is given and much is expected. God can anoint you with a voice people will listen to. However, He will give you a testing period so you will have a testimony no one can deny.

This is essential so no one will question your sincerity and commitment to a higher calling. Imagine the horror of those who tried to hold back to realize due to their actions they have made you more of a threat than they ever imagined.

When you get the anointing of God, there should be no worries, God will never allow anything to truly harm you.

So today, if you want to be powerful, get ready. It will be a bumpy ride but remember: what doesn't kill you makes you stronger and extremely powerful.

O Lord, thank you for this day. Help to me to reach my fullest potential and becoming a voice for those without one. Allow me to trust You and know that You know what is best.

Be the catalyst for change. ☺

DAY 89: Focused

Today is about being focused.

Focusing has never been a problem for me. Sometimes, I can be a little too focused and it becomes a little too much. Focus is about giving something your main emphasis and concentrated quality. If you want the success you have dreamed of, you must learn to focus.

You must possess three qualities to become an incredibly focused person:

Ability to push your personal feelings aside—When you're focused, your personal feelings are no longer applicable. When you're grindin, you cannot allow any other aspects of your life to affect the task at hand. Everything but the task or project at hand is on hold.

Be able to hear from God—Hearing from God is extremely important. God will make sure you're doing the correct tasks. He will also let you know when you're going too far.

Ability to produce under extreme pressure—When you're focused, it doesn't matter what kind of day you've had, etcetera. What is important is producing the needed results. Nothing else matters. So you learn to produce under insurmountable odds.

So today: get focused. Allow yourself to get the frame of mind to create miracles with God's help.

O Lord, thank you for the today. Allow me to have razor-like focus. Help me to push my personal feelings aside, to be open to hearing from you and the ability to produce under extreme pressure.

Be a catalyst for change. ☺

DAY 90: God's Will

Today is about God's Will.

I remember when I was dating my great college boyfriend (i.e. the great love of my life). I was very confident we would be together. However, due to mistakes of youth, that didn't happen.

I began to pray for us to get back together; at the end of the prayer I added, "In your will." I noticed my prayers were not answered in the way I wanted.

As I grew in my faith, I learned when you pray your prayers are answered according to His will. If it's not best for you, it won't happen.

Despite any initial discomfort, God knows what's best for you. Allow yourself to trust you.

God will do whatever it takes to protect you from hurt and harm. This includes not giving you what you want.

When in prayer, I have learned to ask for God's Will despite the caution. God's will is what is best for you and it may not align with what you want at the moment.

So today: Submit to God's Will. Trust Him. He will always have your best interest at heart.

O Lord, thank you for this day. Please forgive me for my sins. Allow me to submit to God's Will. Help me to trust you and have faith in your plans for the my life.

Be a catalyst for change. ☺

DAY 91: Light Versus Darkness

Today is about choosing light versus darkness.

I have, for the most part, a sunny deposition. I prefer sunny days to rainy. However, I do understand they both are equally important. However, you can't allow the rain in your life to overshadow your perspective.

During these tough economic times, it's easy to feel alone. You've chosen to either see the beauty in the world or submerge into darkness.

When you're in a testing period, it's easy to become despondent about life. It's easy to lose your sense of morale and focus. It easy to blame God for you losing control. Don't.

In every growth experience, there's a learning experience. All heartache and disappointment works together for the glory of God.

Some life experiences take years or even decades to reveal their importance. I'm still attempting to process all that happened in my 20s. ☺

We are living in times that are incredibly important to your spiritual growth. Allow yourself to focus on the light instead of the darkness.

So today: Choose Light and trust God. Despite your feelings of loneness and isolation, God is getting ready to do a mighty thing in your life. Step back and allow God to take complete control over your life.

O Lord, thank you for this day. Help me to choose light over darkness. Let me see the beauty in my life. Help me to trust You and lean on You for support.

Be the catalyst for change.☺

MONTH 4

DAY 92: Praying for Others

Today is about praying for others.

I learned the power of prayer for others over my life by accident. I have a friend from law school (only one year, I know, I know, I'm clearly overeducated) and she had just taken the bar.

She was the primary breadwinner for her family and the first one in her family to graduate from college and law school. We had spoken at length about her fear about not passing the bar and what long-term effects that could have on her career.

In Georgia, they post the names of those who passed the bar on the website around 4 pm. So I was working on a government job at the time and she had been on my mind. I began to prayer for her and her family. I prayed for favor for her over the bar.

Then I called her, she wasn't at home but wanted me to check for her. So I had the pleasure of telling her she had passed the bar. We both were crying tears of joy at the end of the call. It was such a special moment.

When I felt the intense power of praying for others, afterward, I received a completely shocking windfall of money that eventually helped me to start my own business.

You're not in the race of life on your own. You're on this path together with humanity. You must allow yourself to lean on others for strength when necessary.

When you pray for others, you can really get God's attention. It also illustrates an unselfish part of yourself that's appealing.

So today: take a little time to pray for someone else. Allow your unique light of kindness to shine and feel the power of prayer.

O Lord, thank you for this day. Help me to step away from my own problems to pray for someone else. Allow me to feel the intense power of prayer in my life and in others.

Be the catalyst for change. ☺

DAY 93: Joy

Today is about Joy.

Joy is the delight, happiness and enjoyment in something or someone.

One of the reasons why I'm so optimistic is because I live my life immersed in God's Joy.

I make sure I face each day with anticipation of an answered prayer, of something good happening.

I celebrate every small victory in my life. Whether it be a financial breakthrough down to a good parking space in the grocery store. I stop to smell the roses, so to speak.

You must work to obtain God's Joy in your heart. It's a process and its doesn't mean you won't have bad days; it just means you'll make a commitment to anticipate good instead of bad.

Life is about choices. If you anticipate something good; then good will happen. However if you'll begin to anticipate something bad; then something negative will occur.

Focus on light and positive. Allow yourself to dream and know breakthrough is just around the corner.

If you're having trouble seeing the positive and allowing God's Joy to enter your heart, start keeping a 'positive journal'. Write down every unique and positive blessing you receive each day and then also write down what you want to be blessed with on the next day. At the end of the day, continue to do this and then cross some of the blessings that come to pass. You'll be amazed by God's movement.

You'll be delighting yourself in God's Joy in no time.

So today: make yourself swim in bliss, become a vessel of God's Joy. It may take some process, but you'll be able to see God's Joy every day in no time.

O Lord, thank you for this day. Help me to become a vessel for God's Joy. Allow me to open my heart and see all of the beauty in the world. Help me to stay focused on Your will and glory.

Be the catalyst for change. ☺

DAY 94: Grindin'

Today is about grindin'.

Grindin' is a intense, rapid paced work. It's difficult to maintain an extended amount of time. It's exhausting.

I have been grindin' for a while now. I have about seven new projects going all at the same time and it can be a bit overwhelming. I have been working all day and almost all night due to business partners in other countries.

Grindin' is when you're working without any breaks or vacation. When you're relentless in your drive and amount of passion you putting into your craft.

When you're grindin', you must attempt to keep your core aligned. Your core is mind, body, and spirit.

You must feed and exercise your body. Make sure you do the same for mind and spirit.

It's important to stay in prayer while you're grinding. Because of the rapid pace it's easy for certain items to get left to wayside. If you're in prayer you become almost instinctive. You will do things that will become almost second nature without realizing it.

To jumpstart your day, try adding a bit of exercise and 15 minute bible study. You will be amazed how it can change the course of your day but also how you handle challenges.

So today: Rise and Grind. While it may be exhausting, if keep yourself focused on God and in stay in prayer, there is no limit where you may go.

O Lord, Thank you for this day. Allow me to stay focused on you, Lord while I'm grinding. Allow me to exhaustion and frustration to get the better of me. Help to understand you have my best interests at heart. Help me to step into my destiny without fear.

Be the catalyst for change. ☺

DAY 95: Favor

Today is about favor.

When I started my masters in public administration at Clark Atlanta University, I had spent one year in law school and I was extremely aggressive. However, all my professors liked me because I was aggressive and I knew my stuff.

While it didn't endear me to my classmates, it helped earn the respect of the professors and boyfriend at the time. I was favored. There are times in your life when you have favor. Everything you touch will turn to gold. You will have the Midas touch. It usually comes after a particularly devastating time.

When you first figure out that you're favored, you're shocked. You've struggled for so long… you cannot believe it. Allow yourself to enjoy it. God blesses with favor when have shown a huge amount of courage, strength, and restraint during a testing period.

So today, if you're favored, enjoy it. If you're waiting, know your time is coming.

I embrace the favor you have given me Lord. Not because I was so good or deserving, but out of clear mercy on my soul. I thank all of those who prayed for me when I couldn't or wouldn't pray for myself. I will also pray for others. Continue to allow the favor to rain down on my life and allow my life to be changed forever.

Be the catalyst for change. ☺

DAY 96: Becoming Resilient

Today is about becoming resilient.

I have learned to be resilient. Resilient is about being flexible, tough and strong. I have learned over my experiences the last couple of years.

During a time when I had two big project launches, my grandmother died. I was at a loss. I have never experienced loss in my family before and it hit me like a ton of bricks.

For the first time in my life, I was unable to perform under pressure. I couldn't think straight. I had become paralyzed with fear.

There have been times in my life things have been so bad I knew only God and I were the ones to get myself out of the situations. So I have become resilient.

Becoming resilient requires that unshakeable faith, belief and prayer. You must believe in yourself because if you don't believe why should anyone else?

While you might stumble from the weight of problems on your shoulders. You might cry yourself to sleep at night but you'll get through this; you will survive.

When you come through a storm you never thought you could live through, you're completely humbled and dependent on God.

So today: allow yourself to become shaped and molded by God. While the process might not be pleasant, it will make you a more awesome self.

O Lord, Thank you for this day. Allow me to weather to storms of life. I feel myself become stronger and more resilient. No one can stop me. With you with me Lord, then who can be against me? Allow me to believe in myself and fulfill my dreams. I will never stop trying to achieve my goals and one day they will be fulfilled. They will be fulfilled because it's my destiny.

Be a catalyst for change. ☺

DAY 97: Instructions

Today is about instructions.

Growing up in Georgia, I was a bit of snotty brat. I hated taking and following instructions. I always like to be put my own spin on the instruction.

Until I got involved in cheerleading and dance team. When you're learning a routine, you must follow the instructions. From that point on, I learned there are certain times in life you need to follow instructions.

There are many Christians who were just like me. We want to create our own version of Christianity and pick out à la carte rules. There's a reason why God wants us to follow all of his commandments. There are rewards for those who do.

God will also love us despite our imperfect nature; however, we must try to follow his instructions when He gives them to us. There's a purpose when God speaks; He provides clear instructions to keep us away from harm and danger.

So today, while you might be sick of authority and rules: follow the instructions of God. While He may not explain the purpose, trust that He has our best interests at heart.

O Lord, provide instruction to me. Help me to know the next stage of my life. I cannot do this without you. Help me to trust despite all of the chaos I see around me. I know you have and will continue to protect my life. Allow me to be in a fiery furnace but don't allow me to be burned.

Be a catalyst for change. ☺

DAY 98: Real Love

Today is about real love.

I have really been in love maybe three times in my life. The rest of the people, I liked a lot.

When I'm in love, I'm extremely stubborn. It doesn't matter what anyone says. I love them and that's the end of it.

Sure, we may argue, say horrible things about each other but no matter, I got their back.

When I'm in love with someone, I treat them like my family. I love my family despite the fact we may get on each other nerves and fight. However, I would never abandon them for any reason.

That's exactly the way God loves us. God loves us despite our sometimes ignorant behavior and always has our back. God is devoted to our needs and wants. He wants the best for us no matter what.

So today: try to love others similarly to the way God loves us. Sure, it's demanding and sometimes thankless but God will bless you immensely for it.

O Lord, thank you for this day. Allow me to be understanding to those I love. The more I love, the more that love is returned to me. I'm treating those I love with the most love and respect. I pray love will fill the hearts of those around me.

Be a catalyst for change. ☺

DAY 99: Relaxation

Today is about relaxation.

I remember my first real vacation as a working adult. It was two years ago. Despite the fact that I worked the entire time, I enjoyed my vacation in South Beach. My girlfriend and I had so much fun.

I was able to allow my mind to drift and relax. It ultimately helped my business because I was able to think more creatively that I ever had before.

Sometimes, a break is necessary in order to relax.

Evil can creep into your life in one of the easiest ways: by getting caught up in the business of life and lacking the ability to relax. Keep your eye on the prize in this race of life by learning to relax when necessary.

God wants you to have the endurance to being able to enjoy the breakthrough that's coming. That is why pacing yourself is absolutely necessary.

The race of life is a marathon not a sprint. While it attempts to force things to speed up, God truly does things on His own time. So while you're plugging away in life, allow yourself some relaxation and recognize God has your back in all situations. So enjoy the ride.

Today: Dare to take a break. Give your mind and spirit a taste of relaxation and watch your creativity soar.

O Lord, thank you for this day. I deserve to relax. As I stop and relax, I refresh my mind, my body, and my spirit. God is my constant Source of inner peace and strength, because I'm part of God and God is part of me.

Be a catalyst for change. ☺

DAY 100: Showing God to Others

Today is showing God to others.

I loved the newest, hottest, up and coming hairstylists. I was definitely at that point in my life; I would jump chair to chair with various stylists without any real commitment.

I would take all of my friends along for the ride. I would rave about a stylist for a while. Then I would become bored with them and move on to the next. My friends would move with me.

I begin to realize I wanted to establish some connections with a stylist at some point. Someone who could get to know my likes and dislikes.

I make the decide to settle down with one stylist. I may occasionally get styled by others but only one person cuts my hair. The moment I began to settle down with a hairstylist, my friends began to do the same. Because I made it a priority to be an example.

I believe exposing God to other people is similar as well. I'm a believer in the idea that you can show someone better than you can tell them. The best way to lead people to Christ is through your example of how to live aligned with His will.

While you might falter or stumble, your ability to get back up and continue on this path of life is important for your own spiritual development but others walk as well.

So today: Dare to be an example. Show someone the Christ who lives in you. How do you show them? By living a God-centered life.

O Lord, thank you for this day. Help me to show people the way to you by living right. Help me to understand and be nonjudgmental. Allow me to see Your works through my positive actions.

Be a catalyst for change. ☺

DAY 101: Getting Lost in the Moment

Today is about getting lost in the moment.

One of my best friends and I are food junkies aka foodies. We absolutely love to eat. This is our thing.

While in college, we made plans to make a trip to the Krispy Kreme donut place close to her house. I drove to her house and then we took her car to the shop. We had so much fun and then she dropped me off at my place.

Once I got inside, I realized I had left a textbook I needed in the car. I went downstairs to get it from my car and realized my car was gone. I immediately thought it was stolen only to realize I left my car at her house.

I had to tell her to pick me up so I could get my car. That's how focused we were on food. As we have gotten older, we have learned to control it.

There are many times in our lives we can get lost in the moment. We can allow all common sense to be thrown by the wayside.

That's why we must focus on God's Ways. God wants us to be able to follow His path and instructions for Daily Living.

While it's difficult at times not to allow ourselves to get caught up in feeling rebellious and frustrated. Don't allow God's sustaining and peaceful spirit to wash over you like a ray of sunshine.

So today, don't beat yourself up when you get lost in the moment and find yourself off track. Brush yourself off and get back into the game. While it might be difficult and disappointing at first, it will be worth it in the long run.

O Lord, thank you for this day. Please forgive me for knowing and unknowing sins. Allow me get back on track when I get lost in the moment. Help me to trust You will always be with me regardless of circumstances.

Be a catalyst for change. ☺

DAY 102: When God is Silent

Today is about when God says nothing.

I went through a horribly mean stage with guys when I would push the limits. I would give guys my number. When they called, I would pick up the phone and say nothing. They would say my name over and over until they hung up.

I thought this was hilarious. Actually, it wasn't. It was cruel.

However, many of us feel God is doing that to us.

We are calling out in pain, asking God to fix our circumstances and we're getting nothing but silence. It's difficult to continue to believe in someone who isn't responding.

While we need to humanize our relationship with God in relation to prayer, this isn't one of those times. God is an all-knowing spirit. He knows our needs before we even say them. He also knows the outcome of any situations because He controls it.

There are many times when God goes silent He's working hard on our behalf. He's working to create that blessing or breakthrough we've been waiting on.

Other times, He's watching our emotional progression in various situations. Sometimes, we're holding ourselves back, not being present in the situation and handing over control to God.

Your emotions must progress in a positive way so God can bless you. God will not bless you until He feels comfortable you can handle the blessing.

So today, allow yourself not to become frustrated when God says nothing when you call. He hears your cries and will respond but all in due time.

O Lord, thank you for this day. Help me not become frustrated when I don't hear from you, Help me to trust you have my best interests and are working hard to provide me with the blessing I so desire.

Be a catalyst for change. ☺

DAY 103: Taking the Joy out of Everything

Today is about taking the joy out of everything.

I had a friend from college who was so picky about her food. She could fault in Jesus LOL. ☺

We were on our first spring break trip and she constantly complained about her food. It was unbearable; everywhere we went, she found something wrong in every situation until eventually we stopped having meals with her.

She later admitted she was super nervous being on her first adult vacation and she was being picky out of fear rather than because there was an actual problem.

True Joy is difficult to create because there are so many negative influences in the world today.

When trying to obtain joy, you must be open to enjoy the life God has provided. Some people are not open to this experience.

Instead of being angry with those who have a habit of taking the joy out of everything (i.e. Debbie Downer), pray for them.

There is something in their life suppressing their ability to see the positive and beautiful in the world. Eventually, through looking at everything with fresh perspective, they will eventually be able to experience joy in their life.

So today if you encounter someone who takes the joy out of everything, allow yourself to pray for God to melt their heart so they can see the beauty in the world.

O Lord, thank you for this day. Please forgive me for all of my knowing and unknowing sins. Help me to see even the smallest joy in my life and help others to do the same.

Be a catalyst for change. ☺

DAY 104: Too Good to be True

Today is about something being too good to be true.

When I was twenty, I went on my first spring break trip to South Beach in Miami Florida.

Three of my girlfriends from college and I said we were going to have the best trip ever. We found a great deal online for a hotel room for $40.00 a night. That meant it would be $10.00 per person and for one week $70.00 in total. This place was going to be amazing. Or so we thought.

We got there and it gave a whole new meaning to roach motel. It was old and decrepit. There was dried blood on the wall. We were shocked and had just driven ten hours in my car so we were totally tired. We decided we would take a two-hour nap and then get up and find another place to stay.

We decided to sleep in the bed because the sheets are always changed but not necessarily the comforter. One of my girlfriends decided to lay under the comforter with shorts and no socks despite our advice to the contrary. At the end of our two-hour nap, she has rash all over legs and feet.

Sometimes in life there are some things that are just too good to be true.

In most situations we all hope for the best. Sometimes life doesn't live up to our expectations. When this occurs, it's easy to be resentful and frustrated.

Disappointment is a part of life and it's essential you learn to deal with it. When life fails to attain hopes or wishes, you must continue to believe life will get better despite the circumstances around you.

So today: when life hands you lemons, make lemonade. Dare to be hopeful. Every situation in life won't end in disappointment and frustration. Trust, Pray and Believe. Speak light into the atmosphere and watch in manifest.

O Lord, thank you for this day. Help me to stay hopeful in the midst of disappointment. Allow me to speak light and hope in my life.

Be a catalyst for change. ☺

DAY 105: The Unexpected

Today is about the unexpected.

When I was in college, my friends and I wanted to pledge a sorority. When at an all-girl school, it's difficult to become a part of a sorority because it too much competition. We decided to attempt to upgrade our status by participating in a talent show.

We decided to be Salt n Pepa and rap 'Push It.' We went and got these awful asymmetrical wigs, cat suits, and riding boots. I came up with great choreography and we were ready.

My girlfriend in the middle was supposed to be Spinderella. There was a crucial part of the routine and she was supposed to drop her body and duck. Then our other friend and I were supposed to kick over her head. Well, she didn't duck far enough like she had done at practice and we both kicked her in her head.

Sometimes, the unexpected happens. When you can have the best laid plans only for things to go haywire. It's difficult to pinpoint when everything went wrong, but it did.

Do not waste time attempting to figure out. Just pick yourself up and get back in the race of life. Life comes in stages of growth and you have to take it in each stage. Each of them is important to your long-term stability.

God will sometimes allow your plans to fail so you can see only God has all of the power. While it may be hurtful, ultimately it will help you to get to the next stage of your life.

It also gives you a testimony so you can be a beacon of life to others.

So today, when the unexpected happens, instead of asking, "Why me?" Ask "why not?" Allow yourself to be a vessel for the Lord and help others bask in the greatness God has to offer.

O Lord, thank you for this day. Help me not become despondent when the unexpected happens. Help me to become a better believer and to know you have my back no matter what.

Be the catalyst for change. ☺

DAY 106: Grief

Today is about grief.

When my grandmother died, she has been sick for a while. She took a turn for the worse and we stayed late into the night with her and then went home.

Prior to going back to the hospice care facility, I wanted to go for my daily run. It was drizzling, which is fine, but began to rain really hard. I continued to run while becoming absolutely drenched.

Then, I begin to feel nauseous and hurled onto the steps of an art museum. I began to feel like I was going to pass out. I ran out of the house with no money, keys or even a phone. So I had to walk back to my house, which was pretty far away. I was utterly alone. Once I got back home, got dressed to go to the hospice care facility. I found out she was already gone and probably passed away while I was out on my run.

Grief is a powerful thing when it hits you. It usually comes with a little friend by the name of guilt. It's easy to see the mistakes of our past and ponder what we would do differently.

Once guilt settles in, the waves of disappointment and disgust in our own behavior set up.

Grief is part of life, especially after a death, however guilt isn't. Do not allow guilt to override your spirit until you feel worthless.

All of us are human and make mistakes. You did the best you could with the tools you had. God knows.

So today if you're grieving: allow yourself to miss your loved one but don't feel guilty for the past. Your heart was in the right place and God forgives you even if it wasn't.

O Lord, thank you for this day. Give me strength during this time of bereavement. Allow me to miss my loved one but not injure myself with guilt of past behavior. Help me to forgive myself, which is the hardest form of forgiveness.

Be the catalyst for change.☺

DAY 107: Curiosity

Today is about curiosity.

My college boyfriend (i.e. the great love of my life) is now married. One of my best girlfriends from college saw he and his wife while on vacation in Myrtle Beach.

She gave me all of the details of how his new wife looked and how he looked now. Even thought I have clearly moved on, I can't help but be a bit curious.

Curiosity is a desire to know, to pry or snoop. Curiosity isn't always a good thing and can lead to further actions. My curiosity about my college boyfriend was out of insecurity and frustration about my own failed relationship. I wanted to be the first to be married but unfortunately that wasn't the case.

When life doesn't go the way you plan, it's easy to allow yourself to be curious to see if your life is better than theirs. This is a no-win situation. We must focus on our game and not others.

So today: move past the curiosity and desire to know. It's not healthy. Focus on God and His healing powers so you can become busy living the life you have always dreamed, instead of wondering 'what if.'

O Lord, thank you for this day. Please forgive me for knowing and unknowing sins. Help to move past the curiosity that leads nowhere. Allow me to focus on my life and not on the lives of others.

Be the catalyst for change. ☺

DAY 108: Going Home Again

Today is about going home again.

I grew up in the suburbs of south Atlanta, Georgia. While I enjoyed my childhood, I always loved coming into the city to enjoy the sites. I vowed when I became an adult I would live in the city.

While I still live in the same city where I grew up, I live in a completely different area with a different lifestyle. A little of Sex in the City with the Hills. With no sex of course. ☺

I love the sights and smells of city living. However, I do still long for the comforts of childhood and suburbia. Less crime, more eateries with mega portions.

It's still good to go home where I'm from. Home is where you roots are and foundation. Home isn't an actual structure but a state of mind where you feel the most content. While we're running in the race of life, it's easy to become lost and lose our way home.

God is part of home and state of mind. He can calm us when we're at a loss, He can be a mother, father, best friend, confidante. He is the best One to talk to in the face of adversity.

So today: don't be afraid to go home again. Allow yourself to rediscover your roots and a time when things were so difficult and not complicated. Get in touch with God. He will show you the path.

O Lord, thank you for this day. Please forgive me for my sins. Allow me to visit home again and allow the good positive experience to wash over me. Help me to see this reconnection allows me to thank you for how far I have come but yet know how far I still need to go.

Be the catalyst for change. ☺

DAY 109: Shock

Today is about shock.

When I went to graduate school, I made another vacation to Miami. During this trip, we had gotten a good deal at a hotel through a classmate of mine who rode down with us. He wanted to come down to visit his son and had placed the entire hotel bill on his credit card and then we gave him cash.

We noticed from the moment we parted with our cash, it seemed our key card wouldn't open the door. Then, by the end of the second day, we got a call that the credit card was declined and we needed to use another method of payment. However, my girlfriends and I had already given my classmate cash. We called him and he told us just to use one of our credit cards. We said no and we were coming to get the money we had given him. He tried to discourage us but we were adamant. We didn't have directions back to his son's house where he was staying and we had dropped him off. He abruptly gave us directions and we left immediately.

We noticed we were going away from Miami and further into the swamps of the Everglades. However, we continued following the directions. Then we came to a bridge with an operator who asked for $25.00 so we could ride through the Everglades? What $%&*!!!!

We eventually figured out how to get back to his son's house and got our money back. He didn't have any money for his portion that amounted to gas, et cetera. So we had to leave a day early. We told him what time we were leaving and he needs to let us know if he was riding back. He didn't want to leave early but we didn't care. So when we didn't hear from him the morning we were supposed to leave, we left Miami without a second thought.

He called four hours later, asking if we were still there. By then, we were already in Tallahassee.

There are times in life went we have shocking experiences. Some of the experiences are good, such as finding the love of your life and some bad, like finding out someone will not live up to your expectations.

While these events can be disheartening, they're strategically placed in our lives by God for a reason. Sometimes the reason is revealed, sometimes it's not. What's important is to take the experience at face value and move past it. Sometimes the importance of a shocking experience isn't its origin but rather how you deal with the situation.

So today, don't allow shocking lessons to rock your world. Allow yourself to learn from the experience but then move on. Handle it with grace and move up to the next level of spiritual growth.

O Lord, thank you for this day. Help me get through this shocking experience but not hinder my mind or process. Allow me to understand all that happens to me. Help me to continue to trust you in this race called life.

Be the catalyst for change. ☺

DAY 110: Expectation

Today is about expectation.

To get my first car, my parents and I had a deal that they would match whatever I came up with. I worked two jobs prior to my senior year so I could drive up on the first day of my senior year in style.

What I didn't count on was not passing my driver's license test. Sometimes, things don't happen the way you would expect.

Expectation is the anticipation of something happening, hope or prospect for the future. It's exciting when you have expectations of something great occurring. What isn't so much, is when the expectation isn't fulfilled. What makes it even more difficult is when God gives you a revelation about it.

Where are you supposed go on from here?

God will sometimes provide expectations to help you get to the next stage of your life. We all need something to believe in and expectations fulfill that job.

It's dangerous for anyone who stops believing or expecting anything out of life. God will send expectations so you will still be on the path of righteous while dealing with a testing period.

No one can take constant bad news. We all need something to believe, to rely on during this race of life.

So today, continue to believe and expect great things, despite whether they have occurred in the past. God has mysterious ways and he knows how our story will end. Allow Him leverage in the process. Trust Him; He will never steer off course.

O Lord, thank you for this day. Help renew my faith in you and increase my expectations. Do not allow me to slip into depression and frustration when expectations are not fulfilled. Allow my faith and trust to increase.

Be the catalyst for change.☺

DAY 111: Annoyed

Today is about being annoyed.

My dad is a great preacher and when I was in college he would go to visit a lot of sick members. The only problem is that he wouldn't accurately tell me how long the visit would take. Of course, by the time it was 11:30 pm at night and I had missed a date, I would be steaming mad.

Being annoyed is a part of life. At some point, a situation or someone will cause you and become frustrated or angry. However, what if it's God?

God has our best interest at heart. However, there will be a time in your life when you become angry with Him when your ideas and His ideas for your life don't mesh.

You may get passed over for that big promotion, new job, or experience devastation in your personal life. This is all part of God's shaping and molding process. It doesn't feel good but it's essential. Imagine feeling your growing during a growth spurt.

However, spiritually that's exactly what's happening. In the spiritual, we consider it part of life but in the physical, we get both easily annoyed and frustrated.

God loves us all exactly as we are right now in this point in our lives. While we may be annoyed with outcomes at times, allow yourself to trust God. Reflect on the times He got you out of difficult situations. Allow the anger to drift and get back on the mend.

So today: allow yourself to be annoyed but only for a second. Then move yourself past it. God has our best interests at heart. Allow yourself to move past and allow your faith in God to carry you.

O Lord, thank you for this day. Help to get past annoyed feelings and emotions of frustration and aggravation. Help me to trust and know God knows what's best for me... more than I know myself.

Be the catalyst for change. ☺

DAY 112: Confidence

Today is about confidence

I was definitely a weird child. I remember in the fourth grade, I went through a stage when I would collect rocks and bones and bring them home. That is, until my Mother told me one day I would bring home a dead dog. That ended my hobby.

My mother wasn't confident in my new hobby.

There will be times in your life when you won't get the support you need for a new project, relationship, et cetera.

These are times when you must show confidence in yourself and in your abilities. Confidence is about helping to foster something, cheer, persuade and support.

Confidence comes from within, not outwardly. You must dig within yourself to build confidence.

Confidence is knowing despite the chaos around you, knowing that situation will change.

Confidence is knowing you can do a job when you do not have experience in that area.

Confidence is knowing you're a beacon of light and anyone who cannot see your light must need glasses.

Confidence is swagger, knowledge that you can make it happen, not because of your intelligence but your desire to succeed.

Remember, the one who endures wins the race, not always the fastest one. ☺

So today, dare to be a more confident self. Strip away all of your insecurities from the past and dare to step into your destiny in a bold new way.

O Lord, thank you for this day. Help me to exude confidence. Allow me not to be distracted by haters and those with no swagger. Strengthen my inner resolve that I can take on anything regardless of anything.

Be the catalyst for change. ☺

DAY 113: Choosing

Today is about choosing.

When in elementary school, we were supposed to look at various musical instrument and told to choose our preferred one. I wanted to play a violin and was set to go. Until my mother got involved and decided I should play the clarinet, the instrument my mother played in college.

The opportunity to make a selection was removed and I was devastated.

However, many times in life, the power to choose is eliminated. It can be at work, home, or even in a relationship. For whatever the reason, the ability and power to choose was taken away from you. This is a crummy set of circumstances for sure.

While it's frustrating, there is a purpose to the madness that you haven't been made privy to.

There are situations in life when you're only given a portion of the big picture. Then slowly, all of the portions of the picture are revealed. Then you'll understand the whole purpose.

It's hard to make accurate and clear choices when you're not aware of all of the perspectives involved. That's when God must step in and make the choices for you. This keeps you for making bad decisions that can follow you for a lifetime.

So today, thank God when He takes over the choosing. This means the next crucial step in your life can't be left up to chance.

O Lord, thank you for this day. Please forgive me for my knowing and unknowing sins. Allow me to give up control so you can make clear choices for me. When you take control, allow me to submit to Your will and know what is best.

Be the catalyst for change.☺

DAY 114: Being Knocked Down

Today is about being knocked down.

When I was in the second grade, I was hanging upside down on the jungle gym and a classmate was playing monster. Monster consisted of her running around on the ground tickling everyone who was hanging upside down. When she tickled me, I started laughing and lost my grip and fell on the ground headfirst.

I was completely thrown off guard. I was knocked down.

On this race called life, there are times in life you will be knocked down. You will be talked about, and lied upon. People will take advantage of you. The blows will come from so many different places; you won't be able to protect yourself.

Rejoice that you're being promoted by God. Anytime God allows such blows to come upon you there is a method to the madness. Allow yourself not to get dismayed by the process but understand God is shaping and refining you into something special. Every blow is building your testimony to be a blessing for others. How can you truly sympathize with someone unless you have been there?

That's why pastors usually have some rather devastating background stories. They must go through so much heartache and pain to understand the plight of their future congregation without judgment. So the larger and bigger the blows, they larger the calling on your life. Know each blow, disappointment, and frustration point is a labor of love. Do not allow Satan to get into your mind and claim it's punishment.

The Lord is in the blessing business and will restore all that's lost to you. So buckle down and get though the experience with the expectations that there's a purpose in it all.

So today: get back up when you're knocked down. Dust yourself off and continue in the race of life. The race is given to those who are patient and endure the race, not to the fastest.

O Lord, thank you for this day. Help me to be enveloped into your love. Allow me to weather the blows of life and to know better times are around the bend if I just believe.

Be the catalyst for change. ☺

DAY 115: Indulging Yourself

Today is about indulging yourself.

My daddy and I have always been close. When I was in college, I would always have a break between 1 pm–2pm; we would talk on the phone and watch in the Heat of the Night or Matlock together. When I moved into my own place, he would wash my clothes and put them away for me in my closet.

I was spoiled rotten. I will admit. However, sometimes you need to be indulged even if you do it yourself.

For those who are ambitious we're constantly marching toward greatness. Working hard to make everything happen. However, we rarely take time to stop and smell the roses.

During life, it's important to allow yourself an opportunity to indulge. This is the permission to give yourself a treat of some sort and to be pampered.

Giving yourself a treat can be instrumental in keeping yourself on the pace of the righteous and ambition.

After my first really big check as an entrepreneur. I decided to treat myself to a jewelry cross from Tiffany and Co. My necklace is so important to me because I gave it to myself; it wasn't from anyone. It illustrated my independence from anything or anyone.

So today, allow yourself to indulge. Indulging isn't taking you off the path, in fact; it's strengthening your pace and stride to ensure you can stay on the path of ambition and righteousness.

O Lord, thank you for this day. Help me to stay on the path of righteous. Allow me to indulge myself as a reward without any guilt or remorse.

Be the catalyst for change. ☺

DAY 116: Isolation

Today is about isolation

While in law school, I felt totally isolated. I was in a new town, not city and all my other friends were in major metropolitan cities and having the time of their lives.

It was such an overwhelming experience. There are many ways to hurt someone but the easiest way for Satan to hurt believers is to isolate us.

Isolation is being separate, remote and in seclusion. It's hard to think when you have no one to talk to and bounce thoughts off of.

It can be a harrowing experience.

Isolation can eat at your mind and your self-esteem. It can make you feel unworthy of love and kindness.

Having an active prayer life is essential when you're feeling isolated. If you don't rely on prayer, you can look for a connection with anything or anyone who can change your life in an instant.

God will never leave or forsake you, even when He is silent. He is still with you; God will also be with you until the end of time.

So on today: step up your prayer life when you're feeling isolated. This will melt those separated and distant feelings. Remember, God is only a prayer a way.

O Lord, Thank you for this day. Help me resist feelings of hopeless when I'm feeling isolated, Help me to understand you're always with me no matter what.

Be the catalyst for change. ☺

DAY 117: Flipping Out

Today is about flipping out.

When I was 16, I would visit my sister, all the time, at Howard University. One visit, she had gotten her coveted refund check and had to cash it. She didn't have a car so we had to walk eight city blocks to the bank only to find it was closing. My sister talked to a security guard attempting to get him to let us in until I was so frustrated I started to rant and rave, yelling at the top of my lungs.

Needless to say, we didn't get in the bank that day.

We all have moments when self-control is gone. They approach you so fast you can't control them. For me, I rev up fast if I really care about you. I have to love you to allow myself to lose control to that level now.

I learned to discipline my emotions years ago. There is a time and place for everything but yet there is really no time to express the white-hot rage that has been building inside of you. A limited amount of control can be done when you've reach the point of no return. However, I can help you bounce back from a flipping out moment.

Forgive yourself. Prayer is an active part of your life but prayer can only scratch the surface of yourself when you're open to forgiving yourself. Forgiving yourself is one of the hardest things to do because we are often our worst critic. Rather than blaming others, we end up blaming ourselves as if we have often caused the bad things that happen to us.

So today: if you had a flipping out moment, forgive yourself. There is no right etiquette when you have a moment. We are all human and our breaking points are different. Ask God forgiveness and then move on.

O Lord, thank you for this day. Help me to forgive myself from all of my unsightly behavior. Allow me to realize I'm human and bound to make mistakes.

Be the catalyst for change. ☺

DAY 118: Distancing Yourself

Today is about distancing yourself.

During my freshman fall semester at Howard University, there had a problem with food fights at dinner. It seems every time I went to dinner, there was always a food fight. Being a southerner, I didn't want anything messing up my hair. Eventually I stopped going to dinner in the cafeteria and ate elsewhere.

I begin distancing myself from problems in the cafeteria. Many times in life, you must protect yourself, and this can come in the form of distance.

Distance is sometimes necessary. You can't continue to place yourself in harm's way without the possibility of getting hurt at some point.

Distance can heal the body and mind. It allows you to process all events and find solutions. Some of the best advice I received was to become a reflective person.

I'm extremely action-oriented. You say something and I'm off trying to make it happen. However, it does pay to wait a second and figure out a plan of action before running into the trenches.

So today allow yourself to began distancing yourself from trouble. While it may seem like retreating or even running away, it's essential to maintain a sense of perspective about life.

O Lord, thank you for this day. Help me to distance myself from trouble. Allow me to take a timeout, so I may stay in the race called life.

Be the catalyst for change. ☺

DAY 119: Living a Different World

Today is about living in a different world.

When I first came to Howard University, I was really something…a bit extra. I was appalled by the lack of air conditioning. The residents in my hall were surprised I came to college with over fifteen big boxes of just clothing and a loud southern drawl. I instantly earned the nickname of 'Whitley' from 'The Cosby Show' spinoff cult hit 'A Different World.'

When God really enters your heart as an adult, you live in a different world. Things you used to like to do, you won't do. You will be a new creature in Christ.

This can overwhelm you and your past life.

It will take some time to find your footing. You must figure out your place in the world all over again. While it can be slightly trying, it's best for you in the long run.

God softly whispers the directions of His will and glory if we just stop and listen. Allow God's mercy and holy spirit to transform you from the inside out.

You will morph into a new person, the person you were destined to be.

So today, if you experience some uneasiness after God has transformed you, relax. It's part of spiritual life. Take it day-by-day. Each day will be easier and more comfortable.

O Lord, thank you for this day. Allow my spiritual to setting in my different world. Help me to bask in the presence of God. Allow me to know and understand you have my best interest in Your heart and I can trust You.

Be the catalyst for change. ☺

DAY 120: Counting to Ten

Today is about counting to ten.

There I was, lying on my bed like a Flag of Action.

A Captain Crunch Granola Bar.

My roommate at Howard University was selfish. She would always lock her snacks in her desk but eat all of mine. The last straw was my sister had brought me a box of Captain Crunch the day before. The next day when I came home from class, the treat was on my bed. It's common knowledge that it takes a lot of tenacity to get down to the treat in just one day. I was filled with fury; she would pay for this disrespect.

Ok, I have a bit of a temper. I work hard to control it. I used to get mad at every little thing like this but I got older and was able to control my emotions.

Sometimes things will occur; they make you so angry you must take a moment to pause.

The pause is a break, an opportunity to make a good decision. It's also an opportunity to allow God to speak to you and guide your steps.

Everything that annoys or upsets doesn't need to be acted upon. However, it takes time and a trained listening ear from God to understand you must count to ten before reacting.

So today: take your time before responding to something angering you. Not only will it allow God to speak to you, it will also provide serenity to enter your spirit as well.

O Lord, thank you for this day. Help me to pause before responding so you may speak to me. Help me to focus on hearing from You instead of the problems brewing.

Be the catalyst for change. ☺

DAY 121: Fantasy

Today is about fantasy.

When we were in eighth grade, my friends and I were absolutely obsessed with the LA rap scene, mostly NWA, Snoop Dogg, and Dr. Dre. We all wore white t-shirts with a plaid shirt on top with it buttoned at the very top. We were totally suburban kids with no real connection with violence but were so hard. Or so we thought.

We got caught up in the fantasy. Fantasies are mental image, impractical idea. A dream is a tangible possibility and a fantasy isn't.

Sometimes in life, when we have a mental image that isn't founded in reality. It's our version of what we want life to be without a game plan.

We'll attempt to make a fantasy become a reality and that's simply not possible. When God puts a vision of destiny in your spirit it will also promote the glory of God not to go against it.

When it's aligned with the Glory of God, it's a Dream or vision, not a fantasy. Fantasy does not promote any positive energy except an escape from the real world.

So today: do not allow your fantasy to overcome your reality. Stay founded in God's will and allow His peace to manifest itself.

O Lord, thank you for this day. Forgive me for knowing and unknowing sins. Help me not attempt to make a fantasy my reality. Allow me to trust you to manifest the right vision at the right time.

Be the catalyst for change.☺

MONTH 5

DAY 122: Spiritual Growth

Today is about spiritual growth.

When I was in the fifth grade, I already had a chosen career path: to be a backup dancer for MC Hammer and travel the world. My friends and I already had a videotape of us dancing to send to him so we could start our chosen career path.

It's amazing how much can occur during our spiritual growth. Spiritual growth involves development, evolution, progress or advancement. Sometimes, what you think you want to do with your life is in stark contrast to what God has ordained for you.

It takes time and growth to be able to see past our needs and allow God to have complete control over our life. Spiritual growth is a process; it cannot be expedited. It's not about the end result; the power is in the journey. Embrace it.

You must also have patience as you grow. Certain life lessons cannot be rushed. You must allow yourself to present in the situations despite how unbearable it may be.

So today: allow yourself to ponder your spiritual growth. Allow yourself to savor the experience. It's the food for the soul.

O Lord, thank you for the day. I thank you for my spiritual growth so I may be a testimony to others. Help me to gain patience to endure this process.

Be the catalyst for change.☺

DAY 123: Progress

Today is about progress.

While in elementary school, I was a cool nerd. While well liked in school, I absolutely loved to read. I was a monster when it came to BOOK IT.

BOOK IT! runs every school year from October through March. The teacher sets a reading goal for each child in the class. A tracking chart is included to make it that much easier. As soon as a child meets the monthly reading goal, the teacher gives him or her a Reading Award Certificate. The restaurant manager and team congratulate every child for meeting the monthly reading goal and reward them with a free, one-topping Personal Pan pizza, BOOK IT! card.

To me, it was the best of both worlds. ☺ I love to eat and read. I was in heaven. I was enjoying the progress I was making.

Progress is the positive development, improvement and process. Progress is a great consequence of hard work.

God will bless us with an ability to see the manifestation of our hard work—to see that all of our hard work has not been in vain. It's a great time in life when you can see the evolution of your ideas, business ventures, or even your spirit.

However, you must learn to trust God during the dark times. Without the dark times, you wouldn't be able to progress. You would remain at the status quo.

Every piece of progress eventually leads to the breakthrough you have been praying for.

So today, if you're in a dark time in suspended motion. Trust God. Allow His urging to lead you in the right direction. He has our best interests at heart.

O Lord, thank you for this day. Thank you for allowing progress to occur in my life. Allow me to focus on every little step so I make it in the race called life.

Be the catalyst for change.☺

DAY 124: Discouraged

Today is about being discouraged.

Growing up, I was the worst runner ever. That's why it's so interesting that now as an adult, I'm pretty good.

I was the slowest in my group. All of my friends in my elementary school clique were faster than me. So much so that I just stopped trying to compete. So when there were races during field day and other activities, I would bow out and be the timekeeper or something. I blamed it on having a heart murmur, but really I was just slow and discouraged.

Being discouraged is a part of life. Being discouraged is when you're less than optimistic, lacking expectation and being overall dejected.

We are all human. You cannot be the best at everything in life. There are times you may not provide less than stellar work. It's part of life.

You may want to exceed expectations only to realize you can't even meet them. This can be a heart wrenching but humbling experience.

However, this is the precise moment when you're in line to receive a miracle. God can provide a blessing about something you know you can't do on your own. When that miracle occurs, you have become a testament to God's power.

So today: don't allow yourself to become discouraged. Pick yourself up and continue to run in this race of life. Run into God's welcoming arms and allow Him to give you the strength to continue.

O Lord, thank you for this day. Help me not become discouraged when life throws me a curve ball. Allow me to have enough patience and faith to weather the storms of life.

Be the catalyst for change.☺

DAY 125: The Wrong Idea

Today is having the wrong idea.

When I became student government president at the end of my junior year. I was like, finally I'm going to impact change in my community. I was super excited until I was informed I didn't get a chance to run anything but rather my advisor made the real decisions.

I quickly became disillusioned and unhappy with my role. All the hard work for nothing.

I had the wrong idea.

We have been confident in the wrong things. We believe certain things will occur when in fact they won't. It's difficult to get past when our blessing we prayed for turns out to be a nightmare.

At times, that blessing can be a nightmare and nightmares can be blessings. It's important to stay focused on God and prayerful in order to keep frustration and resentment at bay.

There is always a method to the madness. It's not our purpose to know God's ways but trust them. God has a unique place for all of our lives and it's up to us to stay on the path of righteous in order to see the plan come to fruition.

So today: do not allow yourself to get the wrong idea because of resentment and disappointment. There is purpose in all things God does. Allow yourself to trust Him and be patient as His plan is being revealed.

O Lord, thank you for this day. Help me not to get the wrong idea about God's place for the rest of my life. Help me to be patient and trust Him.

Be the catalyst for change.☺

DAY 126: It's Your Time

Today it is your time.

When I was in high school, I really blossomed. I really didn't have much luck with the boys until I got contacts and became more active in school. My first real boyfriend was a senior when I was a freshman. It was such a big deal and a real boost to my confidence. All of my girlfriends who were major players in middle school were no longer, once we got to high school. It was my time to shine.

The time has come. There have been so many false starts; it's easy to become despondent and just go through life without any expectations.

Then it finally happens: your breakthrough. It's your time.

When breakthroughs happen, there isn't a parade or fireworks. It's one good thing after another until you realize this is my time.

There are very few times in life when it's your time. When it's your time, you can potentially ruin being in shock.

While in a testing experience, life can be so tough that it's like being in a desert. When you come into your moment, then it seems like your oasis, a fantasy.

It's not. It's a real blessing and breakthrough. Thank God and savor the event. Become a testament to God's amazing capabilities. However, take advantage of all the amazing opportunities God has bestowed upon you.

So today: this is your time. Walk into your destiny. Be a walking testimony waiting on their breakthrough. Help others who are struggling underneath the burdens of this life.

O Lord, thank you for this day. Please forgive me for my sins. This is my time and I thank you for this blessing. Help me to trust there are not problems lurking around the corner and for me to take full advantage of the opportunities around me.

Be the catalyst for change.☺

DAY 127: Shock

Today is about shock.

I got the shock of my young life when the Senior will and testament was printed at the end of my freshman year for the Class of 1994. The most beautiful girl in school and the only African American girl on the homecoming court left me something. I was surprised she even knew who I was. I grabbed the newspaper and was shocked to read she left me my boyfriend.

Apparently, she had been dating him during high school and until I came along. I was so shocked; I didn't know what to do.

Shock is upsetting feelings, distressing, upsetting and completely unexpected. Shock can also be stunning. Sometimes it's experiences in life that are completely unexpected.

There's nothing that can be done to prepare for these experience. These are truly sink or swim situations.

Day-to-day living is your homework assignments and the final exams are your shocking experiences in the school of life. Having an active prayer life and strong belief system are key to passing the testing periods.

Don't question the origin of attempt to understand how or why this situation has occurred. Just allow yourself to focus on making it through the situation with as much poise and discipline as possible.

O Lord, thank you for this day. Allow me to get past this shock of disrespect and disappointment. Help me to remember everyone is human and isn't perfect. Allow me to see I must stay focused on You and divine will.

Be the catalyst for change.☺

DAY 128: Life Changing Events

Today is about life changing events.

I met my high school sweetheart while working at Footaction at my local mall. He was tall, fair skinned with dark hair. Just my type at the time. He brought some FILA stuff and asked for my number.

At the time, I was attempting to figure out who I would take to prom my senior year and was having a bit of anxiety over it. Then he came alone one Wednesday evening and everything changed. We dated off and on for about four years.

It amazing how your life can change in an instant.

Life changing events don't start with great fanfare. They usually begin with a seemingly mundane moment.

Sometimes, when you're in the midst of a testing experience, you look for hope in every situation only to be disappointing by attempting to find relevancy in every situation.

Continue to live life as normal and this life-changing event will come into your life without having to seek them out. These experiences will be effortless and completely created by God.

So today: go out about your daily living. When you concentrate on just daily living, a life changing experience will pop up without any fanfare. Embrace the process and allow yourself to live in the moment day-by-day.

O Lord, thank you for this day. Please forgive me for my sins. Help me to enjoy daily living while quietly anticipate life changing events without succumbing to disappointment and resentment.

Be the catalyst for change.☺

DAY 129: Needing a Do Over

Today is about needing a do over.

When I met my college sweetheart, it was love at first sight, kinda. I was waiting to enter the classroom for my religion class at Clark Atlanta. There was another class prior to ours and this totally hot guy came out. He saw me staring at him and smiled. He was sooooo cute. (Can you tell I'm shallow? LOL) He was about 5"10, brown skinned with a slim build. He looked like Taye Diggs, the famous actor.

So every time this class was held, I would make sure I got there early to flirt with this guy. We began to chat a bit and eventually exchanged information. We both thought the other went to Clark Atlanta but it turned out we had a brother/sister connection. He was a Morehouse man and I was student at Spelman college. Our schools had brother/sister relationships and were across the street from each other. Spelhouse love. It was totally meant to me. Until I found out my best friend absolutely hated him.

We still dated briefly and moved on to other people. We really didn't connect until our senior year and it was great.

There're many reasons why you need a do over. Could be a mixture of bad timing combined with a lot of other mitigating factors.

A do over is an opportunity to go over new ground, to rediscover a gem that inadvertently got left behind somehow. It doesn't mean you can't move on, it's merely giving fresh eyes to an already established alternative.

So today: consider a do over in your life. Listen to the urging in your spirit to reconsider a job, tasks or even a person. Only you know what is deemed eligible for a do over. Allow you and God to guide your path and decision making to know what to do.

O Lord, thank you for this day. Help me have a discerning spirit to make a decision on when to provide a do over. Lord, order my steps so I'm constantly aligned with Your will.

Be the catalyst for change.☺

DAY 130: Living in the Moment

Today is about living in the moment.

So when I met my college boyfriend, he wanted my friends and me to travel with his friends to Miami for spring break. Of course, I found that my best friend hated him so we didn't travel together. His last day in Miami was our first day there. So we decided to hang out after club. We walked on the beach but it was super windy that night. So we just walked around South Beach and then watched the sunrise together. No sex, just the sweet puppy dog love. Everyone was so jealous when I got back and I wished that moment could last forever.

Living in the moment can be a good thing at times. It allows you not to over-think situations and take the fun out of them.

Living in the moment is being present in that instant. Don't think about the past or the future. Just what is occurring right now.

This can also encourage a contentment in life. When life throws you curve balls, you must be able to continue on the path of life without hitting ground each time. You can develop this endurance when you learn to be content in daily living but still anticipating a break through.

This means being able to go to movies, hang out with friends and family. Being able to appreciate the good things in your life at this moment but still focusing on getting to the next level.

You must be able to pay homage to the blessing God has already given you, otherwise why should He bless you when you can't appreciate what He has already done.

So today: live in the moment. Allow yourself to relax in your spirit so you can enjoy the little blessing God gives us daily.

O Lord, thank you for this day. Thank you for the little blessings You give me daily. Help me to enjoy being in Your presence more and living in the moment. Allow me to show thanks for all you have done for me.

Be the catalyst for change.☺

DAY 131: Going for It

Today is about going for it.

When I met my muse, my second great love, I was at a nightclub by my house. This average guy approached me wanting my number and I was ok with it until his friend came over. He was absolutely spectacular, he was sooooo cute but incredibly smart. He was about 5"10, fair skinned with a bald head, which is what I love. He looked like Chico DeBarge to me, so I was instantly attracted. He was totally into politics. It had just come after a disappointing situation where I had to drop out of the mayor's race in 2005 and I was feeling a little hateful. He totally knew who I was and was becoming increasingly more attracted. He expressed interest in running for office some day. However, then I felt like I wasn't ready for him. He seemed to be optimistic and happy that I wasn't sure I was ready. Plus his friend already had my number.

I went out with his friend with the hope of seeing this other guy again. I eventually stopped talking to the other guy because I knew my real emotions would come out.

Then, fast forward two years later. I'm feeling more confident and ready to settle down. I saw him at a lounge and went in for the kill. Was it drama because of his friend? Yes but it was worth it. I didn't care; I'd made a decision to go for it.

During life, there are times when all of us, for various reasons, can become a little gun shy. A little scared to put it all on the line for someone else. I didn't want the situation to be the cause of discomfort or difficulty for ourselves and others.

Nothing in life comes without some form of sacrifice. You can't please everyone, there will always be someone who disagrees with actions or thoughts. Pay no attention to the peanut gallery. You must be willing to go the extra mile and fight for what you want and believe in.

So today, be willing to go for it. Throw caution to the wind and becoming more daring. Allow yourself to push past your discomfort and go after what you want.

O Lord, thank you for this day. Please forgive me for my knowing and unknowing sins. Help me get the confidence to go aggressively after what I want. Help me to understand the only person who is holding me back is me.

Be the catalyst for change.☺

DAY 132: Lack of Focus

Today is about a lack of focus.

When I decided I wanted to be an attorney, I enrolled in the Kaplan prep class over the summer between my junior and senior year. I did decent but not as well as my other friends. I was too busy trying to work and partying that summer. My heart wasn't in it.

The focus and discipline I have now, wasn't always there. I have always enjoyed socializing but I had to learn you must sacrifice for your goals in order obtain true success.

That's the key to ambition. Knowing the right time and project to focus on and become disciplined about.

Allow God to lead your path. He will give you a discerning spirit that will lead you to make clear and accurate decision. While it may be difficult to know how to make a logical decision, go to God under his throne of grace.

Allow yourself to talk to God the way you would speak to a loving parent or grandmother. God loves you beyond our comprehension. He will be there for us and believe in us even when we don't believe in ourselves.

So today, don't be dismayed by your lack of focus. Pray for the Lord to give further instruction and motivation to move into your destiny.

O Lord, thank you for this day. Help me to become more focused and driven. Please order my steps and provide me with vision in this, my race called life, so I will know how to guide myself in my breakthrough.

DAY 133: Hustler

Today is about being a hustler.

I have always been an entrepreneur. When I was in second grade, I would sell wrapping bows that were unraveled and curled to look like streamers and my homemade bookmarks for fifty cents each. I was always chasing a dollar.

The word 'hustler' is considered to have a negative connotation. However, it's not negative; a hustler is an aggressive determined person.

A person with unwavering focus, who is strong-minded and firm.

A hustler is someone who goes in early and leaves later. A person who works two jobs to save up for a business and feed their family. A person who doesn't complain about problems but rather find solutions.

That's a hustler. They will find a way or make one.

Allow yourself to take a hustler persona. Ask fewer questions and just get to work on getting your life on track.

Sometimes, attempting to find the origin of a problems can be a waste of time. It doesn't solve anything and enduring any easier.

However, a quest for 'why' can become a never-ending journey that helps or resolves nothing.

So today: become a hustler. Focus on solutions rather than moaning and complaining about problems. Problems will be with us until the end of time. When our defining moment is how we choose to handle them.

Lord, thank you for this day. Please forgive me for my sins. Allow me to believe in you and your will. Allow me to focus on solutions and not problems.

Be the catalyst for change.☺

DAY 134: Wasting Time

Today is about wasting time.

My senior year in college we would spend hours attempting to get free parking. Spelman college built a parking deck for $3.00 a day but we were too cheap to pay $3.00 or even buy a parking pass. We would wait hours before class so we could park in the free parking space. We even had a script. "Excuse me, are you leaving for the day? May I follow you to your parking space? Thank you."

There are many times in life we waste time by not having a clear logical plan. A plan is an intention, layout, outline or strategy.

Each aspect in life should have a general plan. If you don't have a plan, you'll wander around life without any clear direction. Life without clear direction is sailing a boat without a map—or now, driving a car without a GPS.

God wants us all to be successful and wants to provide us with a plan if you just open ourselves to listen. The only way to listen to God is keep in active prayer life. When you talk to God, you can hear Him as well.

How can you expect to hear from God when you don't spend any time listening to Him?

So today: don't allow yourself to waste time due to illogical and poorly thought out plans. Allow yourself to spend a little time with God and listen to Him. His ways are always best.

O Lord, thank you for this day. Help me not to waste time. Allow me to spend more time listening so my steps can be in order in your divine will.

Be the catalyst for change.☺

DAY 135: Addiction

Today is about addiction.

I always had a fascination with weave from the moment I placed that first track in my hair when I was sixteen years old. I was hooked. It was a ten-year off and on love affair that ended recently last year. Some don't believe we are done but I think I'm ready to deal with other issues instead of being preoccupied with hair related issues.

I was completely addicted to weave. Not just to the hair but the response I received from men while wearing it. It made me feel very confident and attractive. However, I was living a false self.

It wasn't really me but a version of me I thought people liked. Only until I had the confidence to stop living a false version of myself then I realized I was beautiful naturally the way God intended for me to be.

It's easy to become addicted. Some are addicted to food, sex, attention, drugs, smoking, alcohol, or weave. We tell ourselves we don't really have problem and we can stop anytime we want.

By the time we realize the situation is beyond our control, we're deep in the throes of the addiction. Addiction isn't about being weak or out of control. It's about being dependent on something, a need or infatuation. Any time you think you can't live without something is a sign of addiction and compulsion.

What do you do if you find yourself in the throes of addiction? You must forgive yourself. There is a huge amount of shame involved with addiction. Disappointment in your own behavior. Cut yourself some slack. We are all human and, at times, prone to develop habits with ease. Some are positive and others not so much.

Slowly remove yourself from all triggers causing a backslide into the addiction and finally ask for additional help. It could be from anyone you believe who can help you through the situation. A friend, family member or spiritual counselor can get you on the right path.

So today: kick that addiction. Forgive yourself and move on with your life. Pace yourself day-by-day to remove the need from your life. Trust that God will get you out of this situation just as He has before.

O Lord, thank you for this day. Help me to give up my addiction. Please take the craving out of my mind, body, and spirit. Allow me to understand addiction happens to the best of us and you can heal me from anything.

Be the catalyst for change.☺

DAY 136: Jumping Into the Deep

Today is about jumping into the deep.

I never learned to swim. Because I either had glasses or contacts, I never wanted to risk anything happening with my eyes. Sure I will put on a bikini and play around in the water but I will never get past waist deep water, which is very little for me since I'm so short. I just have a complex over water.

Add to my fear after my family members who almost died in Hurricane Katrina and I'm good about not wanting to be around water long-term.

I need to be able to get away from water at any time.

My fear of the water is similar to some of us about jumping into the deepness of life.

While I'm a very inquisitive person, I can be comfortable living a shallow lifestyle with clear surface conversations, friendships, and feelings.

It's become shallow because you're immune to hurt, harm or danger but nothing can touch you because you've shut yourself off from any real significant issues.

However, there are times in everyone's life you must get beyond the shallow end of life and jump into the deep.

Jumping in too deep is pondering life's questions only God can answer. Those questions are even difficult to ponder. Allow yourself to get over the initial discomfort; move past shallowness and into the deep.

So today: allow your jump into the deepness of your conscious mind. There are many things we harbor that inhibit us from being close friends and family, even God. We must allow ourselves to let go so we can experience the intimacy we crave.

O lord, thank You for this day. Help me to move past a shallow lifestyle into the deepness of a fulfilling life. Allow me to open myself up to You and trust You to protect me.

Be the catalyst for change.☺

DAY 137: Being Free

Today is about Being Free.

When I was in band in high school, I hated it. I always had to take off my lipstick to play the clarinet and it sucked. I thought I was too fly at the time. However, my mother wouldn't let me quit. Then, one day, she finally relented after a marathon begging session. I'm not sure what changed but I was glad to be free.

There are some things in life we don't like doing but we have to for various reasons. It could be not drinking, going to work in a job you hate, going to school, etcetera.

However, there's a purpose in doing these trying tasks. There's a lesson to be learned.

God will sometimes send us on assignment to teach us something we will need when we receive our breakthrough. While it's not particularly pleasant, it's needed for us to get to the next level.

So, while the process is restricted, regulated and constrictive, embrace it. If God allowed it, there's a reason for it. Allow your faith to carry you while in a situation you hate. You'll be blessed if you do.

So today: keep plugging away each day. One day you will be free. God has a purpose in every task He assigns to you.

O Lord, thank you for this day. Help me to weather the storms of life while attempting to stay aligned with your will. Help me have faith to trust and believe.

Be the catalyst for change.☺

DAY 138: In Control

Today is about being in control.

I went through a heavy pageant stage in high school. I liked it; it introduced my weave addiction. I never really go far because I'm so short. However, I enjoyed the process and friendships with all of the others girls. Pageant is about being poised and in control.

When I was younger, I was extremely emotional. I wouldn't be able to control myself when I got upset. I still have problems with that when I'm really, really upset. However I have learned to control myself over the years.

Control is about exercising restraint or limits, and ability to manage. God wants us to be able to control ourselves so we can live a true righteous life.

While falling short is often a part of life, we must make an effort to make mistakes less and less frequently as we grow in spiritual maturity.

We work hard on the path of spiritual growth. While it's not pleasant during the process, always remember there's a purpose in all that we do.

God can send us problems as tests in order to determine where we are on the spiritual path otherwise known as life.

So today, work on being in control of yourself and your actions. While it can be difficult at first, it will be increasingly important on the path where God is taking you.

O Lord, thank you for this day. Help me to become more in control of my emotions. Allow me to understand everything works under the will of God even when all has been revealed. Please provide mercy on me when I don't measure up to your will.

Be the catalyst for change.☺

DAY 139: Survival

Today is about survival.

I absolutely adore Carmex. I love it so much I can't survive without putting some on at least three or four time a day. I have at least four to five containers at one time in various places, my purse, bathroom, car, etcetera. So I'm never without one. It's vital to my standard of living.

During these tough economic times, we are all in survival mode. Survival mode is when you outlast your trouble. You cut back to only the necessities and stay focused on getting through day-to-day living.

Being in survival mode helps you to figure out what's a necessity and what's luxury. It's amazing what you can live without when necessary.

God takes us through these tough times to really show us what is important in our lives. These time are character building and humbling at the same time.

What other people are saying no longer matters. What matters is what is in God's heart and direction.

It takes some time to get there but once you get into survival mode long enough, it will come natural.

So today: decide what is a necessity and what is a luxury while in your survival mode. Allow yourself to take only what you need because it helps to refine you as a Christian and is key to spiritual growth.

O Lord, thank you for this day. Help me while I'm in survival mode. I feel ready to give up. Give me the support I need to get past this period in my life and move on to the next level.

Be the catalyst for change.☺

DAY 140: Knowing What is Best

Today is about you knowing what is best.

When I first started my vending business, people though it was such a weird match. They thought I was way too girly to do vending. I explained to them vending wasn't about being girly or not. It was about money. I loved that every time I went to check on a machine, it was payday in cash.

I knew the way the economy was going at the time, I needed another revenue stream. I had already had the experience of being broke in graduate school and didn't want that again.

So I wanted to put every safeguard in place in order to protect myself from any additional harm. That's how my vending business was born.

Doing what's best is doing the best possible thing or circumstances to ensure stability.

When you have negative experience, you never forget the lesson you learned. You will try to do whatever it takes not to have a repeat of that experience.

God will send you the tools needed to safeguard from that experience. While it may seem a little odd to others, you and God know what's best for you.

Whatever is going to ensure your safety of mind, body and spirit, then it must be done.

So today: allow yourself to do what is best for you. While many may not understand it, God does and is directing your path. Allow God to set the tenor of the spiritual ringtone of your life and watch your life ring with promise.

O Lord, thank you for this day. Thank you for guiding me to know what's best. Don't allow me to become distracted by those who understand our plans. Help me to stay focused on you.

Be the catalyst for change.☺

DAY 141: Expect the Unexpected

Today is about expecting the unexpected.

My senior year, I planned a twenty-first birthday celebration for one of my good friends. She had a huge crush on the guy at Morehouse who was extremely popular. I arranged for Him to be her date for the evening, pick her up and show her a good time. When she arrived at the party, she was all smiles because he had given her a dozen roses. I was super excited for her until he pulled me aside and asked to be reimbursed for them.

That was totally unexpected.

On this race called life, there are millions of completely unexpected moments. Some of them good, some bad. What's important is how you deal with the unexpected.

Here are three core rules to help you deal with the unexpected.

Be calm—when the unexpected happens, be calm. There isn't anything worse than flipping out when in a situation commanding a serene spirit. Give yourself a moment to get over the initial shock and then allow God's tranquil spirit to wash over you.

Ask God for Guidance—Ask God for direction of what to focus on first. Go to Him in prayer and allow Him to direct your spirit. Asking God for guidance, will keep you from making foolish mistakes.

Keep a positive attitude—It's essential to keep a positive attitude during unexpected and sometimes shocking events. While you may not understand the purpose in these situations, it's essential you maintain a positive attitude. This allows you to know these circumstances are temporary and to hold on.

So today: always expect the unexpected. While it's not ideal, it's a part of life. Allow yourself to rely on God for strength and direction during this experience.

O Lord, thank you for this day. Help me to deal with unexpected life lessons by being calm, asking You for guidance and keeping a positive attitude. Allow your calming spirit to touch my soul and help in this race of life.

Be the catalyst for change.☺

DAY 142: Mean

Today is about being mean.

My friends and I were prepping for our talent show act while attempting to pledge a sorority. We were so proud of ourselves and ready to give the performance of a lifetime with Salt n Pepa 'Push it.' Another friend in another group wanted to use our wigs. They were performing TLC 'What about your friends?' We thought they had an edge over us because a member of the group was already favored by the sorority. So we told them no.

To be mean is to be unkind, bad-tempered, shameful and nasty. We all have our moments of being mean. None of us are immune.

There are various things to cause a person to act in an unsavory way. For us, it was jealousy and fatigue. It was also the risk that the other group was attempting to take advantage of us.

As people, we sometimes try to take on the role of God. We are not superheroes and our judgment can be fundamentally flawed without realizing it. This is why it's so important to ask God for guidance in all situations.

While you can't avoid human emotion, such as meanness and jealousy, you can ask God to forgive you for your actions and order yourself so when the similar situation happens again, you will also let Jesus take the wheel.

So today: stop being mean. Allow God to order your steps so you're less likely to make decisions off of petty emotion and be closely aligned with His will.

O Lord, thank you for this day. Allow me to keep from being mean and cruel to others in order to protect myself. Help me to rely on God for protection.

Be the catalyst for change.☺

DAY 143: Being Prepared

Today is about being prepared.

One of my best girlfriends was getting married in Houston and I could only be there for one day due to schedule constraints. I flew into town and was in my hotel getting dressed until I suffered a problem, my dress didn't fit. My top was too small.

When I gave my measurements, I went with the measurements saved on my computer from my sister's wedding two years before. I assumed it would work. Wrong! It took two housekeeping maids at the hotel to help zip me into the dress. I couldn't breathe and I looked like the Incredible Hulk.

I wasn't prepared for the wedding at all. There are times when you're unprepared.

When you're unprepared, you're not ready, Ill equipped and untrained. It's a horrible feeling.

Life sometimes throws a wrench into your daily plans; it throws us for a loop. We have to improvise in the process.

It's a lesson to be learned by not being prepared. God sends us this situation to make sure our eyes and ears are continually focused on Him.

It also serves as a wake up to pay attention to all of what's going on around us.

So today: embrace the situation when you're unprepared. Remember, God has a purpose in everything. Allow yourself to see the lesson so it won't happen again.

O Lord, thank you for this day. Please forgive me for knowing and unknowing sins. Help me to become more prepared and stay focused on you.

Be the catalyst for change.☺

DAY 144: Paying the Price

Today is about paying the price.

I was hanging out with some girlfriends eating pizza when I became really sick. I thought the problem was the pizza and thought I had food poisoning but it was my too tight jeans. However, I was determined to wear these jeans and I paid the price by getting sick.

We all pay the price in life. Everything in life has a price. The price is what you're willing to sacrifice to achieve it.

Sacrifice is the loss in giving up something valued, to surrender.

No pain; no gain. You must think long and hard about every choice you make. Regardless of whether you consider it mundane. Even mundane decisions have a price.

You must look to God for strength and direction in order to determine whether the price is worth it. God can provide quiet instructions to ensure you're on the right path.

Are you willing to put it all on the line for this prize? Do you feel this is worth it?

So today: have a good long talk with God and determine if you're willing to pay the price. God is the only one who truly has your best interests at heart. Allow yourself the freedom to speak openly to God and watch Him change your heart.

O Lord, thank you for this day. Allow me to make a decision about whether I'm willing to pay the price. Help me to become stronger in my belief in you and your glory.

Be the catalyst for change.☺

DAY 145: Overwhelmed

Today is about being overwhelmed.

I'm a total sports fanatic. I love football, basketball, golf, even hockey. I love sports because I'm a disciplined person and like to see people who are disciplined like myself reach their goals. It's n overwhelming and inspiring experience to see. I have been reduced to tears more by watching sports than anything else because it's such a pure outpouring of emotion.

While watching sports provides an overwhelming amount of positive emotions, being overwhelmed isn't always a positive experience. Being overwhelmed is being besieged with emotions, inundated, or plagued. It's when you can't think straight and stay focused.

It seems like everyone is pulling on you at once. It's hard to think and make sure you're covering all of your bases in times like this. You just want to get in your car and drive away from it all. However, you can't. There's too much to do and there are too many people counting on you to perform miracles.

You're afraid of disappointing others and also yourself. When your back is against the wall, this is the perfect time to go to God in prayer. God didn't design life to overwhelm us but rather to make us stronger. He wants us to keep our eyes focused on the Hill in which cometh our help.

So today: don't allow life to burden you. While it may be difficult to deal with, just continue to fight the good fight of righteous.

Be the catalyst for change.☺

DAY 146: Feeling the Aftershocks

Today is about feeling the aftershocks.

My parents ended their relationship when I was about seven or eight years old but they attempted to work it over for years afterward. They finally called it quits in the early 1990s. I really didn't think their actions affected me but they did.

Aftershocks are a delayed reaction to a serious event or trauma. When negative things happen to us, we go into protective mode. When we're in protective mode, we're focused on the future and not on the past.

We're proudly marching on the future, stepping over all the leftover problems in the process. However, at some time, they must be addressed or you're bound to repeat problems over and over again.

We must allow ourselves to seek understanding in all that happens in our lives, the good and the bad. This will provide understanding and clarity so we won't make the same mistakes again.

God does take us through certain experiences to refine us and mold us into positive people. However, we must seek understanding in the situation so we won't make the same mistakes again.

Ask the Lord for his grace and mercy to trust Him to handle things you don't understand.

So today: allow yourself to feel the aftershocks. While they may not be pleasant, they're crucial to the personal development.

O Lord, thank you for this day. Help me to feel the aftershocks from all of my childhood trauma. Allow me to make peace with them so I can focus on the future.

Be the catalyst for change.☺

DAY 147: Staying Connected

Today is about staying connected.

I have always had a big family. My dad has seven brothers and sisters so we have always had a lot of cousins around to hang out with at any time. Now we don't get together as much as we should but when we do, it's like a party.

Children, husband, wife, career, dog and life in general. These are just some things that can get in the way of staying connected with your extended family.

While social networking has made keeping in touch easier, we still don't see each other as often as we should.

We have to make a genuine effort to stay connected. This is very similar to our relationship with God.

With so many distractions in our day-to-day life, it's easy to become disconnected from God. While you might be physically present at church, are you emotionally invested and connected?

It's easy to become numb and drift day-to-day due to waves of discontentment growing in your spirit. Add in the disappointment and overall frustration, waiting on a breakthrough can be unbearable.

So today: Wait on the Lord. Trust Him. When He is silent, know He is working on your next blessing and breakthrough. Just focus on staying connected.

O Lord, thank you for this day. Help to stay connected while I wait for my breakthrough. Help me not become depressed due to the wait. Allow my faith to increase so I can weather the storms of life.

Be the catalyst for change.☺

DAY 148: Getting the Job Done

Today is about getting the job done.

I have always been very organized and I believe people have taken advantage of that over the years. I will make sure tasks are completed regardless of emotions. This might have rubbed people the wrong way but hey it's a risk you take asking me to complete a task.

I'm a 'by any means necessary' kind of girl. I'm gutsy and driven with a kick butt attitude. This, at times, can be hard to take. I'm also very action oriented. I'm always ready for action at all times.

God is just as determined and focused as well. He works hard to get the job done for us. While we may not be able to hear or see, just trust that God is always working hard to our behalf.

He is constantly aligning this in place so my breakthrough is ready, and on His time.

In return, God wants us to work just as hard in return for Him. Consider your relationship with God as a partnership. He wants us to all get to Heaven but He also wants us to work toward it as well.

So today: work on getting the job done. God works hard for us and we need to return the favor. Don't allow day-to-day distraction to get into the way of relationship with God.

O Lord, help to get the job of saving myself and others done. Allow me to speak the truth to motivate and inspire others. Help me to encourage change in myself and others.

Be the catalyst for change.☺

DAY 149: Being Yourself

Today is about being yourself.

I grew up in the suburbs where there were an extremely limited number of African Americans in my school. I was the third African American in my Advanced Placement classes. There were times in my life when I didn't feel 'Black' enough.

I would overcompensate by being pseudo ghetto when it wasn't necessary. It took me going to college to get it out of my system. Even though it does come out when I get angry.

I had hard time being comfortable in my own skin due to a lack of strong African American influences around me.

It became difficult for me to understand regardless of what I'm lacking. I don't have be pretend to be something I'm not. I must become comfortable in my own skin.

God makes us unique for a reason. To make us a testament to others that you don't have to be a cookie cutter, and just like everyone else.

Your uniqueness is truly what makes you beautiful. Allow uniqueness to shine through.

So today: be yourself. Don't allow the pressures of the world to overwhelm you. God makes us perfect in our own way. Don't question God's artistry, there is purpose in it.

O Lord, thank you for this day. Help me to be myself. Allow me to be more confident in myself and my abilities.

Be the catalyst for change.☺

DAY 150: A Taste of Home

Today is a taste of home.

Fall semester of my freshman year at Howard University, I had an unusually bad case of homesickness. I attended my first house party in DC and they wouldn't play any southern music. So while I'm a fan of northern rap music, I was disappointed in the lack of southern music. There were a lot of people from the south at the party and we went outside in the backyard and begin to shout the lyrics to our fave southern rap songs. I knew then I wanted to go home.

There are times in life when the burdens are so heavy you need an escape. A place to go where life's troubles are not so blinding and destructive to your mind, body and spirit.

This place is home. Home is considered a safe place, a place of assistance or a place to center. This is where all of us run to when life becomes too much to handle.

Allow God to become your home. Home isn't always a structure but a feeling, an emotion. Allow your God to become your comforting force in your life that will help to continue on the race called life.

So today: Run to the comforts of God in open arms. Allow yourself to sink into the comforts of God. Help his soothing quality help to continue in the race of life.

O Lord, thank you for this day. Please forgive me for my sins both knowing and unknowing. Please protect me from burdens of life and allow me to take comfort in you.

Be the catalyst for change.☺

DAY 151: You Never Know

Today is: you never know.

My sister is four years older than me and was in college during the greatest times in hip-hop while at Howard University. My mother would allow me to attend homecoming with her each year. I remember when I was sixteen, I was in the yard, and I stopped out of shock. Standing before me was Biggie Smalls aka Christopher Wallace in a gold leather jacket. I remembered I ran up to him to get an autograph and was immediately shut down by his security.

Sean Combs aka Puff Daddy was standing there and felt pity on me. He posed with me in a picture I still have. At the time, he was unrecognizable with his dark shades on. However, in my photo, for some reason he put his sunglasses on top of his head in the photo. I thought to myself, no one would know it's him without the sunglasses and wouldn't be worth anything. Boy, was I wrong. ☺

You never know what the future may hold. What you believe is your future could turn out to be very different. None of us can predict the future but we can be guided by God and the Holy Spirit. God knows our total story and guides us through this journey called life.

God takes us through certain trials and tribulations for a reason and purpose. He may not share the purpose with us so we must trust Him. God has our best interests at heart, so just allow ourselves to experience this wild rollercoaster

Today, you never know what the future may hold. Allow God to move in your life and watch your life be changed forever. You never know what God has in store for you.

O Lord, thank you for this day. Please forgive me for my sins. Allow me to trust you to take control of my life. Remove all hesitation and allow me to believe.

Be the catalyst for change.☺

MONTH 6

DAY 152: A Stress Reliever

Today about having a stress reliever.

I have always loved going out. Not just because of music but the vibe of lounges. Regardless of what kind of day you're having, sitting back and hanging out with your friends is always the ultimate stress reliever.

Stress is considered a strain, pressure, anxiety, or trauma. It's something you have very little control over.

When we are in stressful situations, we have a sense of urgency to make the situation go away or at least not feel as overwhelmed.

It's important to have a stress reliever on this journey called life. You must learn not to allow anxiety to overcome your spirit and rock your foundation.

Finding a stress reliever is essential. I have many stress relievers but I believe having them is what keeps me grounded when I'm becoming overwhelmed and increasingly frustrated with life changes.

God blesses but He is also a comforter. God will provide you with comfort when you need it the most. Finding a stress reliever is God's way of giving you comfort.

So today: find a way to cope with all of the stressful situations in your life. While it may be difficult to endure, stay focused on just getting through each day and life will become a little easier.

O Lord, Thank you for this day. Help me to rely on you to resolve the stressful situations in my life. Help to see that you know what is best for me.

Be the catalyst for change.☺

DAY 153: Loyalty

Today is about loyalty.

I was such a huge fan of Trina, a female Miami-based rapper. When she came to Jaguars, a popular hip-hop club in Atlanta one time, I was super excited. She actually was in town for my twenty-first birthday. I was so hyped that someone at the club arranged for me to meet her. What did I say: OMG! I love your music! My friends and I love your music and we bump it our cars * valley girl voice*

Huh? I'm not sure why it came out that way. However, she was gracious and told me she was happy to have me as a fan. I have always been a loyal fan to Trina to this day.

Loyalty is a lost science. It's important to be loyal to some people but not to the detriment to your soul.

Loyalty is about being faithful to a person or ideal. It's also about being trustworthy, devoted and reliable.

During these times, everyone is out for themselves. They will jump on bandwagons without being truly loyal. People love you when you're hot, but are gone when you're not.

You should keep your loyalty in check with God. God is the One who will never turn His back on you, deceive you, make fun of you or otherwise become untrustworthy.

Allow yourself to be armed with God's spirit and stay loyal. God will reward you in a way you couldn't even imagine. Resist the urge to be caught in today's society and become phony with God.

O Lord, thank you for this day. Help me to stay loyal to you and the Word. Allow me to stay focused on your Word and trust in it.

Be the catalyst for change.☺

DAY 154: The Future

Today is about the future.

For most people, we're either spending too much time mentally in the past or focused on the future.

While the past can provide lessons for the future, it's better to focus on the future. The future is when you can use all of your new knowledge to good use. It's the place where you can start fresh and anew.

The future focuses on things to come, potential and can be considered an opportunity.

The future for me during the dark time is what kept me going. When life is less than ideal, you find something to focus on to get you through the tough times.

During tough times, it seems like they go on and on forever. However, in reality they were relativity short periods of time with just a huge amount of discomfort with them.

God will always have good prospects for the future because they are the gas in our spiritual tank to keep us running in this race called life.

So today: allow yourself to focus on the future. Create a place for the future and follow it. Get everything ready so when your breakthrough occurs you will be ready.

O Lord, thank you for this day. Help me to stay focused on the future. Allow me to see good times are coming if I just continue to believe.

Be the catalyst for change.☺

DAY 155: The Life of a Believer

Today is about the life of a believer.

Being a believer isn't always easy. It swings between a little ahead of your time and slight crazy.

To the secular world, you're believing in things that haven't occurred. You're making decisions based on the best-case scenario and not on logic and common sense. You must possess a certain level of stubbornness and tough skin to live life as a believer.

When you're the closest to your breakthrough is usually the darkest and when you feel the most insecure. This is why it's important to be quiet and don't make any rash movements. While it's sooooo difficult to do, it's absolutely necessary.

You must have burning desire for more in your life and be armed with knowledge God is the place where you can get it.

Sometimes, God doesn't give what you need but rather He dissolves the situation so no solution is needed.

To a nonbeliever, that is almost mythical and amazing. For us, it's just a breakthrough. Allow yourself to stay on the path even when you don't fully understand what is going on in your life. We are not supposed to always understand; we are just supposed to believe.

So today: continue on the path of life of a believer. While it may not be the most comfortable life, it's a safe one. You've the security of being one of God's people and He will always protect you from harm.

O Lord, thank you for this day. Allow me to stay on the path of being a believer in you. Help me to stay focused on your will when I don't always understand them. Allow me to check my intelligence at the door because my intelligence won't inhibit my faith.

Be the catalyst for change.☺

DAY 156: Revenge

Today is about revenge.

When I was growing up, I didn't hold grudges but was a bit vengeful. I was like a little demigod. I believed I would extract punishment on you until I feel like I equaled what you did to me. Then you would feel the pain you have bestowed upon me.

Boy was that the wrong way to be. There isn't anything positive about revenge. Revenge is about parceling out punishment, desire for retaliation or payback.

God and His people should always be focused on forgiveness. Forgiveness is difficult even for those who don't hold grudges. While we may not stay mad at you long, we also may not want to be in your presence either as a way of protecting ourselves.

You must resist the tendency to extract revenge on those who have wronged you. What you must do is forgive them and pray for them. Allow God to decide if punishment is necessary and to bestow it.

None of us all perfect. We all have something you have done that has been always positive. So how dare we attempt to pretend we haven't? Whatever mercy you would like God to have on you is what you provide to others.

So today: resist the urge to become vengeful and enact revenge. Not only is it bad karma; it can hurt your relationship with God.

O Lord, thank you for this day. Help me to stay focused on Your will and away from negative energy. Allow positive energy to flow from me.

Be the catalyst for change.☺

DAY 157: Being Creative

Today is about being creative.

I have always been creative. Not just in what I create but how I think. That is why I never worry about competition. When you think creative, competition is no longer a factor because you think so differently than others.

Creativity is the ability to compose new ideas or things, to be inventive and have vision.

Creativity is one of the best gifts from God. It allows you to positively change your environment for all to enjoy.

It allows you to express yourself in way everyone can enjoy. However, you must be in a positive space to be creative.

You can't be creative when you feel frustrated, mean spirited, and just overall hateful.

You allow positive energy to flow into your spirit in order to reach the optimal level of creativity.

God will send a creative spirit in order to help you manifest your destiny. However, you must be listening to God to receive it.

God wants you to live up to your expectations in life but it's up to you to push yourself to make it happen.

So today: Dare to be your most creative self. Allow your mind to roam free as a bird. Don't factor whether something can be done; allow God to take care of that. Just work on performing your product of innovation.

O Lord, thank you for this day. Allow me to continue to be as creative and innovative as possible. Allow me not to be afraid of failure but embrace change. Creativity brings about change and change is what we need to improve humanity.

Be the catalyst for change.☺

DAY 158: Glory

Today is about glory.

Glory is about achievement, splendor, and beauty. It also illustrates credit and praise.

Glory is directly connected to praise and is important within your spiritual experience.

God is responsible for every good thing that happens in our lives. We must give honor to Him for blessing beyond comprehension.

When times are tough, it's truly difficult to see the Glory of God. Don't allow Evil to allow you to become pessimistic and discount God's abilities.

I know it's difficult to get moving when you're hurt, frustrated and just plain worn out. When your spiritual energy is on empty, it's easy to believe God has left you.

God will not leave you. God may go silent but He has not left you. You must learn to trust God from the times He is raining blessings to the months without any really significant breakthrough and everyone is getting on your nerves.

So today, focus on giving God glory for all past things He has done in your life. This will also allow you to get through hard times because you know if He has done it before, He will do it again.

O Lord, thank you for this day. Thank you for giving me your peace and I am giving you the glory for it. Help me to maintain it during these tough times.

Be the catalyst for change.☺

DAY 159: Deceit

Today is about deceit.

Deceit is dishonesty practices and to deliberately mislead. We all have been deceived at some point in our lives.

It's not a great feeling. It usually leads to a huge amount of anger and frustration. It's not your responsibility to exact revenge but rather you must focus on moving on.

Trying to get someone back or understand why the deceit has occurred is wasted energy.

Sometimes, Evil will send deceit to scramble your mind and energy. It's a great tool for getting you to focus on the wrong thing.

Don't allow your frustration about this deceit to build. It will solve nothing.

God will deal with those who mislead you and hurt you. Allow Him to take control of the situation. It's God's battle, not yours.

Try focusing on other aspects of your life that are more positive. Don't allow Evil to throw you off track.

So today, get past the deceit. While it can be frustrating, it's not the end of the world. Move past it and get into the driver's seat of God's car.

O Lord, thank you for this day. Help me to get past the deceit that's in my world. Allow me to trust you and stay positive.

Be the catalyst for change.☺

DAY 160: Feeling Burdened

Today is about feeling burdened.

There are times in my life when I feel burdened down. It seems everyone is looking to me to solve all of their problems.

However, there's no one who's looking out for me. I'm the solution to everyone else's problems but not to my own.

I want to be helpful, but it's becoming too much. This is when you have to ask God for help. It's difficult at times to say no when you're feeling overwhelmed especially for Christians.

You feel like you're disappointing God when you tell someone no. You're not disappointing God and you're also not protecting yourself from exhaustion.

The same people who were pulling on you are also the people who were unavailable to help during your time of need.

You must be real with yourself about your limitation in your life. You also must be wary of people who just want to take and take from you but give little in return. Any time God gives you an inkling of feeling a little bamboozled, pay attention. Trust your gut and intuition; it will never fail you.

Every time I have wanted to tell someone no and I don't, I live to regret it, each and every time.

So today: allow yourself to become unburdened. Dare to say no and say it with confidence. Your piece of mind is far more important than any task.

O Lord, thank you for this day. Allow me to unburdened from all of the responsibilities hanging over me. Allow me to stay focused

Be the catalyst for change.☺

DAY 161: Being Trapped in Captivity

Today is about being trapped in captivity.

When life is difficult it can feel like you're a caged animal in a zoo or circus.

You're only let out to work and then you return to your cage. There is no relief in sight and it just seems to be more and more responsibilities.

You feel everyone looks at you as a moneymaker and not as a real person.

People are counting on you but yet no one has your back. It's difficult to make a decision when you feel like you can't roam to figure out a solution.

You're locked down with no way out. There are times in life where you feel you're captive. You've been held captive by your sins, regrets, guilt and responsibilities. There feels like no way out.

God is patient and forgiving. He knows what ails us and what we need before we even form the words. While it's difficult not to become frustrated or resentment but feeling like you're out of options. Don't.

Talk to God. Helping to talk to God doesn't always change the situation but it helps change how we deal with the situation.

So today: break out of captivity. Allow yourself to become free through God's help. Allow God to shoulder the burden instead of you. Life full time without God is just too much to handle.

O Lord, thank you for this day. Break me out of this cage I'm locked in. Help me to trust that you have my best interest at heart. Allow my faith to carry me.

Be the catalyst for change.☺

DAY 162: Comfort

Today is about comfort.

When I get stressed, I treat myself to something I normally don't eat. My comfort foods are Doritos and Oreos.

While it's not particularly healthy, it's my vice to get through the tough days. However, I'm always up the next morning, running off the damage from the night before.

When the problems of life are dragging you down, there is a need for comfort of some sort. Comfort is there to soothe, console and relieve pressure.

God can also be a needed comforter. God has a unique ability to provide with the support that no human could reasonably be able to give continually.

None of us are perfect and we all have problems. It's unreasonable to think any human would have the capacity to be constantly unwaveringly open and supportive.

That's why relying on God is so important. He can provide you with comfort beyond our human comprehension.

He will provide relief from what is ailing and provide instant relief. There isn't anything more profound in life than to be understood. God can provide the relief we seek.

So today, instead of attempt to rely on man, rely on God for comfort. Allow God to ease your pain and provide a healing balm to your heart.

O Lord, thank you for this day. Help me to seek comfort in you. Allow me to believe that you reassure me and calm my spirit. By seeking your comfort, I will be able to weather the storms of life.

Be the catalyst for change.☺

DAY 163: Making a Commitment

Today is about making a commitment.

When I make a commitment, I stick to it. While sometimes it's easier to drop the commitment rather than stick it out.

A commitment is about a promise, responsibility, or pledge. You make a commitment you should be dedicated, and devoted to fulfilling your end of the bargain.

God made a commitment to the human race so long ago. God promised He would never leave us or forsake, beyond all others. He has held His promise.

We all should make the same commitment to God. Allow yourself to promise to stand on God's word despite all evidence to the contrary. To fight the good fight and stay on the path of righteous even when the other paths look oh so tempting.

God sacrificed a lot for us; we should do the same for Him. Take a big step toward God and give Him your heart. Once you commitment to Him, your life will never be the same.

When it feels like He left you, He hasn't. He's working on aligning blessings for you instead of communicating with you. So when it feels like all hope is lost, remember, God keeps his promises to us. You must believe.

So today: don't be afraid to make a commitment to God. If you allow God to enter your heart, He will change your life forever.

O Lord, thank you for this day. Please forgive me for my sins. Help me to open myself to make a commitment to you. Allow me to trust, believe and take you at your word.

Be the catalyst for change. ☺

DAY 164: Confirmation

Today is about confirmation.

In business, I absolutely adore written confirmation. I do not like surprises. I like to know whether I can truly count on your support. My decisions are based upon it, which is important. Without clear confirmation, all you have is a promise, which can be broken. Confirmation usually holds people to a higher standard and is taken more seriously.

That's the same in our spiritual life as well. Confirmation is also great with God. When God places an idea, proposal, dream or vision into your spirit, it can be an overwhelming experience.

You're not sure whether you should act upon it or not. The best way to do so is ask God for confirmation. God has His own special ways to confirm your idea or vision. However, you must be open and willing to receive.

God knows when we are ready for a change in our lives. When we cannot continue on the path we are on. When we are so despondent and cannot take it anymore.

That is when confirmation is such a blessing. It gives us something to believe in so we can continue in this race called life.

So today: allow yourself to seek confirmation. When God gives you that little nudge, it can be powerful and push on the path to greatness.

O Lord, thank you for this day. Thank you for blessing me with confirmation for vision and ideas. Allow me to stand on your word and continually seek you at all times.

Be the catalyst for change.☺

DAY 165: A Contender

Today is about being a contender.

At all times, I feel like I'm a major contender. I'm someone who is always attempting to get the next level. I will never be comfortable where I am in my life. I will always strive for excellence and to get more out of life.

We should also try to keep ourselves mentally at the contender status. When you're a contender, you're always the underdog. You never have the advantage. You never get cocky. You never relax.

You never know what's lurking behind every corner. You give it your all. Your blood, sweat and tears. You're grindin' when everyone else is sleeping. You're working to achieve your goals and when you've met your goals, you create new ones.

God want us to take the same aggression and put it into staying in focus on the path of righteous. God has a special place for all of our lives and in order to reach that place you must stay driven and aligned with God's will.

Even if you stumble, don't fall. Even if you fall, don't stay down for long. While the path can be treacherous at times, God will bless beyond your wildest dreams if you believe.

So today: stay in the race and be a contender. Allow yourself to run toward the light of God and away from darkness.

O Lord, thank you for this day. Help me to stay in the race of life and be a major contender in Christ. Allow me to trust and believe that all my dreams come through.

Be the catalyst for change.☺

DAY 166: Coveting

Today is about coveting.

Growing up, I always wanted really, really long thick hair. I could only achieve this look through some extra pieces.

As an adult in my early 20s, I really wanted to get married. All my friends were getting married and I felt like the last single person on earth.

I completely understand what it's like to covet. To covet is to want, desire or yearn for.

No one is immune from it. For each of us, there's something we yearn for that we can't have. It's a part of life.

Be careful of coveting. When you began to covet, irrational thinking comes into play.

When you begin to covet, it's difficult at times not to make silly mistakes allowing yourself to slip away from God.

It's essential you allow yourself not to act upon it. If you act upon it, the desire will grow and there is no telling how far you will go for what you want.

So today: allow yourself to covet within reason. There are certain things we all desire. However, don't allow your wants to lead you away from God.

O Lord, thank you for this day. Help me to keep my desire in check and to covet within reason. Allow me trust that God will provide my wants aligned with His will.

Be the catalyst for change.☺

DAY 167: Digging Deep

Today is digging deep.

When I'm running, my first two miles feel great and I'm extremely motivated. I'm able to say hi to all of the regular runners I pass each day. I'm enjoyed the day and slowly waking up. However, on my last two miles, I'm struggling to hold it together. I can barely wave, let alone talk. That's when I have to dig deep.

I push myself, turn up my iPod and finish my run. No matter what. I hype up my endurance and strength to finish. I'm stronger, wiser and overall, a better runner because of it.

Life is similar. When you dig deep, you must pull out what you're made of. You must put all of your other concerns to the side and buckle down. Just focus on the task at hand.

There are times in your life when you have to dig deep. You must allow yourself to have tunnel vision.

Nothing else matters but the tasks you're working on. While this is great for overall living, it's important to get to the next level of life.

So today: allow yourself to dig deep to get to the next phase in life. Push yourself through the pain and resentment to get into the promised land.

O Lord, thank you for this day. Help me to dig deep during tough times. Give me the strength to endure and fight the good fight in this race called life.

Be the catalyst for change.☺

DAY 168: Distractions

Today is about distractions.

Every time I'm working a huge project, a great number of distractions come my way. They're always time consuming and difficult to resolve.

It's so annoyed because just when I've removed one distraction, another one appears.

I've come to realize distractions are something you have to create a plan of attack to handle or it could throw your project or even your life completely off track.

A distraction is an interruption, disturbance, or diversion in life. They come in many forms, in tasks, people, relationships, etcetera.

They're also energy drainers. They get you to take your eye off your goal and onto a situation that's more trouble than it's worth.

It causes more agitation and anxiety more than anything. You must be able to stay focused on your goal and not the distractions that tag along.

So today: remember distractions are just there to cause confusion. Allow yourself to attempt to resolve them, then move on. You will be happy you did.

O Lord, thank you for this day. Help me not to be disturbed by the distractions in life. Allow me to stay focus on my goal and aligned with your will.

Be the catalyst for change.☺

DAY 169: Distressed

Today is being distressed.

When trouble comes back knocking at your door. It can completely change your outlook. You can become distressed by life. Being distressed is to become upset, distraught, troubled, or worried.

You become immersed in the problems and resolving them. It's easy to track when the troubles began but not solve them. You try everything to get your life back to order.

However, nothing seems to work. You're become so frustrated with your techniques that you're close to giving up.

You're distressed.

When you're distressed, you're still attempting to work out a situation yourself and not giving it to God.

God is the only One truly equipped to deal with all of life's problems. Life is too much to handle on your own. Release it and give it to God.

God waits for us to relinquish control but He steps in to help us. He wants to ensure you have given up control and understand He provides all the support you will ever need.

So today: don't allow yourself to become distressed. While you might be shaken at times by life's events, you mustn't allow it to affect your spiritual walk and outlook.

O Lord, thank you for this day. Help me not to become too distressed in the face of adversity. Allow me to remember there isn't anything too big for God or something He can't handle.

Be the catalyst for change.☺

DAY 170: It's Done

Today it's done.

When I start my day, I always begin with a task list. My task list is everything I must complete today. Then I rank them by importance. I know, I know…very type A.

When I have completed a task, I cross it off my list. I can't begin to tell you how satisfying it is. It really gives you a feeling your life is coming together and you can make it after all.

I know it seems weird that crossing something off my task list would be so important but it is to me. I'm completely frustrated when I can't cross something off. To me, crossing the item off means it's done.

Done means it's completed, ended, finished, or ready. It means I can move on the next task on my list.

Life is similar to this. When God gives you a test and you complete it, you move on to the next stage of your life. When you move to the next level, it comes with additional tasks to be completed but it's moving you closer to your breakthrough and your destiny.

So today: ask yourself to finish tasks on your spiritual task list. It will give hope and endurance for the future. While it may not be a fast process, it's a process you'll remember.

O Lord, thank you for this day. Help me to finish all the tasks on my spiritual checklist. Allow me to understand each task's completion moves me closer to a breakthrough in my life.

Be the catalyst for change.☺

DAY 171: When in Doubt

Today is about when in doubt.

I have many times in my life when I doubted the situation, relationship, people and even God. Doubt is hesitation, uncertainty or any reservation about something. Doubt is usually based on past negative experiences.

If something bad happens to us, we have a habit of believing it will happen again. For instance, if I have a bad experience in an outfit, I don't wear that outfit again. If I have a good experience in an outfit, it becomes 'lucky.'

We must all let go of superstitious techniques in life and allow God to work in each and every unique situation.

There are various reasons why you could have a negative experience. You could haven't been ready; it could have been bad timing or just an overall fluke.

For example, have you ever tried to unlock your car door and it doesn't open, do you just walk away from your car forever and say I'm done. Yet we do this time and time again in our spiritual walk.

Only doubt what you feel to be inside of you and then brush it off. Allow yourself to live your life as if each day is the first day of the rest of your life.

So today, remove doubt from your mind. Allow yourself to remember nothing is over and finished until God says it is. Look at every event with a fresh perspective.

O Lord, thank you for this day. Help me to remove my doubt for my mind and spirit. Allow me to see you can handle everything regardless of past experience.

Be the catalyst for change.☺

DAY 172: Early

Today is about being early.

For the most part, I'm an early riser in the morning. I have a million things to do and I have started out fresh in the morning to attempt to tackle my task list.

I also like to get up early, so I can fit my workout in. One of the best ways to start your day off right is with exercise.

Early means something in its first stages, before the expected time, ripening before others.

There are times in your life when being early can win the race. Being early means you're listening to your instinct and allow yourself to be ahead of the curve.

It also saves you from a lot of stress but managing your time properly so you can finish all of your important tasks within the day.

Now if I could be early for my appointment instead of late, I would be a monster LOL. ☺

A lot of times, God will speak to us early in the morning as well. There is such a tremendous amount of peace in the morning hours. There are many people who will stay up late at night but there are limited numbers who choose to be early risers.

So today: become an early riser. Watch how productive you become when you allow yourself the time to finish all of your tasks when your mind is the most sharp.

O Lord, thank you for this day. Help me to become an early riser so I can have more time in my day to connect with you and my destiny. Allow me to discipline myself so this can occur.

Be the catalyst for change.☺

DAY 173: Empty

Today is about being empty.

When the mayoral campaign ended, I was empty. I put all I had of myself into the campaign; I had nothing left to go on. I didn't know how to begin again; I had sacrificed so much I really didn't have a place for afterward. I gave myself to everyone, which is very dangerous. You should keep a little of yourself from consumption.

During the holiday months, I was so mentally drained I don't remember a lot from them. Literally, I just slept all day and night. Very much like Carrie from the Sex and the City Movie. I loved to sleep when under pressure. You can't feel emotions when you're asleep. You can't feel disappointment, angry, resentment, despair. All you feel nothing and empty.

When your life is becoming too much to handle, it's easy to want to feel nothing but it sure beats feeling bad. You must resist this. You have to be present with all of your emotions, good and bad.

The experiences may not be the most pleasant, but they are vital to your spiritual development and testimony. Become a beacon of light for others by forcing yourself to deal with your emotions and then get past them.

So today: don't allow yourself to stay empty. Slowly allow yourself to feel again. It's important for you to stay emotionally present in all situations both good and bad.

O Lord, thank you for this day. Help to remove the empty feeling I have. Allow me to believe life will be better than what is now in front of me. Allow me to trust, hope and believe.

Be the catalyst for change.☺

DAY 174: Excuses

Today is about excuses.

I'm not really big on them. I believe it's a way of getting out of being accountable for your behavior. It's an attempt to justify something— something you're usually not proud of.

In the business world, I will forgive you for not fulfilling your portion of a deal. However, I may decide not to work with you again.

In life, the unexpected happens. However, you can plan so that when the unexpected happens, it doesn't affect everything.

When you don't fulfill your part of a bargain, be prepared not to work with that person again. This is a consequence of the excuse.

When you want to be a Boss, make it happen. Bosses don't give excuses, a boss creates miracles. A boss is someone who understands they must perform regardless of the circumstances.

That's different between a top person in your field and being a legend. If you want to be a legend, you gotta work for it and there are no shortcuts for hard work.

At some point, you have let all the silliness of being an underachiever go and get on the path of greatness. You should need someone to push you to the next level. There must be inner resolve inside of you to make your destiny come to pass.

So today: don't give excuses. Perform or move out of the way. There are many hungry people out here willing to do whatever it takes to get to the next level.

Lord, thank you for this day. Help me to perform and not give excuses. Allow me to have the stamina to get to the next level in my life.

Be the catalyst for change.☺

DAY 175: Express Yourself

Today is about expressing yourself.

I have always been a very expressive person. You will know what I think about something—good and bad.

I don't get involved in other people's affairs but if you ask for my opinion, I will give it to you. I'm honest to a fault. Especially about business.

If you want to be a leader in the world today you must be willing to truly express yourself. Not in a fake or phony way. People can spot phoniness a mile away and it won't help you.

You have the show the world the real you. There is someone out there that gets you and is motivated by your actions.

There have been times I felt a little unmotivated and an email from a Twitter fan would boost my spirits. It helps me to feel like I'm really making a difference.

Convey your real thoughts and emotions. While it may be difficult because of the worry of looking like a fool, eventually the way you feel about others will matter less and less.

You cannot please everyone but what you can do is be an authentic self and live your life to the fullest.

So today: Dare to express yourself. Allow the world to see your light. While not everyone may like your light, your light is unique. It's important for you to allow it to shine.

O Lord, thank you for this day. Allow me to express myself fully without fear and over analyzing. Help me to stay focused and aligned with your will.

Be the catalyst for change.☺

DAY 176: Don't Faint

Today, don't faint.

There have only been a couple of times in my life when I almost fainted. One of the funniest was when I was about ten or eleven. My family had decided to attend the fourth of July parade in downtown Atlanta. I had been eating ice cream all day and didn't have any water and it was extremely hot.

I felt fine and then I notice everything I was seeing was in black and white like an old-fashioned movie. I knew something was horribly wrong. I went to my mom and she didn't pay me any attention. Then my dad looked at me and told her to look at me again. They sat me down and then gave me so water. I was a little shaky but fine.

Now that wasn't the first time I had a lot of ice cream outside in the hot streets of Atlanta. However, it was the first time it didn't agree with me.

You can't worry about when something unexpected has happened. However, what you must worry about is getting past it.

Evil will send us trouble to throw our game. We allow ourselves to get so wrapped up into the situation; we realize are have completely thrown ourselves off of our personal game plan.

So today don't faint. We must work at the first sign of trouble; take in the spiritual nourishment of God's words and prayer. While the situation may not be completely pleasant and ideal. We can get through it with God's help.

O Lord, thank you for this day. Increase my endurance in this race called life. Help not to faint under problems of this world. Allow me to stay focused on your will.

Be the catalyst for change.☺

DAY 177: Farewell

Today is about farewell.

Farewell is when you depart, exit, leave. It's when it's time to move on to greener pastures. There are times in your life when it's time to bid certain aspects of our lives farewell. It may not be a negative situation but rather a situation with people and things we've outgrown.

When we outgrow something and we continue to stay in the situation, it can become dangerous to our spiritual health.

God is attempting to take someone beyond where they are now. However, nothing moving on you is limiting yourself and God. You're also dwarfing your blessings from God because you're not following His instructions.

While it may be love, pity, regret or just plain out laziness from keeping us from moving on, it's truly holding us back from getting to the next level.

While it may be difficult and slightly uncomfortable, it's necessary.

God gives all of us assignments. Some assignments are short-term or long-term. When the assignment is completed, it's time for you or that person to move on. God is taking you places everyone may not be assigned to go.

So today: farewell to certain aspects of your life. If you want to be a legend, you must make sacrifices. With those sacrifices, it means some people may not be able to continue on your path to greatness. Trust in God and continue on this journey called life.

O Lord, thank you for this day. Please forgive me for all knowing and unknowing sins. Allow me to bid farewell to those who no longer fit into my life plan. Help to trust and believe there is a purpose in all that God commands me to do.

Be the catalyst for change.☺

DAY 178: Fear

Today is about fear.

There is always fear when doing something different or out of your comfort zone. Fear signifies apprehension, worry, and trepidation. It usually connects to a loss of control.

It's common to feel fear in certain situations: loss of a job, a devastating loss, or anything shocking and completely unexpected.

However, you cannot allow fear to control your mind and your decision-making. God already knows your life story and the ending (you win). Since we don't have a copy of the book, when trouble shows up, we must learn to live in shaky times.

God said He will protect and keep you away from all hurt, harm and danger. Now that doesn't mean you want to have problems, heartbreak, or experience despair. It means you feel less than five percent of what experience is but won't be harmed. You may not get frostbite but it doesn't mean you won't shiver from the cold weather.

So today: allow yourself to step past fear. The fear you feel is merely because of unknown elements that exist in your life right now. Rely on your experience when you felt this way before and God pulled you out of the situation.

You know God can provide aspiring miracle but you take your foot off the gas and give God the wheel.

O Lord, thank you for this day. Help me to let go of fear and worry. Allow me to focus on your miracle making track record so I make it in this race called life.

Be the catalyst for change.☺

DAY 179: Fellowship

Today is about fellowship.

Being someone who has grown up as a believer, I haven't placed a lot of emphasis on fellowship until now as an adult. I think I took it for granted and I have enough people praying for me that I didn't notice trouble that was avoided because of it. That is, until I became an adult.

Now, as an adult, true Christian fellowship is critical to your spirit walk. You place yourself in an environment where you're being held accountable for your actions, good and bad. Someone to help you to understand why living a good and just life is important. Why trying to live in the world and in the heavenly quarter is spiritually dysfunctional. At some point, one is going to outweigh the other. The world has so much power; it's easier to succumb to its temptations.

Fellowship isn't about being judgmental or critical but rather being a group of likeminded people who can understand all of the problems you're experiencing. There's a certain amount of friendship and society. It's like being in a special club. ☺

God wants us to connect with others on this spiritual walk. You can't live out your life alone. You need the help of others for spiritual strength and to be a beacon of strength to others. That's truly what fellowship is all about. Even thought I hate the word. It's so churchy to say I'm *fellowshipping*, but rather I'm just hanging out. Ah, but I digress. ☺

So today: allow yourself to fellowship more with those on a similar path as well. Be a confidante for them and allow them to be that for you as well. You can't make it in this world alone. You must reach out to others.

O Lord, thank you for this day. Help me to fellowship more with others on my spiritual path. Allow me to stay focused on my right and just path.

Be the catalyst for change.☺

DAY 180: Stop Fighting

Today is about stop fighting.

Fighting is a part of life. You fight with family, you fight with friends, you fight to get to the next level of your career. There are various aspects of life where fighting is permissible. However, too much fighting can wear you out. Too much fighting calls you to wrestle a lot with issues that are not really important. Most of the fighting is a struggle for control. Sometimes, it's better to allow someone to have control to save your sanity.

God is trying to take you somewhere you dreams can't even measure up to. While pushing to that next level, the fighting is bringing you back to earth with a thud.

The purpose of fighting is to do nothing more than throw you off track and shake your spirit. Your goals and legacy is too important for you to allow negative energy to get the best of you.

While standing up for yourself is important, allowing yourself to be drawn into an unsavory situation by argumentative people isn't a good usage of your time.

It took me a long time to realize some people's main purpose in life is to irritate. Don't allow them to win. Will yourself not to respond to their strange tactics.

So today: stop the fighting. It's not positive and nothing more than a deterrent. God wants more for you and you must be willing to ignore those who're working to get you off track.

O Lord, thank you for this day. Help me to control my anger and keep me from getting into petty arguments (fights). Help me to stay focused on you and have strength to ignore anything that's not going to help while pursuing my goals.

Be the catalyst for change.☺

DAY 181: Filth

Today is about filth.

While I was a little messy when I was a child, I'm definitely a clean freak as an adult. I cannot go more than about two days without making sure my house is spotless. While I do know how to clean, there isn't anything like a cleaning from a professional.

I truly believe, when my house is spotless, I can think clearer. I truly believe in the idea of an alignment of mind, body and spirit.

Filth is foul dirt, smut and muck. We have all been to someone's house that was filthy. You know times when you have to use the bathroom, until you get into the bathroom and you no longer have to go? Or you go to someone's house for dinner and their kitchen is no dirty you're no longer hungry.

Now, that's filth. However, this is a very sensitive subject. A subject that many don't want to discuss. While it's difficult to allow yourself to determine whether or not you're clean, you already know the answer inside.

Our spiritual life is similar. We all know what areas in our lives we're struggling with; we just don't want to face the problems.

It's easier to sweep it under our spiritual rug and pretend it doesn't exist. However, we know it's there. We know what's ailing us. We don't always have to tell the world our troubles but we do need to fess up to God so He can help get us on track.

So today: allow yourself to really see the filth in your lives. None of us are perfect. There's always something we can't stand to work on.

O Lord, thank you for this day. Help me to see and fix the filth piling up in my spiritual life. Free from the burdens of sins and allow me to get back on track.

Be the catalyst for change.☺

MONTH 7

DAY 182: Fleeting

Today is about fleeing.

When life gets to become too much, it's easier to flee instead of fighting.

Fleeing is when you escape, take off, and run away. Fleeing gives you an opportunity to figure out your plan of action before doing something you might regret later.

There are times when I'm extremely angry. I get silent and remove myself from the situation. That's when I'm so upset that I'm sure what I might do. So it's better for everyone to remove myself and get a cooling off period.

When the unexpected happens and you don't have a plan of action. Fleeing. Fleeing gives God some time to speak with you and tell what your next step should be. You must give God time to speak to your heart and spirit. He's a little busy with the world you know. ☺

Fleeing might not be the easiest course of action for those like me who are a little scrappy. You must resist 'standing up' for yourself or letting them know 'what's up' Don't do it, it's not worth it and can potentially make you look bad.

So today: flee when necessary. Fleeing can allow you to save face in the midst of overwhelming circumstances.

O Lord, thank you for this day. Help me to know when to flee during this journey called life. While it may be difficult, I help to restrain myself and God to fight my battles.

Be the catalyst for change.☺

DAY 183: Follow Me

Today is follow me.

I have always been a natural leader, I can lead people to heaven and darkness, I have done both. This primarily comes from being a persuasive person. Even when my train of thought isn't particularly positive, I will explain in such a way to causes people to pause and reconsider their point of view. Much is given, then much is expected.

When you have the blessing that people will follow you, you must be careful. When people follow you, tremendous responsibility for their well-being fits squarely on your shoulders.

You must be sure your actions are always above board so you don't invoke God's wrath for leading God's people down a garden path. While there are times you want to do your own thing without that responsibility, it's tough.

No matter what you're doing and where you are, there is always someone watching. While at times it might feel as if you're free, you really aren't. In the digital age in which we live, please understand, you never really escape responsibility as much as we all would like to.

From a business perspective, you must protect your brand. If your brand is positive, you make a concentrated effort to keep from allowing yourself to be involved in unsavory conditions.

God gives all of us spiritual gifts. If your spiritual gift is the ability to lead, you will always be considered a role model. You must remember there's someone on this globe imitating your every move. So for your own piece of mind, make sure your actions are as positive as possible.

So today: don't be afraid to be a leader and have people follow you. However, remember it does come with responsibility and you must take it seriously.

O Lord, thank you for this day. Help me to be a just and positive leader. Allow me to lead people to promise and not to destruction.

Be the catalyst for change.☺

DAY 184: Foolish

Today is about being foolish.

When you're being foolish, you're not being sensible, not showing good judgment and seeming ridiculous. You're being silly and completely irrational.

People like to blame foolishness on various other behaviors such as drinking, anger, etcetera. However, regardless of the origin, the result is the same: you're looking quite foolish.

Being foolish will happen to us again. We're prone to do things that don't illustrate a healthy dose of common sense.

While you can't avoid looking foolish, you can make the aftermath bearable by doing these key things:

Apologize immediately. If your actions have affected those around, apologize. No excuses. This will help resolve the problem immediately.

Stop any idiotic behavior. Stop doing actions that caused you to be foolish in the first place. Don't continue this behavior. It digs a deeper hole for you to crawl out of.

Pray. Whether it was your fault or if someone else's actions caused you to look foolish, ask the Lord for guidance. The only way to receive guidance is to pray. Prayer is the direct cell phone number to God that He always answers. Even if He doesn't answer, He will text you to let you know He will call you back later.

So today, while it's difficult, being or acting foolish happens to the best of us. While the situation may not be ideal to have a game plan when it happens to you, you will be prepared. ☺

Lord, thank you for this day. Please forgive me for all of my knowing and unknowing sins. Allow me to bounce back from foolish behavior and move on with my life.

Be the catalyst for change.☺

DAY 185: Forgetful

Today is about being forgetful.

Forgetful is being absent minded, neglectful, scatterbrained, and dreamy.

Usually, it's considered to be a negative attribute. However, I would like to give a slightly different perspective. When you're attempting to forgive someone, you must become slightly forgetful.

You must allow yourself to let go of the hurt and pain the person caused. If you don't, you'll never be able to successfully forgive them.

I'm sure you've heard the quote "I will forgive but not forget." If you can't forget, then you never really ever forgave the person.

When you forget, you're giving that person or situation a clean slate. Like there is no history that you're going to bring up every time you're in the heat of an argument you can't win.

Many relationships have failed because one person or both people in the relationship can't forget the past and move into the future. That's called holding a grudge. All these activities do is ensure you will be alone and bitter.

So today: learn to forget. If you willing bestow the forgiveness Christ gives us every day, be serious and forget what occurred as well. This will give you and that person a new lease on life,

O Lord, thank you for this day. Help me to learn not only to forgive but forget. Allow me to give understand that you give to us on a daily basis.

Be the catalyst for change.☺

DAY 186: Fulfilled

Today is about being fulfilled.

Being fulfilled is when you're satisfied in achieving goals. When you're content, happy and pleased with your life.

I would like to reach a point in my life when I can say I'm fulfilled. I don't think I'm there yet. I have yet the start a family as well as allow my career to be in a place for me to feel comfortable.

At times, I do worry my standards are a little too high. Not with men ☺ but rather about when I will feel I'm at the point in my career when I've made it.

I believe you've made it when you have no student loans. So, I think that's a reasonably attainable goal.

Whatever your place of fulfillment is, we must work in this life to get there. We must learn to be happy in life.

I know there have been times when I look back at that time in my life, I should have been happy but I wasn't. I believe you have to fight to be happy just like you have to fight for anything else in your life.

You also must believe fulfillment is attainable for you. So many people don't believe in fulfillment because they don't believe they deserve to be happy. Everyone deserves to be happy despite your past.

So today: focus on becoming fulfilled. At some point in your life, your life is enough. You should be satisfied and content. Work hard to reach that place.

O Lord, thank you for this day. Help me to become fulfilled in my life. Allow me to understand I have to work at happiness and contentment just like anything else. Allow me to stand on my faith so I may reach my goals of fulfillment in life.

Be the catalyst for change.☺

DAY 187: Giving

Today is about giving.

I absolutely adore giving gifts. My family grew up that it's more important to give than receive. We always attempt to outdo each other with our gifts.

I had to learn over time and through trial and error, everyone doesn't grow up with the same mantra.

Some people are just naturally cheap. Not everyone knows how to receive a gift.

Nothing makes me more mad than someone who is ungrateful for a gift. They think you have ulterior motives, when all you want to do is make them happy.

Or the opposite end of the spectrum is when their expectations for gifts are too high and they don't even acknowledge you in return.

For example, If I get you an iPad for your birthday, would it be too much to ask for a phone call on my birthday?

God loves to gives us gifts as well, blessings. He loves to shower us with blessings but He has to make sure we are ready to receive them.

While we all want to be blessed, we have to make sure we're strong enough to receive them and not self-destruct in the process.

That's why God will hold blessings for a time to ensure we are mature enough to handle them.

So today: Dare to be giving and allow God to the same to you. Allow yourself to be strong and mature enough to receive blessings God is giving.

O Lord, thank you for this day. Help me to become more giving and also be mature enough to handle all of the blessings God has for me.

Be the catalyst for change.☺

DAY 188: Appearances

Today is about appearances.

It's easy to put on appearances. To give assurance that life is great for you, even when it's not.

Once you start putting on appearances, it's difficult to stop. You'll dig a deeper hole for yourself and push yourself into further isolation.

There is no worse place to start putting on airs than at church. Church is the one place where you should be able to release yourself without judgment. Where you should be able to express yourself. However, if you start keeping up appearances, it can make your life a living hell.

As a preacher's kid, my family was extremely proficient in keeping up appearances until my parents got divorced. Then everything fell apart. I learned from that experience, you must be careful in putting yourself in situations where you feel like you can't freely express yourself in church.

If you've gotten yourself into appearances, you must break the cycle. Stop caring so much what people think. It's better for them to know you have trouble in your household than for you to lose your mind from lack of release.

So today: allow yourself to stop keeping up appearances. Not only is it not healthy; it can truly be dangerous to your spirit. Allow yourself to break free and be your authentic self.

O Lord, thank you for this day. Help me become more authentic and less fake. Help show my true self, warts and all. Allow me to grow closer to you in the process.

Be the catalyst for change.☺

DAY 189: Too Busy for God

Today is called too busy for God.

I have always been active in Church. However, as I have gotten older, I have learned I must watch my extracurricular activities at church.

Church is like being in high school. We all go to class (church services) and then we go to our extracurriculars such as cheerleading, dance or sports. Extracurricular activities in a church are ushering, choir practice, youth ministry, etcetera.

Like high school, it's very easy to get caught up in the extracurricular activities. However, there are no safeguards like in high schools. If you didn't handle business in class you can't participant in the extracurricular activities.

There is no rule like that in the church and what's worse, you can easily crowd God out of your life be being too busy doing God's work.

You won't realize it at first but you will become increasingly stressed when you enter the church. Then you find yourself having less and less time to attend services and spent in prayer.

Before you know it, you have allowed yourself to become separated from God and that can lead to sin playing a prominent role in your life.

God will always prefer you spend quality time with Him rather than allow yourself overwhelming church committee work.

So today: make sure you're not too busy for God. Make sure you always attend your church services to feed your spiritual soul so you won't run out of nourishment during your extracurriculars.

O Lord, thank you for this day. Help me not to become too busy for you. Allow me to have balance in my life so I won't be separated from you.

Be the catalyst for change.☺

DAY 190: Being out of Order

Today is about being out of order.

While there are a lot of great stewards of church, there are some that are not. Remember, church work is similar to a hospital and less like heaven. None of us is perfect and it's always something we are struggling with.

Some church members are better at hiding negative behavior. Some of my biggest times of struggle are when I spent a lot of time at church. While being heavily involved in one church, I saw more than I really needed: sexual harassment, gambling, and a clear lack of respect for God while still on the church grounds.

There are huge numbers of bigots who identified themselves as Man or Women after God's heart.

I have had plenty of run-ins with 'Church Saints.' I remember when I wasn't celibate and I was arguing with a boyfriend while on spring break. I remember while I was upset with one of my girlfriend's irritating friends aka a 'Church Saint,' said to me, I wouldn't have had those problems with Him if I had lived right under God's will. True statement' bad timing yes. I always disliked her from that point on. She was a virgin back then. I just found out recently when she made that comment, she actually was no longer a virgin and was pretending to be one. Now that makes me angry.

God's love is pure and never judgmental. Anyone who uses God's name to hurt anyone is someone you should really question if you want to be around. I'm not here to judge. However, you should be careful if you place anyone on a pedestal. At some point, they may take a tumble.

You must understand you must not put your faith in man but rather in God. Man can fail you quiet easily and put you in a place where it makes it difficult to recover.

So today: don't allow yourself to get out of order when things are not always what they seem at church. Take bitter with the sweet and always keep your eyes focused on God.

O Lord, thank you for this day. Help me to keep realistic expectations of all of the Lord's people. Allow me to remember they're human and prone to make mistakes like the rest of us.

Be the catalyst for change.☺

DAY 191: Watching Your Motives

Today is about watching your motives.

While we all like to enjoy doing things for God's Kingdom. There is a little bit of ego involved as well.

We all like to be needed. We like be the savior of an event. We like to find a niche where everyone comes to you if they need help with it.

However, you have to keep your motives as pure as possible.

Have you ever seen the little old lady at church who constantly complains about all of the work she has to do for the church? She sometimes works for church or sometimes she doesn't. She pays very little attention to anyone because she is so busy doing 'God work.'

She's putting on a show. She's complaining so people will be aware of all of her hard work for the church. Her goal is the incarnate Jesus, long-suffering and willing to sacrifice her personal life for the greater good of God.

However, that isn't what happens. Instead of seeing her that way, we just see her as a complaining mean old lady who we all wished would shut up.

So today: Don't create a persona at church. Just be yourself. Good, bad and ugly. Allow yourself to be noticed without you talking about it.

The only acknowledgment you really need is from the Lord.

O Lord, thank you for this day. Allow me to stay focused on your will and watch my emotions. Help me to understand, God wants us to do everything for Him and not for man or to receive praise.

Be the catalyst for change.☺

DAY 192: Keeping Secrets

Today is about keeping secrets.

When you a keep secret, it can be very difficult to do. If you're like me, I'm such a straight shooter; it's really hard for me to keep a secret. However, I have learned over the years.

A secret is something that isn't widely known, undercover and covert. Keeping a secret isn't necessarily a bad thing; it can protect your blessings.

All the people who you come into contact with do not wish you well. There can be a bit of jealousy under the surface. That's why you must be careful who you share your dreams with.

Some people are angry for various reasons: a dream failing, frustration with a relationship or life in general. They didn't succeed and so they do not want anyone else to succeed either.

Or they just don't want someone to succeed before them, which is worse. These people will not only work hard to kill your dreams but also undermine your spirit to make you feel stupid or unrealistic for wanting more for your life.

There's a method to God's techniques on blessing us. We don't know it and He shouldn't have shared it. We should concentrate on the end result of the blessing. God will bless us all in due time and on His divine schedule.

So today: try to keep some things secret: your big dreams. Allow them to take shape and become ironclad before you share. This can get your dream to soar with very little interference.

O Lord, thank you for this day. Help me to be careful about sharing me dreams with everyone. Protect my dreams from harm from others who are jealous. Allow me to continue working away on my dreams despite any delays that might occur.

Be the catalyst for change.☺

DAY 193: Habits

Today is about habits.

We all have them and some are healthy and some are not.

They can become part of a routine. A habit is a regularly repeated behavior pattern, practice or tradition.

I'm a creature of habit. I'm very predictable; I go run in the morning. Every Wednesday, I go to Wednesday evening services. I go to the grocery store after church, and get eyebrow waxed every two weeks. Yep, a creature of habit.

Make spending time with God part of your habits. When you're new in your spirit walk, the most difficult thing to do is get used to attending church and prayer on a regular basis. It will seem like every Sunday morning, it's rainy or you will always end up staying out too late on Saturday night. Something makes it difficult to get up in the morning.

You must not allow Evil to infect your mind, body and spirit. Habits are created usually without thinking and to usually the most convenient. For example, I don't do grocery shopping until Sunday. It's usually the best time because there's a small waiting time and ensure that I'll attend church in the morning because otherwise I won't have food for the week.

So today: allow God to become part of your life and a habit. He should be a center item in our lives and we should work hard to maintain it. Once you make God a habit, your life will never be the same.

O Lord, thank you for this day. Help me to allow you to become a habit and critical fixture in my life. Allow me to stay focused and aligned at your will.

Be the catalyst for change.☺

DAY 194: Bringing it to a Halt

Today is about bringing it to a halt.

I had a friend who all she wanted to do was go out to clubs with me. She wasn't really fun and she had a habit of rubbing guys the wrong way when we were out.

I know a lot of people and she would be able to meet guys from me. However, I was getting little out of hanging out from her but irritation. A lot of interaction was pity for her despite her attitude.

So the day came when I needed her to work on a important project for me and she waited until thirty minutes before to tell me she couldn't do it. I went out the night before to be nice to her.

Then, she had the nerve to ask me if I wanted to go out after she had left me in a lurch that had potential to cost me millions of dollars. I politely said no, I called our friendship to a halt at this point.

Sometimes, you must call a halt to some things in your life. You must let people know they can't continue to use and belittle you in their own ways. While there might be good in that person, you must distance yourself from the person for your own sanity.

People don't know their limits unless you provide them. Place rigid boundaries in your life and watch how things will began to fall into place.

So today: think about people and projects that need to be halted in your life. By halting people or behavior, it allows God to send positive energy and people into your life.

O Lord, thank you for this day. Allow me to be strong enough to remove people or projects from my life that are no longer relevant. Help me to rely on you as I march bravely until the unknown.

Be the catalyst for change.☺

DAY 195: Headstrong

Today is about being headstrong.

I have always been headstrong. Being headstrong is the first cousin of stubborn. Those who are headstrong are determined, willful and pigheaded.

There is very little anyone can tell me when I've made up my mind on something. I know what I want it in life and I make decisions based upon that.

Even if I fail, I will fail with dignity. Because of this trait, I'm someone who has very little regret in my life. You live your life in regret with you always prone to listen to every bit of advice that comes your way.

You have to question people's motivation when someone offers you unsolicited advice; a lot of people are hateful and want to bring your spirit down.

Every single one of my biggest triumphs came immediately after someone decided whatever I was working on wouldn't happen. That's ultimate payback. ☺

So where would I be in my life if I had chosen to listen to every person who thought I was taking too many risks and my idea wasn't doable.

You win some, you lose some. It's all the numbers game. You must continue to plug away and at some point you will strike it big.

So today: allow yourself to continue to be headstrong. Believe in yourself; don't count on others for support. There's no great pleasure in knowing when you're successful that you don't owe anyone and your belief in God and yourself sent you into the destiny you had always dreamed of.

O Lord, thank you for this day. Help me to continue to strive to get to the next level in my career, regardless of what haters say. Allow me to ignore negative energy and focus on the positive. Help me to trust, hope and believe.

Be the catalyst for change.☺

DAY 196: Bringing the Heat

Today is about bringing the heat.

I'm creative, and innovative. I usually don't worry about competition because I think so differently that no one really attempts to do the same things I do at the same time.

I bring up the degree of hotness so much so that my ambition can be almost unbearable.

We all must work hard to bring the heat. We must constantly allow ourselves to exert mental pressure in order to step into our destiny.

Being at low energy will not get you to the next level. High energy and clear confidence in yourself will. You must believe in yourself and be unwilling to compromise on your future. You must be willing to do whatever it takes to reach your goals.

This isn't always easy. Does this mean you will get discouraged? Yes. Does this mean you will have doubts? Yes. You will have moments of non-belief. We all do. However, you must be willing to brush yourself off and continue to fight the good fight against all odds to step into your destiny.

When blessings come, it doesn't mean they will come easy. It doesn't mean you won't say no two or three times. You will have to swallow your pride and dignity to get the deal finished.

This is part of business. You have to know when to bend.

So today: bring the heat. Allow your white-hot burning ambition to shine through. Do not dissuade you. Turn that 'no' into 'not yet.' Fight for your dreams to come through.

O Lord, thank you for this day. Help me to bring the heat and do not get discouraged. While my situation may look bleak. Believe in yourself and watch everything change in an instant.

Be the catalyst for change.☺

DAY 197: Help

Today is about help.

Help can be difficult for those like me who are prideful and have experience that when we ask for help, not only did the help not come; they jerked you around in the process.

I have learned, the only person to truly run to for help is God.

God truly knows our needs and desires. He understands all the pressure we are under and when we are at our wits end.

God can feel our hearts and know when we are pure at heart. He will take care of us whether we deserve it or not.

Allow yourself to relax in the presence of God. Allow Him to become your best friend. Tell God things you wouldn't tell anyone. Get into a close bonding relationship with God. This will allow you to trust and be able to stand on His word.

It's difficult to stand on His word when your whole world is crumbling. When it feels like there is nowhere to turn and the situation is hopeless, that's exactly when God steps in.

He is the only One you need to talk this over with. He is great at keeping secrets. With God, you don't have to worry about Him blabbing your business to everyone, or being jealous of the strides you're making. God is like a supportive parent pushing along you the path of greatness.

So today: ask God for help. Regardless of previous experience with man, speak directly to God and ask for Him to cover you. When you petition God for help and spend a little time with Him, watch Him put your life into overdrive.

O Lord, thank you for this day. Help me to let go of pride and ask you for help. Allow me to trust and believe You can make my destiny come true.

DAY 198: Humiliation

Today is humiliation.

During mayoral humiliation. I experienced enough humiliation to last me a lifetime. Not only did many treat me with contempt because I was not open to being bought, the man I loved (my creative muse) was working on the rival—and ultimately the winning—team.

I didn't believe I could live through it all. I often questioned where I went wrong in my life.

I was very frustrated with life in general and didn't know where to turn. However, I came out of the situation stronger. I've survived my worst nightmare, endured constant public humiliation only to become a completely different person, a humbled person.

I have a whole new understanding of infamous versus fame. When you're famous, even locally, it's positive; when you're infamous it's negative. A lot of people know who you are but just don't get you. It's easy to side from one to another; it's part of being in the public eye.

I'm actually thankful for the experience. It strengthened my faith and allowed me to be unshaken by criticism and problems.

So today: embrace the humiliation. It allows you to become a refined and more dynamic self. You will have incredible faith in yourself and God at the end of the process.

O Lord, thank you for this day. Allow me to endure this humiliation so I may move up to the next level in my life. Help me not to become frustrated and allow me to remember everything works together for the glory of God.

Be the catalyst for change.☺

DAY 199: Idleness

Today is about dealing with idleness.

Idleness is about not working or not in use, running without applying power, passing time aimlessly.

Being idle happens between stages in your life. You can be in-between jobs, relationships, or dreams.

You feel like you're living to same day over and over like in Groundhog Day. It's difficult to sit idle without going mad. It becomes incredibly difficult to keep your spirit up.

So how do you deal with idleness in your life? Find a plan for the next stage. When there's a lull in my schedule, I always keep busy by planning the next stage of my life.

I'm always looking for future homes. I create business plans for future business. I create a life plan for myself so I'm not drifting through life aimlessly.

The best thing about idleness is that it gives you an opportunity to truly think about what you are, and we are going without pressure or stress.

Some of the best ideas come when I'm not under duress, or some crazy timeframe. It's hard to maintain and think creatively when you're grindin'. Grindin' is when you implementing your ideas, idleness is when you conceptualize them.

So today: thank God for the idle times. It gives you a rare opportunity to think without pressure about what you really want in your life.

O Lord, thank you for this day. Thank you for the idle times because they help me to organize my thoughts and dreams. Allow me to stay focused and mindful while on the path of righteousness.

Be the Catalyst for change. ☺

DAY 200: Doing the Impossible

Today is about doing the impossible.

Impossible is a situation without an easily reliable solution, something difficult, unattainable, or deemed out of the question.

I love to achieve the impossible. I've been able to complete the impossible but unable to do things that most Americans do. Go figure. ☺

When attempting the impossible, it's essential you have God on your side. God is the best guide and will direct your path.

You must believe nothing is impossible with God's help. Difficult yes, impossible no.

Things that seems impossible become easy to complete as you work toward them. It's always a long walk away from the finish line but just a jump from the middle.

God uses impossible tasks to test our faith. If you can believe in spite of what is in front of you, God can trust you more and bestow bigger blessings. You will have shown you can handle it.

So today: ask yourself to believe you can achieve the impossible. Put your hand into God's and jump out of your comfort zone. Allow yourself to do something you never imagined and see how much strength you have stored within yourself.

O Lord, thank you for this day. Help me know nothing is impossible. Allow me not to become discouraged in the face of challenges.

Be the catalyst for change.☺

DAY 201: Don't' let the World Define You

Today is about, "Don't let the world define you."

People love to place others in boxes or categories. Everyone is guilty at some point of stereotyping others.

Sometimes it's easier to stereotype someone than it is to take the time to actually get the know them.

I've worked hard not to allow the world to define me. It's difficult not to allow other perspectives to effect you but you mustn't allow it.

Stay focused on your day-to-day living and being the best person you can be.

This doesn't mean you won't have bad days and exercise poor judgment. It merely means when setbacks occur, you won't allow yourself to be beaten down from them.

You must rely on the inner strength and resolve to get past those moments. Allow your determination to shine through and now that God has your back no matter what.

So today: don't allow the world to define you. Rebel against the powers that be and live your life according to God's word and not man's. God will never fail you and faith should always rest in Him

O Lord, thank you for this day. Help me not be shaken by the world's perspective of my life. Allow me to rely on inner resolve and strength while climbing life's hurdles. Help me to ensure that God continues to be a central aspect of my life.

Be the catalyst for change.☺

DAY 202: Slow Down

Today is slow down.

I'm a methodical spender. I plan all my spending sprees even down to groceries.

My sister is an impulse shopper; when she sees something, she will say, "it's only a dollar." So I have to buy a thousand of them.

It's never something she was coveting. It's easy to buy something she just came across at the mall or some other store.

She has to slow down. We all must slow down.

My problem area may not be shopping but I'm wa-a-y-y-y too action-oriented and it truly scares pragmatic people.

When you say you have an idea, I can have a business plan in a day. I'm always easily excited and don't worry about having too much on my plate. I just get a bigger plate. Just like a gluttonous little girl, my mind is bigger than my stomach.

While I can do all of these various projects. I have to learn to finish the first couple of them and have them stable before moving on the new one. I must learn to slow down.

Slowing down isn't about being lazy and idleness. It's about taking time to look at all sides of a situation so you can anticipate all problems with ease.

God will sometimes forcefully slow us down so we can have a better game plan in place so we won't be hurt in the process.

So today: allow yourself to slow down without being resentful. Think of it as a pit stop on your road the greatness. God will always ensure we will win in the end.

Be the catalyst for change.☺

DAY 203: Pushing Through the Pain

Today is about pushing through the pain.

So I've been training since January for Peachtree Road Race, running four miles a day six days a week. I've been feeling pretty good but my neighbor who is an avid runner (running the Boston Marathon) said I need to run the route prior to the race so I can get used to it. He suggested I ride Marta Transit Station to Lenox Station and then run back to my house. #$%^^!!!!!

I knew he was right but I had been dreading it. With only three weeks left to train, I decided to buckle down and do it.

So today, I was up at 6:00 am riding Marta to Lenox. There were bumps along the way. For instance, like not knowing how to actually ride Marta. (What is a Breeze Card?) I finally figured it out and I was on my way.

I was running pretty good and did well the first five miles of the race. The last mile is when I fell apart. My iPod died and then I started to feel a little faint. I walked two blocks and then pushed through to finish. I finished in one hour and thirty minutes first try. That's rough about fifteen minutes per mile.

When I finished, I was soaking wet, and my feet were on fire. However, I was really proud of myself.

We have moments like this. There was something we always wanted to do and we achieve our goals and we're glad we pushed through the pain.

God has big plans for our lives but we must be willing to do work hard to achieve our goals. Does that mean every day will be happy? No but you must concentrate on the sunny days and continue to run this journey called life.

So today: push through the pain. Remind yourself daily there is purpose through all the blood, sweat and tears. Keep plugging away and trust God will come and will be right on time.

O Lord, thank you for the day. Help me to push through the pain of light so I may step into my destiny. Allow me to see the significant in all that happens. Help to stay in the fight despite the circumstances.

Be the catalyst for change. ☺

DAY 204: Going the Wrong Way

Today is about going the wrong way.

When training for the Peachtree Road Race, it took me so much time to determine which streets are good to run and which are not.

I finally got into a groove and found a running route I felt comfortable with.

This is the way life is at times. We spend a lot of time searching for the best route to our destiny. We try a couple of routes only to up on a dead end street.

We become frustrated with all of the running around with no real direction. At the precise moment we feel we can't take it anymore. God comes in with waves and waves of stamina and endurance.

Use God as your personal GPS navigation system. Allow Him to order your path. He already knows your destination (i.e. destiny) so allow Him to plan or route the action for you to follow.

God does not want to suffer any unnecessary harm or trouble. He wants us to be happy and live up to our full potential.

He does squeeze us however. So what is in us will come out of us. The squeezing process does cause some discomfort. However, the benefits outweigh the discomfort.

God has big plans for us and all you have to do is show up, trust and believe.

So today: stop going the wrong way and get back on track. While it seems strange and nothing seems to go right, keep pushing and don't turn back. God will provide the unique route for you while you run in this race called life.

O Lord, thank you for this day. Help me to stay on path or give me a path to follow. I'm so tired of trying to make it in life on my own. I need you to take control and give me the comfort and direction I need to get to my destiny.

Be the catalyst for change.☺

DAY 205: Indignant

Today is about being indignant.

Being indignant is one of my family's biggest jokes. We also joke about various people becoming indignant. Indignant is angry at unfairness, being offended, and resentful.

With all of the various pressures in life, it's not difficult to become indignant. It will sometimes feel like the world is totally against you.

Every time you take one tiny step forward, you have to take nine steps back. It seems you will never get to walk into your destiny. That it will be a dream deferred.

This is usually when the most movement is taking place behind the scenes. The darkest moment in the span of a day is just before dawn.

Life is similar. Just when you think I can't take anything else or nothing but bad stuff is happening and you just mentally give up, God sends you a lifeline.

God will not allow you to get caught in a situation where you have no option. God is always an option for you.

So while you can't control feeling indignant, you can control where you go for help to remove these feelings of resentment and frustration.

Today: Dare to let go of being indignant. Always remember it's the work of Evil attempting to get your attention. Resist the temptation to pour in energy that isn't worth your time and effort.

O Lord, thank you for this day. Allow me to resist the inclination to become indignant. Help me to stay focused on you instead of the petty problems of life.

Be the catalyst for change. ☺

DAY 206: Inheritance

Today is about inheritance.

Growing up I always loved Disney movies, particularly the ones with a princess in them with an inheritance. However, my family isn't wealthy, so there would be no inheritance.

So my all time favorite movie is Willy Wonka and the Chocolate Factory" because it's about a boy who actually inherits the Wonka Chocolate Factory due to the kindness in his heart and his belief that something good would happen to him.

There are an extremely limited number of people who will have inheritance in their lifetime. There is just more debt in the world than fortune. For those who are just unlucky enough not to get or win an inheritance, we are all heirs…to God's Kingdom.

God can unlock all of the wealth you can imagine if you believe. God can bless you beyond your wildest dream if you allow yourself to believe your breakthrough is coming if you can just hold on.

I know you're wondering, why it seems some are being blessed more than others are. The people you're seeing blessed, you don't know what they had to sacrifice to get there. You don't know their lonely nights, tears, and dark moments.

We're paying a price for our blessings. Don't worry about whether those blessed are paying the price. Just focus on your own breakthrough and it will reach you sooner.

So today: work on trying to unlock your inheritance from God. You can unlock your inheritance from God by living a God-focused life and truly believe your breakthrough is coming if you stay focused on the righteous path.

O Lord, thank you for this day. Allow me to believe you will provide me with an inheritance. Allow me to understand all my earthly desires are available if I just believe.

Be the catalyst for change.☺

DAY 207: Making Inquiry

Today is about making inquiry.

With my first business, it took me so time to find office space. I looked around for a long time but it was difficult for me to find a place I really liked.

Either places looked horrible or they were completely out of my price range. I was looking at places for three weeks and wasn't any closer to my goal.

I eventually just decided to wait because I was so disgusted in the spaces available.

Not because there wasn't anything available but because I have unrealistic expectations. I had to create this great amazing place in my mind that was in my price range…. The only problem was, it didn't exist.

That happens to us in life. We create in our minds what something we want looks like and when reality doesn't live up to our expectation, we become disappointed.

That's why we have to keep an open mind when we make an inquiry. Making an inquiry is the act of asking, official review, questions or query. An inquiry is merely stating you would like additional information about a particular topic.

So today: allow yourself to make an inquiry to God. Keep a fresh and open mind so God can provide to you what you need and not necessarily what you want.

O Lord, thank you for this day. Help me to have realistic expectations about life and life's plan. Allow me to stay focused and aligned with Your will.

Be the catalyst for change.☺

DAY 208: In an Instant

Today is about in an instant.

I'm extremely impatient. I want everything instantly. I don't like to wait for anything. I'll try to push everything forward to ensure I meet my personal deadlines. I usually don't care about other's timeframes unless it aligns with my own.

This is the wrong type of attitude.

Growing up and living in a digital society, we want everything instantly. We don't like to wait for anything. You can see the frustration on everyone's face when a text, web page or fax takes longer than a second to load.

Even at church, if the service lasts longer than two hours, half of the church congregation is ready to leave.

While quick and high speed is convenient, it's not always accurate. Most rumors start because the quick passing of inaccurate information.

We must attempt to develop patience in order to get quality and prompt service in all aspects of life.

There are certain things in life we must learn to savor. One of those things is spending time with God. God can fulfill all of our needs but it's on His time and with His process.

While His process may not be as fast as you would like. He is always right on time.

So today: work on pushing for quality and not on instant service. While immediate blessings are great, they can be short lived. Be willing to wait on the substantive blessing that may take time but has potential to change your life forever.

O Lord, thank you for this day. Please forgive me for all knowing and unknowing sins. Give me patience so I can wait on you to provide the breakthrough I have been dreaming about.

Be the catalyst for change. ☺

DAY 209: Feeling Invisible

Today is about feeling invisible.

When you're feeling a bit discouraged, you can feel invisible. It seems no one cares about you or is concerned about your welfare.

When friends were going through tough times, you would check on them and make them feel cared about. When you need them, you don't hear from them.

When you're on top, everyone wants to be your friend. When you're down, there isn't a soul around.

It's difficult to have a positive view of life when you feel invisible. When you're invisible, you're unnoticed, undetectable or concealed.

We all must feel a connection with the world. We need to believe the world notices we exist and more importantly, would miss us if we weren't around.

God can provide us with the connection we crave. We can pray to God to send us a connection with another so we make the best of our lives. We can't make it through life all by ourselves. We need someone else to make us feel whole and comfortable.

So today: ask God to make you visible. Allow Him to send true friends and confidantes to make you feel connected to this world and beyond.

O Lord, thank you for this day. Help me become connected with others. Allow me to open myself to the possibilities of life.

Be the catalyst for change.☺

DAY 210: Taking a Journey

Today about taking a journey.

We are in some stage of a journey. Life is filled with journeys from one stage to another.

A journey isn't anything more than a trip with a purpose in mind, a lesson to be learned. It can also be a process of development of your soul.

God is taking you somewhere you have never been before. You don't know how to prepare for it even if you should mention your journey to others.

Sometimes, it's better to keep your journey status to yourself until it's completed so it won't be disrupted.

Evil can slip in like a thief at night to rock your core and cause your journey to become stalled or even not to finish.

Life is the passage of time. What you do with time is solely up to you.

So today: allow yourself to get on your spiritual journey. Help yourself to see the purpose in all that occurs on your journey. Stay on the path of greatness and watch yourself easily step into your destiny.

O Lord, thank you for this day. Allow myself to rely on you while at various stages of my journey. Help me to weather the storms of light to threaten to take over mind, body and spirit.

Be the catalyst for change.☺

DAY 211: Justification

Today is about justification.

Does it seem like more than ever we have to justify our behavior?

In today's society, it seems like more than ever, everyone wants details and information about our life and path.

We are all addicted to the entertainment blogs and rumor mills. We want to know everyone's secrets while working incredibly hard to keep our own secrets at bay.

There is a clear foundation of nosiness overall, just silliness due to some stress of economy we are all feeling.

We don't owe anyone any explanation or reason for our behavior but God. Don't allow others to infiltrate your space and life with constant pestering.

There are times in your life you must stand up for your rights. You can take the constant annoyance only for so long.

God is taking you places He doesn't want you to share with others. He also needs your complete attention and allow others who attempt force to justify your behavior is taking away of tasks that God has ordinate.

So today: Dare to ignore them. Don't allow yourself to be drawn into silliness but justifying your behavior. You're good enough as you are right now. You don't have to force yourself to describe your life to make others feel comfortable with life under the pretense of caring. It's not caring and it's just plain nosiness.

O Lord, thank you for this day. Help me to remove people in my life who pester and just plain annoy me. Allow me to shift my focus to God's will instead of allowing others to impose their will on me.

Be the catalyst for change.☺

MONTH 8

DAY 212: Making up for What's Lacking

Today is making up for what's lacking.

There is always something I'm lacking. I may have noodles and sauce but no turkey ground beef. Or I have the perfect pair of shoes with no dress. Or I have a great career with no man. It's always something. ☺

It just seems like we're always dealing with a lack in some area of our lives.

We must all learn to live with less or find a way to make up for a deficiency.

We develop a way to cope with a deficiency. Some of us go into the light and other retreat into darkness.

We have certain areas in our lives that aren't the best. What we must do is stop focusing on the negative and begin looking at the positive.

While everything is surely not perfect, it's definitely livable if you keep your eyes on God.

God will send us tools to help us with the deficiencies in our lives. He won't put more on you than you can bear. He didn't say it would be smooth sailing or that you wouldn't feel discomfort in the process but you will not be harmed.

So allow today: makeup for what is lacking in your life. Stay focused on the good and allow God to take care of the rest.

O Lord, thank you for your day. Please forgive me for my sins. Allow me to make up for what's lacking in my life and yet be thankful for what I have.

Be the catalyst for change.☺

DAY 213: Letting go of the Drama

Today is about letting go of the drama.

We are such a drama-filled society. We have become addicted to conflict and drama. I think we have because we can see clear resolution after loads and loads of conflict. There have been many people who have fostered and contributed to drama in my life.

I keep wondering why it seemed like drama-filled people kept entering into my life. I was becoming so sick of the drama. Then I took a look in the mirror. I believe I became addicted to the drama subconscious. I have a habit of only seeing the good in people and ignoring the rest. You must look at the total person and make a decision of whether that best is good for you or toxic.

I realized I must make changes in my life and decided to cut people out of my life.

These were people I felt more pity than love. That I have questioned in my mind many times, why am I friends with them? Once I made the decision, my life has become better because of it.

God wants to take you places and allow you to step into your destiny. However, He can't bless you until you let go of some of the drama in your life.

When you build a brand, the brand is affected by not just you but the people around you. While you may be able to control yourself, others don't understand the empire you're attempting to build and can sabotage it. Don't allow this to happen.

So today, let go of the drama in your life. Allow God to send you even tempered people who will support you but also help along the path to greatness. You can't make it in this world alone. However, you don't want people around who could wreck all of your hard work.

O Lord, thank you for this day. Help me to let go of the drama in my life. Allow me to give people a chance to see the havoc they have caused in my life and for you to send others who won't. Help to rely on You and not try to resolve this myself.

Be the catalyst for change.☺

DAY 214: Meditation

Today is about meditation.

Meditation can be used in your life at every stage. Meditation is deliberation, consideration, and reflection.

Meditation is a great tool to focus your energies so your mind, body, and spirit can stand in the right area. It's being present in what is going on right now instead of allowing your mind to drift to the past and future.

When God requests for you to meditate on something, He's requesting for us to think and ponder about something. Usually it made reference to His words. God's words are very powerful and can unlock your mind. It can help give you direction and focus but you must spend time in the word to receive it.

Spending time in God's Word (i.e. bible study) is an important way to start your day. God can't control how Evil seeps into your life however spending time in God's word can help change how you deal with situations.

God will always give us directions and it's located in His word. However, you must be willing to read His words in order to unlock the power of it.

So today: spend a little more than usual meditating on God's words. He has a lesson in them for each of us. We must open the book to receive them.

O Lord, thank you for this day. Allow me to spend more time in your words. Touch my heart, mind, and spirit. Help me to stay focused and don't allow me to stray off from the plan you have given me.

Be the catalyst for change.☺

DAY 215: Think it Over

Today is called think it over.

I have always been a person who thinks incredibly fast on my feet. I don't need time to mull over a decision because I'm completely in or completely out.

Now my muse, the most significant love of my life, is completely a different story. He has such a pragmatic way of thinking.

It seems he struggles over very little decisions. I bet he struggles at McDonald's over what to order unless he has ordered it before. LOL ☺

However, it's because of his chosen field, law. It's important for him to look at all sides of an argument—much to my dismay at times.

He clearly allows this way of thinking into all aspects of his life. After three years, we are reaching the end of the road.

I believe guys know whether they can marry or not within the first six months and the rest of the time they're stalling.

I also believe there is an inability of him to grow up and become an adult. Getting married and having kids is an adult behavior, something we run from.

However, I'm prone to do a bit of running on my own. It's hard for me to put a stop to something I really want. Its hard-core negotiation with no expectations.

I can do it in business but not in personal life. So the time has come with us to either move on or move to the next level. Now I must state my position then step back and give it some space. Allow him to think it over without getting offended.

There are sometimes you love someone who's a bit hesitant in making a decision about commitment. You can't make the decision for them; they must make it on their own and on their own time.

So today: allow them to think it over. Be patient. Regardless of what the future may hold, you must be willing to allow them to make a decision they feel comfortable with.

O Lord, thank you for this day. Allow me to stay patient while waiting on my breakthroughs. Help me to stay focused on you while I wait.

Be the catalyst for change.☺

DAY 216: In for the Long Haul

Today is about whether you're in it for the long haul.

Women are always quick to say we're so ready to get married. Women want the wedding and being the center of attention.

We want to be able to say: "My husband and I... "or to have someone to come to at night. To know we are not in life alone.

However, I'm not sure women are ready for what marriage holds.

Think of marriage like buying a home. If you don't take the time and really research your home, that could have long lasting consequences.

When you pick a mate, this is the person you will be with for life. You may see death of family together, financial difficulties together, unemployment together, etcetera. So when I believe women should pause and consider: is this person a partner for life, or a great partner for right now?

Sometimes, God will pause or stall a blessing to give you the opportunity to really consider if this is really what you want.

Allow yourself to really ponder if this is who you really want or are you just so focused on finishing the goal you've gotten to a place of, "by any means necessary?"

No one is perfect. However, you want to make sure you have the same lifestyle and value system. This will become a major issue if you don't handle it now.

So today: really think about whether you're in this for the long haul. Do you really think you can be with a person despite life's challenges?

O Lord, thank you for this day. Thank you for allowing me time to decide whether this person I love is really for me. Allow me to see all aspects of this person so I can be sure our relationship will stand the test of time.

Be the catalyst for change.☺

DAY 217: Turning a Blind Eye

Today is about turning the blind eye.

I have a habit of only see the best in people instead of seeing the total person.

I may see the fact that the person is a gifted musician but yet they can't get the gig of their dreams because they never follow through on leads.

A person may be a genius but has a raging addiction problem. She is a great publicist but is extremely unreliable.

I have a habit of turning the blind eye.

There are some times in life when you're walking straight into danger. God will try to warn you in various ways.

However, we often ignore the signs because we have personal feelings that have gotten involved. Whether it's relationship or new business venture, it's easy to allow your feeling to be vested.

Turning the blind eye can be detrimental to your life. Not only does this situations completely catch you off guard, they also wreak havoc on your reputation and brand.

So today: stop turning a blind eye. Face the problems head on and try to resolve them. While you may not like what you're seeing, it's necessary for you to be aware of so you can make an informed decision.

O Lord, thank you for this day. Help me see everything and stop allowing myself to see what I want to see. Allow me to find comfort in you when I'm disappointed beyond belief. Help me to stay focused on being aligned with your will.

Be the catalyst for change.☺

DAY 218: Willingness to Deliberate

Today is about being willing to deliberate.

One of my lifelong dreams is to become a contestant on Jeopardy. It's one of my favorite shows. My favorite part is at the end with the final question and all of the contestants are given an opportunity to deliberate with famous theme music.

When you deliberate, you're giving yourself an opportunity to reflect, mull over, ponder and think about something.

I believe deliberation is necessary in every aspect of your life. I know I'm someone who does not do it very often but I'm attempting to learn.

There are certain decisions in life requiring you to deliberate. God wants to give you an opportunity to see His vision and to hear from Him.

Deliberation allows Him to speak to us in amazing and powerful ways.

God wants the best for us. He is constantly working hard on our behalf to ensure we are able to reach our potential and live out our destiny.

Allow God's words of wisdom to seep into your mind, body, and spirit. Allow Him to use deliberation to help to make major decisions in your life, such as whether or not to purchase a car or even whether you should marry someone in particular.

So today: be willing to deliberate. Free your mind and allow yourself to soar with God by your side. God wants the best for us and you must allow Him to speak to your heart to ensure you stay in step with Him.

O Lord, thank you for this day. Help me to spend more time in deliberation. Allow me to rely on you more than ever to help me to make sound business decisions.

Be the catalyst for change.☺

DAY 219: Regrets

Today is about regret.

I'm someone who, when I make a decision, I'm willing to stick to it. For better or worse. However, I study all things about a decision before I make it so I will decrease my likelihood of regret.

Regrets are tiny pieces of doubt in your mind about a decision you have made. These pieces can wreak havoc on your mind, body, and spirit.

We all have one life to live. We will try to cram millions of years of living into our lives so we don't miss out on any aspect of life. Any time I have hesitated in agreeing with something, I have always lived to regret it. God gives us intuition for a reason.

Allow yourself to trust your instinct and know when to say no. While there may be some discomfort in potentially disappointing others, you will be happy with yourself in the long run.

So today: live without regrets. The only person you must answer to is yourself and God. Trust God when He sends you cues about whether you should do something or not. Allow yourself to pay attention to any urging in your spirit so you won't have any regrets later.

O Lord, thank you for this day. Help me to listen to you more so I decrease my regrets. Allow me to trust and stand on Your word in all situations even in the most mundane.

Be the catalyst for change.☺

DAY 220: Underestimated

Today is about being underestimated.

I love being underestimated in business. That means they never see you coming.

They don't understand what a threat you are. They lower their guard and never think for a second they are telling their secrets to a major contender.

When you're underestimated, it's easy to go into stealth mode. That's when you can make major moves without arousing suspicion.

However, being used to being underestimated does that. It can feel like a slap in the face to all the hard work you have placed in your craft.

There are various reasons why people are underestimated but you can drive yourself crazy wondering why you're not worthy of others respect. Don't.

Being an innovator is something everyone doesn't always understand. You're usually ahead of your time and seen as a little strange. Embrace the strangeness but that's what makes you so unique.

Just focus on achieving your goals and you will have the last laugh. However, remember all those who doubted you.

So today: embrace being underestimated. Thank God that you're able to make some of the biggest moves in your life under the radar. Find solace in the fact that at some point your time is coming and people will know just how innovative you are.

O Lord, thank you for this day. Please forgive me for all knowing and unknowing sins. Allow me to thank you for being underestimated. Help me to see the value in making major moves without anyone noticing. Allow me to stay focus on my goals and believe one day all my hard work will pay off.

Be the catalyst for change.☺

DAY 221: Not a Good Fit

Today is about not being a good fit.

I'm single and I have dated many good men in my life. They were special in their own ways. They had great jobs, attractive and rising pioneers in their field of expertise. The only problem: they were not a good fit for me.

A good fit for you is someone who you feel comfortable with. A person who will fit well in your life. A person who you share the same value system and lifestyle.

Most importantly, someone who isn't difficult to maintain. Trust me; there are some high maintenance men out there.

So while these were great men, I had to pass on them because they didn't align with my life.

God gives us discerning spirit in order to determine what is best for us. Trust this gift, Sometimes all isn't what it seems.

That cute accountant might have his stuff together but that underemployed government worker is giving you the butterflies. You could find out that accountant had criminal legal troubles while the underemployed government worker doesn't. However, you couldn't see from first glance. However, when I met the cute accountant, I knew he was off and I couldn't place what was wrong.

So today, allow yourself to determine who is a good fit in your life. Trust your discerning spirit to figure out whether this person will easily become a part of your life.

O Lord, thank you for this day. Help to figure out who is a good fit in my life. Allow me to trust the urging of my spirit from you. Help to believe all things work for the glory of you.

Be the catalyst for change.☺

DAY 222: Leave me to my own Thoughts

Today is about leaving me to my own thoughts.

I'm independent thinking and not easily swayed by public opinion. I've usually made up my mind prior to any in-depth discussion.

While I try to avoid, I am a businesswoman at heart and I'm always focused on being my brand.

I am astute in knowing when someone thinks they're getting something over on me. Which is fine because, I'll give all the information and leave out one key detail and let you figure it out yourself.

However, most of the time, I don't need anyone to help to come to a decision. I already know what my plans are.

What I do need is time to think things over without any interrupting. You can tell when I am in thought mode because I have a habit of retreating from the social world to grind and do what's necessary to get the job done.

There are times in our lives we become so caught in day-to-day living, we miss opportunities left out of our thoughts.

We must make sure we spend time immersed in our thoughts so we are clear about all of the decisions we intend to make. Don't allow the hustle and bustle of life to interrupt your thinking process.

So today: allow yourself to spend a little time with your thoughts. Don't be so quick to fill your day without a lot of things to do that give the break needed.

O Lord, thank you for this day. Help me stay focused on You when I'm left to my own thoughts. Guide my decision making so it's always aligned with your will.

Be the catalyst for change.☺

DAY 223: Some Experiences are Priceless

Today is about some experiences being priceless.

Some things in life are priceless. These are items that have occurred that have such an emotional attachment to them there is no amount of money that can purchase them.

Time spent with loved ones or the birth of a child is deemed priceless.

The time I spent with my grandmother is now priceless. Particularly the night before she passed, she had been floating in and out of consciousness for about a week. My mom, sister and I were the only ones left in the room very late at night. She opened her eyes and really looked at us and she looked so tired. My mom told her she could go now if she wanted. I couldn't say anything because I was being selfish and I didn't feel that way at the time. I wanted her to stick around and fight. She nodded and went back to sleep. She died at seven the next morning.

The ability to be there for those last moments with grandmother was priceless.

While we're constantly focused on this money and making sure to get the next career wise, we still must acknowledge we must make time, for those items are priceless.

So today: allow yourself to spend time on some items that are priceless. Spend time with loved ones; hang out with your friends. Life is just too short to put off making time for those bolstering those emotional connections.

O Lord, thank you for this day: Thank you for giving up those priceless experiences. Help me stay centered on your will so I can continue to have more of those life-changing experiences.

Be the catalyst for change.☺

DAY 224: Don't Become Detached

Today: don't become detached.

When I'm into someone, I'm totally into them. I can spend all day and all night with them. There isn't anything they can do wrong. I'm completely and totally smitten.

However, when I'm done or just not interested. There isn't anything you can do right. I've become detached and feel nothing for you. Once you reach the point of no return with me, there isn't anything you can do to woo my back.

We all can become detached from friends, family, jobs etcetera for various reasons. Some times out of lack of interest, sometimes out of protection.

After we have been hurt so much, we take special precautions to ensure we won't get hurt again and one of those solutions is becoming detached.

The only problem is, once you employ this technique, it's not easy to turn off. It's a long-term effect. If you're detached for a long period of time, it can help to foster a numbing of your emotions that you feel nothing for anyone, even when you want to.

So while it's a highly successful technique when needed, be careful; you become numb and begin not to care about life.

So today: be careful when you employ the detachment technique. While it can be helpful, don't allow it to change the course of your life or cause you to become indifferent to things you once held dear.

O Lord, thank you for this day. Please forgive me for known and unknown sins. Allow me to only be detached when absolutely necessary. Help me to know when to turn it on and off. Allow me to stay focused on You for guidance and strength.

Be the catalyst for change.☺

DAY 225: Being up Front

Today is about being up front.

I'm completely a straight shooter in business and personal. You will know where I stand, good or bad.

I really don't like to keep secrets but rather I keep information on a need to know basis.

However, I'm upfront even with that. I feel like the worst thing to feel is when someone wasn't clear with you about their plans. You will be allowed to put your faith in someone or something with a shaky foundation. Once this happens, you'll make it your life's purpose not to do the same to others.

However, being upfront has its benefits:

No one can accuse you of tricking them. They had a clear idea of what they were getting themselves into when dealing with me.

There are no surprises. With surprises, you can place clear concrete plans for the future that are founded in heavy doses of reality.

It's honest. There are very few places in life you can find true honesty. Not cruelty but still honesty. When you're upfront with someone, there's trust there because of the honesty. No one likes to be jerked around, so it's such a blessing to have someone being completely honest and transparent with you.

So today: strive to be more upfront. While it might not be pleasant and it's definitely more trustworthy. God has a hand in all of our lives. Being upfront is manifest of God's Love. Share it, embrace, and believe it. Don't jerk people around.

O Lord, thank you for this day. Help me become upfront with people in all aspects in my life. Allow me to see the positive energy this action will bring to me.

Be the catalyst for change.☺

DAY 226: What about Your Intentions?

Today is, "What about your intentions?"

My father loves that statement. Growing up, he would ask all of my boyfriends that question and relished in watching them stammer out an answer.

He believed if they couldn't answer the question that meant they couldn't lie quick on their feet and their intentions were not good. Unfortunately, he was right every time.

Your intentions say a lot about you as a person. Your intentions are your motives, aim, or purpose for that event, person, or venture.

We all have intentions; however, they are not always positive. Most of the time, we would rather not share them.

We must ask God to give us a discerning spirit so we can figure out others' intentions.

God will send you the tools so you can remove yourself from danger but it's up to you to listen. God will always provide signals before we enter a landmine.

While, at times, it may be difficult to decipher, it's worth the effort to attempt to figure it out.

So today: ask those in your life to state their intentions. Allow yourself to see where you fit in their lives. While you may not like what you discover, it will be beneficial to your development.

O Lord, thank you for this day. Please forgive me for my sins. Allow me to discern the intentions of those around me. Help me to have strength to accept what I discover.

Be the catalyst for change.☺

DAY 227: Staying Away From the Victim

Today is about staying away from the victim.

I have one girlfriend who has the worst luck ever. All of these horrible things always happen to her all the time. She always seems to be in one crisis or another all of the time. We have all tried to help her but it seems like the mountain of problems is even too much for two people to handle, let alone one.

However, with further inspection, you begin to see the problems she keeps being involved in are part of her own doing. For instance, someone keys your car but you fail to tell us you were dealing with someone else's boyfriend. So, that could be the cause of the problems.

She's a professional victim. Beware. ☺

You must be careful with anyone who is constantly a victim in every situation. I'm sure you know someone in your life just like this. They always state, "this isn't my fault" before you even ask questions.

We are all human and we make mistakes. In every situation, there's enough blame to go around. There isn't anything that's completely innocent in every situation. At best, you're guilty of enabling the problems you're now having.

Be careful with these pros. They have enough power to not only drag you into their mess but also knock you off your spiritual walk in the process.

So, today, be careful of the professional victim. Allow God to give you the right questions to spot them. Allow yourself not to become meshed into the situations that are spiraling way out of control.

O Lord, thank you for this day. Help me to become a better person. Allow me to discern a professional victim and move away from this problem. While I will continue to pray for them, help to see their hand that they have in their problems.

Be the catalyst for change.☺

DAY 228: Empowering Yourself

Today is about empowering yourself.

To empower yourself is to make yourself more confident, assertive or to inspire.

I work hard each day to empower myself. Some things in life are negative; you must work hard to see the positive or you won't survive on this journey called life.

You must work to set your mind free and be willing to explore all of the possibilities God has for you in life.

There are three ways to ensure you empower yourself:

Stay positive. Happy people are easy to be around and to do business with. They are able to see the silver lining in everything and positive energy/things are drawn to them. Dare to become more positive on a daily basis.

Stay in prayer. God has wonderful opportunities for us that He is just dying to tell us but you have to talk to Him to find out what they are. Allow yourself time in prayer so you will know what direction to go.

Be realistic. We have a habit of shooting for perfection. Perfection doesn't exist. Allow yourself to be realistic in life, your expectation, or your will.

So today: Dare to empower yourself. Place positive energy into the atmosphere; watch what you get in return. God is always watching us to ensure we're striving for our potential. Allow yourself to build; all of this is possible and watch your life soar.

O Lord, thank you for this day. Help me to stay focused on your will. Allow me to empower myself by staying positive, being realistic and staying in prayer. I believe you will bring me what I need to step into my destiny.

Be the catalyst for change.☺

DAY 229: Mistakes

Today is about mistakes.

In seems, in today's society, we're so afraid of making mistakes. With so much poverty, job loss, and overall despair lurking around every corner, most people just want to go to a place where they can maintain their lifestyle at best.

I'm guilty of this. I have made mistakes but I don't like being embarrassed. It seems everyone harps on it, since I rarely make them, which makes me even more sensitive and self-critical.

Unfortunately, mistakes are the best feedback possible. They will teach you more about yourself than positive energy will.

Mistakes will show you who is really riding with you and who is pretending. It shows who really believes in the dream and who is just frontin.'

Mistakes reflect an error in judgment or misunderstanding. While it can be embarrassing, mistakes teach us a lot about ourselves. We know instantly where we need to focus.

So today, allow yourself to be ok with mistakes. Mistakes are a part of life. Embrace them. They will ultimately help you on your path to your destiny.

O Lord, thank you for this day. Allow me to embrace my mistakes of past, present and future. Help me to understand their purpose, so I may not continue to repeat them.

Be the catalyst for change.☺

DAY 230: Lifting Yourself Up

Today is about lifting yourself up.

Right after the mayoral race, I was completely crushed with no backup plan and no motivation to do something. The sting of defeat combined with my disappointment in others' actions was just too much to bear.

I retreated more and more into myself. I didn't want to eat, drink or work out. All I wanted to do was just sleep. I don't remember anything from the last two months of 2009.

I was so depressed; I requested that my family not celebrate Thanksgiving and Christmas at all. I just sat alone in my dark condo talking to no one and watching a DVD box set of the Simpsons series.

There are times in life when you must lift yourself up. With these tough economic times, everyone is struggling with something. People are caught up in their own dramas so you have to encourage yourself.

God will sometimes isolate you so you can see what's really important in life. He will make sure you have no one to rely on but Him.

Keep in constant prayer. Prayer is the direct lifeline to God and will allow you to feel that intimate connection that will keep you running in this race called life. Prayer also will give you hope and confidence to face each day with the expectation that life will be better if you continue to believe.

Prayer can allow waves of urging in your spirit that you can make it and you're more than the circumstances around you. God will began to direct your path so you'll know clearly and succinctly of what to do.

So today: lift yourself up. Ask God to help and direct your life. Allow yourself to trust Him and watch your life slowly begin to show signs of progress.

O Lord, thank you for this day. Help me to continue to lift myself in prayer. Allow me to stay in communication with you so you can help to weather the storms of life.

Be the catalyst for change.☺

DAY 231: Being Selfish

Today is about being selfish.

Being selfish is about looking after your own desires and self-interest. There are times in your life when you're close to getting to your breakthrough and you must stay completely focused on yourself.

If you're a football player, when the playoffs begin, you don't relax; rev it up.

You have to be selfish with your time, your body, and your spirit. You'll not get to the next level in life if you don't become focused on yourself and your dreams.

When you're truly in the presence of God, He will give you vision for your life. This vision will excite your spirit and you will be bursting forth with ways to make your vision become a reality.

However, in order for your vision to become a reality, you must buckle down. Manifesting a vision takes hard work, perseverance and faith in yourself.

That's why, certain times, it's ok to be selfish. You must be your biggest advocate and only you know how important your vision is.

Don't always count on others to have your back but rather focus on getting the job done yourself.

So today: allow yourself to be selfish when you're pursuing your dreams. God has given you a vision and He wants you to put in the work to help it come to fruition.

O Lord, thank you for this day. Allow me to become selfish and focus on myself. Help me to have the strength to manifest my vision into my reality.

Be the catalyst for change.☺

DAY 232: Evolving

Today is about evolving.

When you're evolving as a person, you're developing or changing gradually. It's natural to evolve as a person as you get older. However, it's a process that also allows your life to change as well.

While in college, I was such a party girl. I loved hanging out socially; career aspirations came second. We would go out every night to events or parties in Atlanta. Then we would take road trips to other cities for a change of scenery.

Now, fast forward ten years later, I'm a completely different person. I no longer feel the need to hang out all of the time socially. I will occasionally, once every couple of weeks and definitely don't stay there long. Before we would stay until the event ended. Work is more important that my social life, so my motivations are different.

When your motivations begin to change, that means your values are changing as well. Things and people who have major significance in your life no longer are as important.

When you allow God truly to enter your heart, He will help to lose interest in things that will not help you on the path to destiny. He slowly urges you toward things that will help you get to the next level in life.

So today: allow yourself to evolve. Progress is good for the mind, body, and spirit. Let God enter your heart and watch Him change your life for the better.

O Lord, thank you for this day. Help to evolve as a person and remove anything from my life that inhibits my destiny. Allow me to have enough faith and belief to get to the next level.

Be the catalyst for change.☺

DAY 233: When Desperation Sets In

Today is about when desperation sets in.

Desperation isn't something anyone seeks. It happens through a misguided attempt to make something happen that's having the results you would like.

The times in my life when I became desperate, are when I have become too emotionally attached to a situation or person. Whatever, it wasn't going well, so I'm attempting to resuscitate something that was dying.

That's when my passion and competitive spirit comes out. That's when I go really hard. It's really not a good look. I can become really unattractive fast.

Sometimes, we must allow life to occur. Every story in your life isn't meant to have a happy ending. While this hurts, it's important to your development. Sometimes, you can learn more from a bad experience than a good one.

The best thing to do when you feel the desperation kick in is to give up control and give it to God. God can pick up the slack when life becomes too much to handle. It may seem all you need to do is to apply some pressure and work a little harder to achieve your desired result.

That, in fact, is the last thing you should do. Applying less pressure is always better. Allow people to make the decision on their own. It also saves your dignity and peace of mind in the process.

So today, don't allow the desperation to set in. Resist the urge to apply pressure when you should just let go and let God handle it. God has our best interests at heart; so just allow Him to handle it for you.

O Lord, thank you for this day. Allow me not to become desperate. Help me to rely heavily on you to solve all of life's problems. Allow me to believe what is good for me will be without a lot of prodding on my part.

Be the catalyst for change.☺

DAY 234: Time for Spring Cleaning

Today is time for spring-cleaning.

I love to live in a clean environment. While I don't necessarily like to clean but I do like the feeling of knowing my home is clean and everything is washed and put away.

When it was time for spring. I changed my air conditioner's filter. Then I switched my closet from winter clothes and boots to summer clothes and sandals.

We must do the same emotionally and spiritually.

Many things exist in our minds that we must work hard to remove. Bad memories and situations don't merely just disappear; you must work hard to remove them.

We can harbor trauma from situations that occurred years ago in our minds. We can relive the situation over and over hoping to see purpose or significance in the situation.

It takes time to see significance in your life and it might be years to be revealed. However, you can't allow yourself to keep the situation of emotion or spiritual DVR until you figure it out.

When you don't remove negative situations from your mind, it's difficult to move to the next level.

So today: do a bit of emotional/spiritual spring-cleaning. Allow yourself to remove thoughts and practices in your life that are dated. Help yourself to move past hurt and pain and move to the next level.

O Lord, thank you for this day. Please forgive me for my sins. Allow me to remove any thoughts and memories that are no longer applicable. Help me stand on your word and be able to continue in this race called life.

Be the catalyst for change.☺

DAY 235: Surviving a Spiritual Avalanche

Today is about surviving a spiritual avalanche.

I went through of period time between law school and graduate school when I wasn't really sure what I wanted out of life.

I have just finished my first year and was doing my internship at Fulton County's DA office. It wasn't that the law was the answer for me. However, what should I do?

For the last two years of college, I had been prepping from law school only to get there and not really like it. Combined with fact, I was living in a small town and away from all of my friends.

I was feeling really isolated and alone. It seems when I was talking with my friends, they were out having the time of their life, and I was stuck in a hick town.

I was caught in a spiritual avalanche. A spiritual avalanche occurs when suddenly a large number of issues threaten to overwhelm you. They amass very quickly and come in like a rushing flood.

You become paralyzed with the fear of the unknown and how things got so bad so quickly.

Getting caught in a spiritual avalanche is a part of life. However, you must learn how to survive it. Surviving an on slot of problems requires large doses of faith. Faith that life will get better; Faith that God will send relief, Faith that you're more than the circumstances around you. Faith in yourself that while you're down you're not out.

So today: have faith in yourself to get out of this spiritual avalanche you're in. Continue to trust and believe and watch your life change for the better.

O Lord, thank you for this day. Please forgive me for all knowing and unknowing sins. Allow me to understand that there is purpose in all problems but have faith in spirit to survive them.

Be the catalyst for change.☺

DAY 236: Chaos of the Mind

Today is about chaos of the mind.

I absolutely hate chaos but it's what I live now in my life. There are constantly things going on because of all of the projects I'm working. People are always unreliable and hard to manage. They make you believe they have everything under control only to realize they don't have things under control at all. It makes life very difficult and frustrating.

This chaos eventually bleeds into my mind. I can't relax and it gives me major anxiety. It always causes me discomfort to know things are still hanging over my head and not done properly. Combined with negative feedback, it makes me want to scream.

Chaos sucks. It really seeps into your spirit and causes major irritation in your life. I prefer things in my life to be positive and energetic but it's not always the case.

We must learn how to deal with the chaos attempting to infiltrate our spirit. Evil will send chaos to get into your mind to cause you not to be able to strategize. Once the chaos is in your mind, you'll fixate on attempting to resolve everything instead of creating a plan and then slowly removing all of the problems, one by one.

So today: don't allow chaos of the mind to get you down. God can solve all of our problems in due time if we just believe He can. He may not come every time you call Him but He will come right on time.

O Lord, thank you for this day. Allow me not to become stressed when life doesn't go my way. Allow me to become calm and allow me to stay relaxed and allow God to fix everything.

Be the catalyst for change.☺

DAY 237: Throwing out the Trash

Today is about throwing out the trash.

When I became a homeowner, I discovered a plus to condo living immediately, a trash chute.

I was completely overjoyed, especially for a neat freak like me. This door with a trash chute where you can throw away all of your trash day or night. So no dragging your trash out to the corner or throwing it away when you leave the building. If I decide I want to have a cleaning spell at 2 am, I can and throw things away with little problem to me.

Some of us need to spent time throwing out the trash in our life. Trash can take on many forms. Trash can be discarded material, garbage, waste, debris, or just general nonsense.

Trash is something that no longer has a place in our lives and needs to be removed. However, there is a little part of us that doesn't want to let go because it's part of our identity.

However, it's inhibiting your growth. God will stop you from making any movement forward until you clear out some of the trash in your life.

God wants us to be happy and to achieve our goals. However, He does have some requirements to ensure we stay on the path of greatness. One of those requirement is that we completely rely totally on you. You can't move forward and still attempt to make it happen on your own. God is a jealous one; He doesn't want anything above Him.

So today: let go of some of the trash in your life. These items are not good for you and become toxic in your life. While it may be difficult to allow yourself to remove them.

O Lord, thank you for this day. Please forgive me for my sins. Allow me to let go of some of the trash in my life. Help me to rely on you to remove these items and people, what is truly best for me.

Be the catalyst for change.☺

DAY 238: Holding On

Today is about, "why are you holding on?"

I have a habit of not letting go of things that are no longer applicable in my life. I have a box of VCR tapes I can't play because I no longer have a VCR player. Yet I'm still holding on with thoughts I would have someone convert them to DVDs. That has been at least three or four years.

So what are you holding onto and why?

We all have something or someone we're holding onto with bloody fingers. Whatever the reason, it's not healthy and it's creating a toxic environment to you.

God will send you guidance to remove things and sometimes we don't listen. It's difficult to just let go and act like these items don't have significance to us.

God has a replacement waiting but He can't give it to you until you put down the other one. God doesn't do even exchanges. You must trust in the Lord that He will send you what you need.

So today: stop holding on. Let it go. Allow God to send you exactly what you need exactly at the time you need it. Help yourself to believe and rely on past situations that God provided.

O Lord, thank you for this day. Allow yourself to believe God has a replacement for me so I let go of things that no longer serve a purpose. Increase my belief so I may get through any period of time between the removal and replacement coming.

Be the catalyst for change.☺

DAY 239: Burying the Dead

Today is about burying the dead.

We all carry around a lot of dead spirits. We keep photos, text messages, letters of past relationships. We keep documents from past jobs.

We all have regrets about something in our lives. We become consumed by our mistakes and always spend time walking down memory lane thinking about what could have been.

It's done. You have to bury it. When someone or something dies, you must go through the grieving process in order to move on. Grief allows you to express your regrets and the fact you will miss this thing or person that was once in your life. Then you must find closure so you can move on.

You will not be able to get to the next level in life unless you bury the open memories of yesterday. Open memories are memories with some type of expectation the future can change in any moment.

Close the memories and allow the fragments of your past to exist with no expectation of them affecting your future.

So today: bury the dead. Let these memories not only be buried in your mind but also in your spirit. Allow yourself to close a door so you can open another.

O Lord, thank you for this day. Please forgive me for your sins. Allow me to let go of the past so my future can enter my life.

Be the catalyst for change.☺

DAY 240: Breaking the Cycle

Today is about breaking the cycle.

We have habits we need to break that are part of family lineage. On my dad's side, all of the women marry men with personalities that pale in comparison to theirs. Sometimes, I believe it causes some misery on both sides. I want to break the cycle and I want to make sure I marry someone who is an equal partner.

There are many other areas in our lives where we must make an effort to break the cycle. A cycle is a repeated sequence of events.

Our parents, while they loved us, are not perfect people. They did the best they could with the tools they had. We must work hard to learn from the mistakes they made so we can stop the cycle and not continue the mistakes.

We know these issues are not positive; yet we don't address it and treat it like the norm.

God will allow you to see the pattern of events, so you can stop it from happening again. This is God urging you in your spirit, so you can stop it for future generations.

So today: break the cycle. Allow yourself to see what areas in your life need to be changed.

O Lord, thank you for this day. Please forgive me for my sins. Allow me to recognize what habits in my life need to be broken. Help me to remove all cycles in my family that are not healthy and toxic.

Be the catalyst for change.☺

DAY 241: The Power of Fasting

Today is about the power of fasting.

A fast is when you abstain from food or drink, or something else you do on a routine basis.

Fasting is powerful when you want to hear from God. Fasting is excellent when you need God to show immediately or when you're making a big decision.

I'm such a foodie, the mere thought of fasting was difficult to comprehend let alone do.

However, I really wanted to hear from God about a particular issue I decided to do my first fast. I kept trying to close on my home in 2007 and it seemed like nothing was going right. That was over three years ago. I definitely recommend fasting.

Will it be difficult? Yes, particularly the first day. I always end up going to sleep really early on the first day of the fast because I can think about little else. Each day gets easier and you can really hear from God without any distractions.

You will get an answer. Be careful, it might not be what you wanted. However, you will receive one. It would be bad news but rather instead of going one direction, you will be told to go a different way.

Sometimes, it comes like a blinding light and then sometimes it comes at the end of a fast. It will be showers of blessings coming from various places.

So today: allow yourself to see the power of fasting. Fasting not only provides direct answers from God that you have been looking for but it brings you closer to God.

O Lord, thank you for this day. Please forgive me my sins. Allow me to let go of my inhibitions and try the power of fasting. Help me to keep on the path of righteous so I may become stronger in my walk with you.

Be the catalyst for change.☺

MONTH 9

DAY 242: Spiritual Awakening

Today is its time for Spiritual awakening.

I'm definitely a morning person. However, as I'm getting older, it takes me a little longer to get up in the morning if I haven't had enough sleep. I will push snooze on my cell phone at least five times before I get up.

Once I'm up, I have a positive attitude. However, it does take work. ☺

We all have to make an effort to create a spiritual awakening. With all of the busyness in our lives combined with the pressure of economic times, it's easy to get asleep at the wheel of life.

Everything becomes automated and you begin to go through the motions. You must make an effort to wake your soul.

When you have an awakening, you receive a renewed attention to something. A stirring, arousing feeling building in your spirit.

In order to have spiritual awakening, you must spend a little time with God. Spending a little time with God will help to allow your spirit to soar and yearn for more stability in your life.

So today: create a spiritual awakening for yourself. Spend a little time with God and watch Him give you an urging in your spirit that you have never felt before.

O Lord, thank you for this day. Please forgive me for my sins. Allow me to get a spiritual awakening to jolt my spirit of my stupor. Help to increase my faith and believe so I can develop a better relationship with you.

Be the catalyst for change.☺

DAY 243: A Person of Character

Today is about becoming a person of character.

We all are born with character; it just hasn't been activated. Character is your distinctive quantities, nature, and moral fiber.

Character defines what you're willing to do in your life. How far are you willing to go?

When things aren't going well, it's easy to become desperate and start taking desperate actions. That's when you character will show. When you show what you're truly are made of.

God wants us all to be a people of character and keep our values in check, even during tough times.

We all must make an effort to give our problems to God. This will allow us to keep our moral fiber in check.

When you're too vested into your problems. You will attempt to move God along or "help Him" God doesn't need our help. We think we're helping but we're really in the way. Step aside and allow God to take control of your life completely,

So today, allow yourself to become a person of character. Trust God and give up control to Him. While relinquishing control can be a difficult thing, it's necessary in order to become a person of true Character and Christ-like.

O Lord, thank you for this day. Help me become a person of character. Keep me close to your heart and allow me to let go of complete control in my life.

Be the catalyst for change.☺

DAY 244: God's Love

Today is about God's love.

We all need love. However, a particular type of love, unconditional love. While we would like to assume we can get this from close family and friends, God can always provide the type of love we need.

There isn't anything we have to do to obtain God's Love. All we have to do is exist. God loves us despite all of our transgressions. He loves us when we are down and loves us when we are up.

God loves when we are positive and He loves us when we are negative. God loves us at any stage of our lives.

We must believe we are worthy such love. Sometimes, the reason why you never received unconditional love is you don't feel you deserve it and you run from it.

Don't run. Stay present in the moments. God loves you because you're special—simply because you're you. Don't allow past issues of self-esteem to keep you from basking in the love that feeds your soul.

So today: allow yourself to be shrouded in God's love. He truly cares for you regardless of your past, present or future behavior. Just take God's hand and give Him your heart. Trust Him and believe.

O Lord, thank you for this day. Allow me to embrace your Love. Help me to know in my heart, I'm truly worthy this unconditional love. Help to trust and believe with your grace and mercy, nothing is impossible.

Be the catalyst for change.☺

DAY 245: Released

Today is about being released.

Although I love going to church now, there was times when I didn't. Growing up as a preacher kid, I thought I was wasting my life away in church. I was so jealous of the other kids who could go to one service and go home. They didn't have to stay at church all day and they didn't have to go visit the sick in the hospitals. ☺

My dad went on a sabbatical from the ministry when I was twenty-two. I felt like I had been paroled. It was a great feeling. I got to visit churches, something I really never got a chance to do before. I also would only go to one service and then go home.

To this day: I love going to the 8 am service, so by 10:30 I can go back to sleep. That was something I never got the ability to do when I was younger. I loved being a regular person and a preacher kid. It's been a great feeling as an adult.

I felt like I was being released. Many of us Christian feel the same but in a slightly different way.

When God truly enters your heart, it will give you a spirit of comfort and relaxation that you have never experienced before.

He will give you a calmness you have never felt before. This is because you've given up all the control and are willing to take a back seat to God.

So today: allow yourself to be released from all the anxiety of life. Life can easily become too much to handle and you must let go of control before it overwhelms you.

O Lord, thank you for this day. Please forgive me for my sins. Allow me to release my control over my life and give it to you. Help to have faith and to believe life can get better soon.

Be the catalyst for change.☺

DAY 246: Building a Strong Infrastructure

Today is about building a strong infrastructure.

When you're in business, you want to make sure you have a strong infrastructure. Infrastructure is the basic organization of your venture. There are certain key items you need in the business, like an accountant, attorney, and web designer.

Your spiritual life is similar. There are certain items you need in order to have a strong infrastructure:

A strong prayer life—Having a prayer life is essential in your spiritual life. This is your lifeline or cell phone to God. You must not only use it often but also be comfortable using it.

Having a church you call home—I believe this is important regarding support. We all need support and you can't make it in life on your own. You must open yourself up to having a closer relationship with other believers and it starts with having a church you call home.

Having Strong Faith—You must continually work at your faith. There are many things in life that can shake your faith. You must shake off the problems of life and continue to work to keep your faith intact.

With these items, you will slowly begin building the infrastructure needed to weather the storms of life.

So today: build a new strong infrastructure. By getting a strong prayer life, church home and having a strong faith, you can have infrastructure that you crave.

O Lord, thank you for this day. Please forgive me for my sins. Help me to get structure in my life. Allow me to have strength to continue to fight the good fight in this race of life.

Be the catalyst for change.☺

DAY 247: Hitting a Brick Wall

Today is about hitting a brick wall.

While I'm an innovative and creative human being, there are times when the pressure of life gets to me so much I can't produce creative products. I can only deal with administrative aspects. It's very difficult to deal with both creative and administrative tasks at the same time. Is like cooking your food and eating it all at once.

This is when I usually hit a brick wall. There are times when I just break down under the pressure of life. I try to push through but nothing is happening.

This happens to many of us spiritually. We're working hard to stay in the Christian race, it seems the more we try to live right, the more waves of problems threaten to overtake you. It seems like it's always something negative going on and for an extended amount of time there isn't anything positive to latch onto.

This is when you hit a spiritual brick wall. You begin to question why you work so hard to stay in this Christian race when everyone around is being blessed and they aren't saved.

Don't judge yourself based on what's going around you. The devil will use something to get into your mind and allow you to feel like God has forgotten about you. He hasn't. God blessing us on his schedule and necessary timeframe.

You must develop patience to stay in this race and wait for your breakthrough.

So today: when you hit a brick wall...be patient. Patience is a virtue that takes time to develop. Even the strongest Christian has frustration in certain areas of their life.

O Lord, thank you for this day. Help me to develop patience when in a testing period. Allow me to reflect on the times in my life where are brought me out and they will do so again.

Be the catalyst for change.☺

DAY 248: Becoming Weary

Today is about becoming weary.

If you live long enough, you can become weary in this race called life. This isn't so much a physical exhaustion but a mental exhaustion.

There are times when it seems you're in one major testing period but there are mini tests within one major period.

That's when true weariness sets in. It's not that you don't believe God will bring you out. However, rather you don't know if you can hold on. You're not sure if you can make it day-to-day.

It's like drowning in a pool when you can't swim. At first, you're kicking hard to stay at the top of the water but after a while, physical exhaustion sets in and you sink slowly down to the bottom.

God isn't only the provider of blessings but also strength as well. There are times in life you feel like you can't make it anymore. This is a great time to ask God for strength. He will take the emotional loads you have been carrying and give you the peace that passes all understanding.

God will renew your mind, body and spirit. He will give you fresh perspective and pep in your step that will help to fight the good fight in this race called life.

So today: allow yourself to shake off the weariness in your spirit. While it may be difficult to get past the emotional exhaustion, allow God to give you patience to stand against waves of disillusionment.

O Lord, thank you for this day. Please forgive me for my sins. Allow me to be able to have patience in my life when I feel weary. Help me to see myself as God sees me. As a warrior.

Be the catalyst for change.☺

DAY 249: People who Just Don't get It

Today is about people who just don't get it.

Let's face it. Some people don't just get it. They don't understand God has our back; He blessed us thus far and will continue to bless us in the future.

They didn't get here by themselves and they received help along the way. God will continue to protect until the end of time.

We all can become lost in this race of life. Some of it's our own unbelief; sometimes it's that life's trouble just became too much to bear.

However, how you handle yourself in the process can become a real issue

God will let you be a beacon of life for others who are lost. However, you must be careful that you don't lose yourself trying to save them.

We all have our own demons we have to contend with and fight on a daily basis. So it can be detrimental to our spiritual health to take on the problems of others.

Sometimes, you have to disengage yourself from others who tap your energy. We all must hit rock bottom when we realize God is the center of our lives and the one we must rely on. We can't go through this process for someone else. This is a solo trip.

So today: some people don't get it. Don't go down with the sinking ship. Remove yourself and pray for them from afar. Don't allow people to re-enter your life until you're sure they have a strong enough foundation in the Lord.

O Lord, thank you for this day. Without allowing them to shake your foundation, allow yourself to pray for others going through a difficult time. Help me stay focused on you.

Be the catalyst for change.☺

DAY 250: Saving Yourself

Today is about saving yourself.

While I'm not an animal lover in the sense that I have a dog or cat, I always picked up strays.

What type of strays? Various people are at their wits end. I attempt to help each and every one despite my own personal situation.

However, some people are in a space to be helped. They must want a quick fix, which I can't solve. If I'm going to help you, I'm going to do it the right way and not cross the line.

However, people will give you the song and dance on the fact they want to get their life together but once you begin to help them, their actions don't mirror their words.

You've put yourself out there and used all of your contacts to help this person but yet this person seems unaware of all of the trouble you have gone through on their behalf.

This is when you must save yourself. You can help people but only as much as they want to help themselves. God will give you a discerning spirit that will touch your spirit and let you know how far to go.

You can always pray for those who need help but you must be careful when allowing yourself to become involved with those who are lost and don't want to be saved.

So today: save yourself. While it's an admirable quality to be a good Christian and help others, you must be careful that you don't go over the edge.

O Lord, thank you for this day. Please allow me to help others while not sacrificing myself in the process.

Be the catalyst for change.☺

DAY 251: Vulnerable

Today is about being vulnerable.

We have a persona we project to the general public. This persona is usually much tougher than we feel inside. We hide our feelings with dark hateful feelings instead of getting to the root of the problem.

When you're vulnerable, you're open, exposed and susceptible to many things.

You're also being incredibly brave. It takes a lot of guts to live your life being vulnerable.

You're willing to share yourself with the world, despite the darkness that exists. While it's difficult for people to see the real you, it's refreshing and helps feed others' souls with your testimony.

By being vulnerable and sharing your experiences, good bad and ugly, it allows you to become a beacon of light for those struggling in darkness.

There is strength in being vulnerable. It means you're not living your life in a shroud of secrecy, lies, and deceit. You're attempting to run this race called life in a spirit of positive energy.

God wants you to be honest and vulnerable with Him. In order for God to help to step in your destiny, you must be willing to let off any insecurities and stand before Him as the real you.

So today: allow yourself to be vulnerable. While it may not be the easiest process it can definitely be the most rewarding.

O Lord, thank you for this day. Please forgive me for my sins. Allow me to become vulnerable and show people the real me. Help me have the strength to do this so I can be a beacon of light for others.

Be the catalyst for change.☺

DAY 252: Pretending to Agree

Today is about pretending to agree.

During the mayoral campaign, I had a lot of yes men…aka butt kissers. People who won't give you their real opinion but just tell you what you want to hear.

They also saw their own selfish ambitions and not truly what was best for me.

Then, you have people who were totally unsupportive. They made sure they were always just out of grasp of being helpful.

While both groups are equally annoying, the first group is far more dangerous. They led you to believe something that isn't true.

In life, you need someone who is going to ride with you. If you don't ride, cool. While it hurts, you know not to count on them for anything at all. You can pay them back with success. The best revenge is living well.

However, when you're being told one thing, when you find out they feel totally different, it's gut wrenching when it catches you off guard.

You feel disillusioned and filled with hatred.

God will allow you see these individuals for what they are so you will not trust them again and also to ensure you watch out for anyone who exhibits these qualities and attempts to enter your life.

So today: be careful with those who pretend to agree. These are not your friends and can do more damage than those who are outright unsupportive. Rely on God for support and don't allow this deceit to seep into your spirit.

O Lord, thank you for this day. Please forgive me for my sins. Allow lack of support not to be taken into my mind, body, and spirit. Help me to rely on you for all of the support I need.

Be the catalyst for change.☺

DAY 253: Helping me to See

Today is to help me to see.

My muse had an alcohol problem for as long as I knew him. However, I didn't realize how bad it had gotten until I had thrown a drink on him and watched in horror as he got kicked out of the event.

He was never going to love me because he was in love with others. Their names were Hennessey, Ketel Vodka, Patron and Southern Comfort. He's a raging alcoholic and needed help if we were ever going to be able to be together.

I'm such as optimistic person; sometimes I'll ignore situations that are unpleasant rather than deal with them directly.

This can have disastrous results in time because by the time I have really looked at a situation, it's really in bad shape.

The Lord will place things in your life for you to see and experience in order to make you a better person. For you to be a testimony for others.

However, when it's uncomfortable, we tend to look away and focus on something else instead of what's in front of us.

Don't allow yourself to see the true state of your situation. There's a purpose in why God wants to see this. It's not to hurt you or make you feel bad about yourself.

So today: ask God to help you to see what's in front of you. Then Trust Him. There is purpose in everything in life and all works for Glory of God.

O Lord, thank you for this day. Please forgive me for my sins. Help me to really see the situations needing my attention. Pull me out of my fantasy world and force me to see the reality of a situation.

Be the catalyst for change.☺

DAY 254: Tolerance

Today is about being Tolerant.

I remember I was dating this guy; I really didn't like him. It just seemed a little nice. However, his pace was really slow, the way he walked, talked and thought.

I'm such a fireball of energy; this clearly wasn't a match made in heaven.

The final straw was he took me to the airport and I almost missed my flight because he was driving so slowly. That was the end of the line for us.

While I'm a nice person, I'm not sugary. I will let you know how it is. I guess it's too much of me watching Scarface, and Casino.

I can be tolerant but for a small period of time. This is clearly an area of my life I need to work on. When you're tolerant of others, you're accepting, patient and understanding.

Be tolerant on this journey called life. We all have different life experiences, so we see situations differently.

We mustn't discount other perspectives just because it's different from ours. Christians, in particular, are known for being the most critical and judgmental.

We have to work hard to eliminate the urge to be critical. It doesn't foster openness and vulnerability. God wants to see values in others, even we don't want to.

So today: allow yourself to be more tolerant. Not just in other people but of yourself as well. Things may not be the way you want them but they're how they are supposed to be right now.

O Lord, thank you for this day. Please forgive me for knowing and unknowing sins. Allow me to become more tolerant and learn the significance in all viewpoints in this race called life.

Be the catalyst for change.☺

DAY 255: Sidestepping Trouble

Today is about sidestepping trouble.

Growing up, I was such a rambunctious and rebellious child; I was often in trouble.

I remember while I was a junior in high school, I went to a teen club called the Warehouse in Atlanta. Everyone always had one friend whose parents let them run wild and you were jealous because your parent wouldn't let you do whatever you wanted.

Everyone knew I had a curfew of 12:30 am. We had to leave by midnight so I could be home in the house at 12:30 am.

I was having such a good time, I decided to be gangster and not leave until 1:30 am. I was sweating bullets when I got home.

The next morning, my mother asked what time I have gotten home the night before. However, before I could say anything, my stepfather at the time spoke up and stated he heard me come in at 12:30. Then he smiled at me. We were buddies every since.

My stepfather helped me sidestep trouble.

Many times in life, we're being rebellious and out of control. We want to do what we want whenever we want. We then leave ourselves open to trouble in our lives.

Then God steps in to keep us from getting in trouble. God bestows mercy and grace upon our souls that aren't always the cleanest.

Sometimes God knows we're struggling under the burdens of life we're carrying. It seems no help is ever coming. That's when frustration and resentment reach the boiling point. Slowly take off the loads of doubts and overwhelming feeling and give them to God.

So today: thank God for helping you sidestep trouble. God is in the blessing business and thankfully, He blesses based on His mercy and not on what we deserve.

O Lord, thank you for this day. Please forgive me for my sins. Thank you for providing mercy on me when I've reached the end of my rope. Allow me to shoulder the burdens of life while maintaining a positive attitude.

Be the catalyst for change.☺

DAY 256: Pettiness

Today is about being petty.

It's easy to become petty when you're under stress. You become very motivated to ensure you're getting a fair shake until exercising a bit of kindness.

Petty is when you become narrow-minded, trivial, grudging and small-minded. When you're being petty, you allow your circumstances around you to crowd your judgment.

Sometimes when you're in this race called life, you will make a mistake. We are all human. However, what becomes dangerous is when you start to feel that whole is against you.

Then you become to take an advantageous stance. You must sure you will get what you deserve and no one going to cheat you out of anything.

This is an overwhelming stance to take. You can constantly be the protector all the right and holy by your perspective. Not only will it turn you into a parole officer; it will cause you to lose some faith in humanity and its good works.

While you might meet people who are not in the same place as you in their spiritual walk, you don't have drop down to their level. You must stay at your level and help them rise to meet you.

Show others the kindness that God has bestowed on you. Kindness is like a smile; it's contagious when you spread it around.

So today: resist the urge to be petty. Believe in positive energy and hum a race. Don't allow yourself to become trifling just because someone was little treacherous with you. Just Pray for them and move on.

O Lord, thank you for this day. Please forgive me for my sins. Help me not allow pettiness to get best of me. Allow me to choose light over darkness and spread kindness around. None of us is perfect so help me to become more understanding of others.

Be the catalyst for change.☺

DAY 257: Keeping Your eye on the Prize

Today is about keeping your eye on the prize.

When I become committed to do something, I'm completely focused on it. There is no stopping me. I don't allow myself to get caught up with other things.

For example, for the Peachtree Road race, I have given myself enough training time. I run four miles a day, six days a week rain or shine. I run when I'm tired, I run when I'm frustrated. I run when I don't feel like it, I run when I'm bubbly. I run no matter that.

I keep my eyes on the prize. The prize is for the feeling of accomplishment knowing I was able to finish my task.

God will give us a vision He wants to complete. He will provide the tools to get there. However, it's up to us to keep the motivation while on the path to greatness

There are obstacles and challenges along the way but you must not allow it to shake your spirit.

You must stay positive during the face of adversity. Wait for God to give a second wind in the spirit so you can complete your tasks.

Today: keep your eye on the prize. Don't look long term because it's something that can be overwhelming. Just do it day-by-day and watch yourself transform.

O Lord, thank you for this day. Allow me to keep my eye on the prize. Allow me not to feel frustrated in this race called life. Help me to be able to pace myself, so I can reach my vision.

Be the catalyst for change.☺

DAY 258: Prospering

Today is about prospering.

To prosper means to flourish, succeed financially or do well. During these tough times, you're considering prospering when you're able to sustain your lifestyle and decrease it.

We all will prosper but not the same way or at the same time. You might prosper in your personal life. You may have the life women dream of: a husband, two kids and a house with a picket fence. You might prosper in your career: you may be a leader and expert in your field of expertise.

Prospering isn't about financial success; I believe it's a state of mind. You can manifest anything if you believe. We can't wait on others to motivate us but we must become the motivating force in our own lives.

While there may be times when we become overwhelmed; you mustn't allow the sure drudgery of life to take you down. If you're going to prosper, you must be willing to put your head down and get to work.

Don't worry how well others are doing in life. Don't become dismayed when it feels like you're falling behind. It's just a set up for you; you're next in line for a miracle.

So today: allow yourself to prosper in many ways. While it may not seem like it to others, God will provide everything you need on this journey called life.

O Lord, thank you for this day. Please forgive me for my knowing and unknowing sins. Help me to prosper in every area in my life and be willing to wait for this amazing time. Allow me to exercise patience so I can see and implement my vision.

Be the catalyst for change.☺

DAY 259: Enhancing

Today is about Enhancing.

While I'm not a girly girl, I'm not really big on makeup. However, I'm a beast when comes to skincare.

I believe skincare is way more important than makeup. Good skin will make you positively glow. I use all Aveda products, every moisturizer, mask, and cleanser.

I believe this is vital to enhancing your appearance. We all want to look our best so we work to enhance ourselves.

However, enhancement doesn't just stop with our appearance. We also work to enhance ourselves; professionally, and even spiritually.

When you enhance yourself, you're working to improve yourself, increase clarity, and boost yourself.

Just as we all spend thousands of dollars on enhancing ourselves physically with clothing, hair and nails or with a bachelor's, master's and doctorate degrees professionally, we should spend a little more time spiritually.

When you seek to enhance yourself spiritually, we must first figure out what our spiritual gifts are. Spiritual gifts are things such as the ability to pray, prosperity, etcetera.

Once you figure out your spiritual gifts, allow yourself to cultivate them. God gives you these gifts in order for you to be a blessing to others.

So today: allow yourself opportunity to enhance yourself spiritually. We must make an effort to figure out the God given talents. Then we put these talents to good use and become a blessing to others.

O Lord, thank you for this day. Please forgive my knowing and unknowing sins. Allow me be spend time enhancing the lives of others with my spiritual gifts. Help me to see sharing my gifts with the world can help bring others to Christ.

Be the catalyst for change.☺

DAY 260: Learning to Thrive

Today is about learning to Thrive.

Throughout my life, I have learned to thrive in situations that would have killed other people.

I have always made the best of lackluster situations. I have an uncanny ability to calm my spirit and remove all distractions so I can reach my goals no matter what.

As you continue to live, you will realize how easy it is to thrive in the best circumstances. The question is, can you thrive when nothing is going right?

Can you thrive when you're in over your head? Can you thrive when other parts of your life are crumbling? Can you thrive when you're physically and emotionally exhausted?

This is when you see if you can really cut the mustard. When you thrive, you grow, bloom and succeed. It takes an eye locked firmly on God to thrive under less than ideal circumstances.

So today: learn to thrive under less than ideal circumstances. Don't allow your obstacles of life to consume you. Obstacles are not permanent and can be moved if you rely on God's will.

O Lord, thank you for this day. Help me to thrive regardless of what is going on around me. Allow me to keep my eyes on You while I continue on this journey called life.

Be the catalyst for change.☺

DAY 261: Don't Lose Sight of Where You're Going

Today, don't lose sight of where you're going.

While I'm a creative person, I'm an extremely pragmatic person when it comes to shopping. When I shop, I'm so focused and I have a plan of which stores I will be going into, etcetera. I even have a route because I'm always on time constraints.

However, my sister and mom are completely different. I can't stand shopping with them. They wander all around the mall in search of good deals. There has never been a store they won't go in.

They participate in the Black Friday each and every holiday season.

It's easy to get caught up in the happiness of shopping. However, don't lose sight of where you're going.

Life can work in a similar way. We can get so caught in day-to-day living we slowly meander off track.

It doesn't seem never is a big deal. You would be fine on your spiritual path living your life and then you would begin working on weekends so your only day to sleep late is Sunday. You take a part time job in addition to your full time job and you have to work on Sunday. The little things become big things once you start to accumulate them. They can begin to affect your walk and how you handle things.

Faith is a slippery slope. You must work hard to keep your feet on the ground or you can easily lose your balance.

So today: don't lose sight on where you're going. You must work to stay on the path of righteousness.

O Lord, thank you for this day. Allow me to stay focuses on you while running this race of life. Help me not become distracted by day-to-day living.

Be the catalyst for change.☺

DAY 262: Making the Right Decisions

Today is making the right decisions.

When you make decisions to remove people from your life, it's not easy. There are various reasons why you want to keep them around. It could be convenience, pity, or common interests.

However, once someone shows his or her true colors, there's nothing you can do. You just have to deal with it. Don't allow yourself to become emotionally invested in the situation.

God does allow us to feel an urging in our spirit when it's wrong. The assignment has ended for some people in your life and you must move on without them.

You may feel guilty because you had to clean house. However, cleaning house is necessary for where you're going.

You've got to lighten your load. You become too laden down with other people's problems and crises that have nothing to do with you.

Wish them the best and move on. You can't allow yourself to miss out on a destiny God has for you by continuing to carry friends who are no longer good for your spiritual health.

So today: make the right decisions. Listen to the urging in your spirit. Allow yourself to see what you're doing is wrong. Sometimes, you must close a door before God can open another.

O Lord, thank you for this day. Help me to become strengthened during these times of making tough decisions. While it may seem selfish and uncaring, you must allow yourself to move on with your life.

Be the catalyst for change.☺

DAY 263: Building a Team

Today is about building a team.

When I start a business venture, I always build a team. A Team is a number of people organized to function cooperatively as a group.

Each person in the team has a particular function that helps guide the success for the venture. Each member of the team must be willing to support each other to make the venue a success.

Therefore, for your spiritual world to be a success, you must build a team as well. This team's main focus is to ensure you all make it to heaven and live out your dreams. The team will support each other and keep each on track. Each team member has a function: you may be the person who prays in the group or biblical scholar, etcetera.

However, it's difficult to build a team like this. It will take time. You see a lot more posers. Posers who tell you they have certain experiences but in reality, they really don't.

Don't try to rush the process. Allow yourself to pick up team members little by little over a span of years until your team is complete.

So today: build yourself a spiritual team. A team of people who will have stayed on the spiritual path. While the members are hard to find, continue to search, they will be worth it.

O Lord, thank you for this day. Help me to find likeminded souls who I can build a spiritual team with. Allow me to stay focused on You in order to determine Your discerning spirit.

Be the catalyst for change.☺

DAY 264: What's Limiting you Right Now?

Today is about what's limiting you right now.

When I first began the process of buying my home, it almost ended before it even started.

I had horrible credit from college. I didn't have good credit or spending habits and had to pay for the mistake.

The lender told me this wasn't my time and I should continue to rent. However, something in me flared up. I wouldn't allow anyone to tell me except God, when it was or wasn't my time.

To this day, I hate when anyone tells me I can't do something because "it's not my time"

So I did my research, worked, and removed all the issues off of my credit. In fact, I did so well, I opened a business helping people do the same.

Don't let anyone or anything hold you back from your goals.

Only God truly knows what is best for you. You must question the motives of anyone else who speaks negativity and darkness into your life.

So today, ask yourself: what is limiting you right now? The answer should be nothing. You must work hard not to allow dream killers and haters to influence your world.

O Lord, thank you for this day. Allow me to push past any limitations in my life. Allow me to stay focused on your will and glory while disregarding anyone who speaks darkness into my life.

Be the catalyst for change.☺

DAY 265: Losing Hope

Today is about losing hope.

Life is difficult. We can work really hard for a business or venture only to realize it fails. You can usually bounce back after the first failures. However, if this is your third or fourth failure in a row in causes you to lose hope.

When you lose hope, you just stop caring about anything including life. It's easy to get sick of losing and being disappointed. Everyone else's life seems to be going well except yours.

You may ask God why me? It seems like nothing I do goes right. I only seem to specialize in disappointment and regrets. You're getting sick of putting a positive spin on things that are really bad.

When you find yourself losing hope, immediately go into prayer and ask for peace. Peace can surpass all understanding. It will help you realize despite everything that's going wrong, you will fight to see another day.

With each passing day, there are new opportunities for blessings. Failure isn't a death sentence but feedback. It also builds your character and testimony. How could you really appreciate the good times if you hadn't experienced the bad?

So today: don't lose hope. Take a break and relax one day with limited strategic thinking. Allow yourself to gain a fresh perspective. Having a fresh perspective can allow you back into the game of life with more creativity than before.

O Lord, thank you for this day. Please forgive me for my sins. Give me peace when I lose hope. Lord, I'm feeling broken, help me to rely on you to get through this trying time.

Be the catalyst for change.☺

DAY 266: The Pitfalls of Getting Your Way

Today is about pitfalls of getting your way.

Growing up, I was a spoiled brat. I pretty much got my way regardless. I worked hard to get my way too. So I believed if you worked hard in life, you would eventually get your way.

Not necessarily. The first time I was denied. I guess I must have been around sixteen years old when I didn't win my first bid to become student government president as a sophomore. The position is normally held by a senior and I knew this but didn't care. I wanted my way.

So when the senior class decided to push their candidate and they won, I was crushed. I felt like my life was over. I wanted to stop going to school. I was angry and I'm not a good person to be around when I'm angry. I spent my junior year mad at the world and rebelling against the system that disappointed me.

However, now when I look back on the situation, I probably wouldn't have taken it so hard if I had experienced disappointment prior to that moment.

While it was awesome being a spoiled brat, it handicapped me in some ways. I didn't hear "no" enough as a child. I also picked up some wicked habits from this. For example: I learned from my family I could be persistent enough and wear someone down into giving in to my desires and me. However, persistence doesn't pay sometimes.

So today: be happy for the disappointments. They build you as a person and help you handle life's challenges, as you get older. While not pleasant, they are essential to developing coping mechanisms during this race called life.

O lord, thank you for this day. Allow me to appreciate the disappointment as well as the triumphs in life. You can't appreciate the sunny days unless you experience the overcast. Help me to stay focused on your will while weathering the storms of life.

Be the catalyst for change.☺

DAY 267: Vengeful

Today is about being vengeful.

Growing up, my mother was the disciplinarian in our family. It seems like my whole young life was filled with mother's yelling at me about my behavior.

I got sick of it when I was probably around seven years old and I decided to teach her a lesson.

My mother was cooking dinner on a Saturday night. I wanted a cookie and she snapped, telling me no. She shooed me out of the kitchen. I became vengeful.

My mother had to bake a cake for church the next day and she had just enough sugar to make it without having to go to the store. So what did I do? I poured salt and pepper in the sugar container and swirled it around.

When my mother saw it, I thought she was going to kill me. My dad thought it was hilarious.

I was being vengeful. Being vengeful will never cut whether it's a seven-year-old little girl, or an adult. It's not positive. Being vengeful is unforgiving, resentful and ruthless.

You must resist the urge to retaliate when frustrated. Allow God to fight your battles. When God is in the midst, He can handle all the situations in your life if you give over control.

O Lord, thank you for this day. Help me not become vengeful when angry. Allow me to seek you to calm my spirit while on this journey called life.

Be the catalyst for change.☺

DAY 268: Taken Advantage of

Today is about being taken advantage of.

When I first moved into my home, I wanted to start painting immediately. I would get a reasonable quote over the phone. When I actually got to my place, the price would increase by $1000.

I was a victim of my neighborhood prestige. I live in downtown Atlanta so there is a perception of wealth that's unrealistic.

There isn't anything worse than being taking advantage of. It makes you feel disgusted with humanity.

Don't allow isolated incidents to affect your perception in life. God wants us to be empowered and stand up for ourselves.

God allows us to see what areas of life need to be improved. He will continually show us these problem areas until we are forced to make needed adjustments.

God doesn't show us these things to hurt us but rather because He loves us so much and doesn't want anyone disrespecting us. God is like an overprotective parent who we all need and want.

So today: stand up for yourself. Don't allow anyone to take advantage of you. Using your discerning spirit will show what areas you need to concentrate on.

O Lord, thank you for this day. Please forgive me for my sins. Help me stand up for myself while on this journey called life.

Be the catalyst for change.☺

DAY 269: Elevating Yourself

Today is about elevating yourself.

After my grandmother passed, I was paralyzed with grief. However, I continued to work because I had to. The work was very therapeutic because it allowed me to concentrate on something other than the grief I was feeling.

I knew I have to make it somehow, I have to work to elevate myself beyond the life I have right now. To elevate is to raise, increase, enrich, and inspire someone or something.

I was feeling so low I knew the only way to go was up.

Sometimes, God will squeeze like a lemon. The squeezing process provides precious juice so our spirit can spring forth. This allows you to be elevated and be on the path of greatness.

There is a purpose in all bad times in your life. They're usually what really motivate you. It forces you to make the necessary changes in your life. It helps to become forward thinking and to inspire yourself and figure out what you really want from your life.

So today: elevate yourself. Get out of the passenger seat of life and get into the driver's seat. Make yourself the master of your destiny and change your life forever.

O Lord, thank you for this day. Thank you for allowing me to see the areas where I need change in my life. Help me to stay in constant prayer and have the faith to face adversity in my life.

Be the catalyst for change.☺

DAY 270: Finding Your Identity

Today is about finding your identity.

I don't believe you can really figure out who you are until you've experienced some hardships in your life.

Hardships help refine you as a person and really show what you're made of. It forces you to focus on what you believe is really important.

God provides guidance so we can achieve our goals in life. It will help with your capacity to grow based upon your faith. The more faith you have, the more you'll grow as a person of Faith.

God can see your new self. He can see the power you have. He can see what impact you will have on your community, this nation and the world.

However, you just step out and start acting on your belief. Stop waiting to walk into your destiny, step into it now.

When you step out and walk into destiny, God will show you the identify you're supposed to have.

Your uniqueness will be what will make you powerful and it won't be things you think are attractive about you; it will be the things God ordinates for you to do.

God will send you the help you need. It's not over until God says it is. Don't allow the world to throw you away. Give yourself to God and watch Him change you forever.

So today: become a new creature with God. Allow yourself to become refined by God. God is taking you somewhere but you must be able to trust God.

O Lord, thank you for this day. Please forgive me for my sins. Allow me to become the person I'm going to be.

Be the catalyst for change.☺

DAY 271: I Told You So

Today: I told you so.

In relationships, I always stay and try to work it out. I'm been taught you don't leave people when it gets tough. You must stand behind them and the relationship.

However, I have friends who always tell me it's time to let it go. I always ignore them because ultimately I know what's best for me. I just have to believe God will protect me.

So the relationship ends and then they are the first to say to me, "I told you so."

If you want to be my friend, you must never say those words to me. My challenging area of my life is my relationships. So I'm definitely sensitive about it.

What I expect from loved ones and friends is understanding. I don't harp on you when you make bad career situations.

God doesn't do this to us.

God knows when we're not making good decisions, and when things aren't going to work the way we would like. Yet, He gives us dignity in the process.

So today, give your loved ones the respect they deserve. Don't hit them with, "I told you so." Give them nothing but understanding while they go through the process.

O Lord, thank you for this day. Please forgive me for my sins. Help me understanding to others who are going through testing periods. Allow me to stay focused on you to weather the storms of life.

Be the catalyst for change.☺

MONTH 10

DAY 272: Painful to Accept

Today is about something painful to accept.

When my grandmother died, it was almost too difficult to bear. I didn't want to believe she was really gone. I didn't want to believe I would never have an opportunity to talk with her and laugh with her.

That she would never see me get married, or have children. My mind couldn't process this level of grief.

There are certain times in life when you will experience a blow that's difficult to expect. Your mind won't allow you to accept what has occurred because it's too painful.

That's when you must run to God's welcoming arms and allow yourself to enveloped in his love.

God is will send his comforter, the holy spirit, to provide you with peace during this process. While you may understand why something is happening in your life, God will allow you to relax and run on to see what the end will be.

Don't try it figure it out. Everything that occurs in life may not have easily identifiable meaning. Just allow yourself to get through these trying times and allow God to take care of the rest.

O Lord, thank you for this day. Help me to ensure the pain for things I don't understand. Allow me to rely on you more for strength during these trying times.

Be the catalyst for change.☺

DAY 273: Life Changes

Today is about life changes.

My college boyfriends and I had really a lot of fun back in the day. We had real dates; I forced guys to think creatively. However, the best dates were when we went to basketball and hockey games. Nothing says love and caring like a little violence. Just Kidding ☺

Life was so simple back then. The Clinton Administration years: years of excess wealth and low gas prices. ☺

Now there's unemployment, strict conservation and shifting priorities. You're lucky if you get a guy to take you out to dinner let alone be creative on dates.

Now we're dealing with a whole new set of issues. It can be overwhelming at times.

God doesn't put more on us than we can bear. You must have courage to talk through the storms of life.

Courage is innate in us; it comes out of you similar to integrity and character. When your back is against the wall and you're force to sink or swim, that's when your courage will appear.

Allow your life to get back to simpler times. Have the courage to fight for a better life.

So today, take your life changes in stride. We all go through various phases in our lives. Don't allow outside forces to effect you internally.

O Lord, thank you for this day. Help me not become despondent and frustrated while going through life changes. Give me the peace to endure.

Be the catalyst for change.☺

DAY 274: Startling

Today is startling.

When I was seventeen, I had my first car accident. My mother and stepfather were out of town and I was staying with one of my mom's friends. So I snuck out of the house and went to a club. However, not too far from her house, I hit someone—failure the yield the right of way. My great night of clubbing was ruined.

My night took a starling turn.

Life can't be planned. It can be estimated but estimates are not always correct.

God has a way of getting our attention when our behavior isn't above board. We will have consequences for our behavior. God deals with cause and effect. You will reap what you sow

However, you can always get back on track. Ask forgiveness for all sins and get back into the game.

God forgive us all no matter what we have done because we all have fallen short and some understanding.

So today: don't allow startling events to take you by surprise. Embrace them. They help to build character and will increase your testimony.

O Lord, thank you for this day. Allow me not to become dismayed when startling events occur. While I may not understand them, help me to endure them and so they can strengthen me as a person.

Be the catalyst for change.☺

DAY 275: Having an Imagination

Today about having an imagination.

I have always been imaginative and loved to read. Reading has always been a form of escape for me.

I remember the book fair in elementary was the equivalent to me of the Beatles invasion. I remember my mother and I would argue for days about how much I could spend at the book fair. My mother would give me about $30 and I always wanted $100 but considering most of the books were like $7 it was kinda a waste.

I was a faster reader. Which is why I ended up in school so long. So it was a waste of money for anyone to purchase a book for me that I would be finished reading in less than two hours. I'm library girl and still go to this day.

I believe having an imagination is critical when you're trying to step into your destiny.

Having an imagination means you have the ability to visualize and use your mind's eye. That means you can create something out of nothing.

Imagination is something that can't buy, whether you have one or you don't. God can provides us with an imagination that will allow us to reach our destiny through guidance.

So today: allow yourself to explore your imagination. Don't become so beaten down by life that you lose your ability to dream. You must never lose your hope and your ability to dream. These two items will help you into your destiny.

O Lord, thank you for this day. Allow me to explore my imagination. Help me to figure out what my destiny is. Allow me to shake off resentment and frustrate so it won't inhibit the creative process.

Be the catalyst for change.☺

DAY 276: A Legacy

Today is about a legacy.

My former stepfather was a hard working man. He worked his way from construction worker to a union representative. He also helped me to see the inside of politics due to his work. I got a chance to see how his work effected people's lives. I knew then no matter what my chosen career, I must work and help people.

Everyone will have a legacy and it's generally affected by other people. All the loved ones, family and mentors who gave you a tiny piece of their lives, helped to shape and mold your legacy.

Your legacy is your heritage, tradition and inheritance. While your earthly family may not have left you an inheritance, your spiritual Father made you an heir to His kingdom.

Crafting your legacy should entail figuring out what is important to you. Once that has been decided, you should go forward creating it by having a place to reach your destiny.

So today: Create a legacy. Allow yourself to have a plan that not only will help you but future generations and the community at large.

O Lord, thank you for this day. Please forgive me for my sins. Help me to create a legacy for myself so I can walk into destiny. Allow me to stay focused on your Will.

Be the catalyst for change.☺

DAY 277: A Sense of Accomplishment

Today is about a sense of accomplishment.

I loved working at Footaction as a teenager. It was a teenage girl's dream: great pay and access to cute guys all day long. I was in heaven. However, I did learn how to hustle. While we did have base pay, we did get paid on commission for our sales. So I learned to use my bubbly personality to make money. That's when things really started coming together for me.

It's great when you're able to feel like you've accomplishing something in your life. There are times in life when it gets so rough you never think it will get any better. Then slowly but surely, things begin to take shape and get better.

When God is removing us from a testing period, He will do so in waves. It will be one good thing after another building with intensity. God will allow you to slowly get used to the blessings raining down upon you so you will be able to handle to new and exciting changes in your life.

It's a great feeling for a testing period to end, but it's sad when people self destruct at the beginning of their breakthrough because they can't handle it.

Continue to ask God for his strength during this time. You and God have been waiting a long time for this. Don't allow yourself to lose it at the end through a buildup of resentment and frustration.

So today: enjoy your accomplishments. There are very few times in our lives we truly get a chance to enjoy God's bountiful blessing. Allow God to bless you without question.

O Lord, thank you for this day. Please forgive for me sins. Allow me to enjoy my accomplishment and be able to handle the blessings you have bestowed upon me.

Be the catalyst for change.☺

DAY 278: Needing a Helping Hand

Today is about needing a helping hand.

My first adult job, I hated. I didn't like my boss and didn't think I had the support needed. I definitely needed support because I really didn't know how to work. I had worked in extremely small offices prior to this so I never paid any attention to the office politics in a job environment until then. However, at the point when I realized it, the damage had already been done.

There are things in life we all need a helping hand with. We're not all knowing and we do make mistakes.

It's fine when you need a helping hand and it's provided. It's not cool when you're requesting help only to get none.

This can very difficult to deal with, it will feel like you're sinking in quicksand. It feels like there's no one to turn to.

There is and that's God. God can send you the insight necessary to help. God will send you the angel you need or be the angel Himself.

God allows his love to rain down on you with nuggets of insight so you can get out of the situation you're in.

So today: don't worry if you don't get the helping hand you need. God will send the help you need and nothing else matters.

O Lord, thank you for this day. Please forgive me for my sins. Allow me to become more trusting in you and be willing to stand on your word.

Be the catalyst for change.☺

DAY 279: Be Careful What You Wish For

Today is be careful what you wish for.

I remember I wanted an internship so bad I didn't get it. Then, weeks later after accepting a position, I received an offer for an internship I wanted so badly. So I ended up with two internships at the same time with double the money.

There has been many times I won the race when I thought I didn't and vice versa.

You can't predict God's will and the story for your life. Only God knows the total storyline.

God will sometimes withholds something from you not to punish but to enrich and make it bigger than it was before. God can also give you something that will feel like a blessing but it's really a test (i.e. a possible nightmare).

That's why it's important to stay in constantly prayer with God. God will provide you with guidelines so you can know what to do next in this race called life.

Think long and hard about anything you put your energy behind. There isn't anything worse to pray for a blessing to come to pass only to realize this wasn't what you really needed or wanted.

So today, be careful what you wish for. God knows what's best for you and He will send you a lesson when necessary.

O Lord, thank you for this day. Please forgive me for my sins. Allow me to think more about my prayers, wants and desires. Help me to stay aligned with Your will and glory.

Be the catalyst for change.☺

DAY 280: Atonement

Today is about atonement.

When I was five years old on Easter Sunday, I woke up in a weird mood. I wanted some Fanta soft drink for breakfast and my parents weren't having it, particularly my mother.

I was annoyed and determined to get what I wanted. So the moment we got to church, I ran down to the corner store and got a Fanta soft drink. Then I celebrated on the side steps of the church by tap dancing. However, then my mother found me and I was finished.

I had to atone for my sins. Atonement is to apologize for my sins or to make penance.

We all become extra and selfish. We want what we want regardless of the consequences. We enjoy ourselves during the process until we get into trouble.

God doesn't give us rules to make our lives difficult. He provides us rules and guidance to protect us from harm. God is like a protective parent who wants you to live up to your expectations.

So when we do overstep your bounds and allow yourself to become a bit rebellious under God's will, we must ask for forgiveness.

God will always forgive us when we request. There is no procedure, a little dance, or special circumstances you have to use to obtain God's forgiveness. All you have to do is confess your sins.

So today: Allow yourself to atone for your sins. Ask for forgiveness and confess your sins to the One who keeps us from falling.

O Lord, thank you for your sins. Please forgive me for my sins. Allow me to confess my sins and then get back in this race called life.

Be the catalyst for change.☺

DAY 281: Miracles

Today is miracles.

When I transferred to Spelman college, it was a miracle. I had been told by Spelman I had to wait until the end of my freshman year before I could transfer. I didn't want to wait. I knew it would be more competitive.

So I must have persisted for them to consider me at the end of my fall semester. They said if I had a 4.0 they would. I ended up with a 3.8, which I was frantic about but I decided to stand on God's word. I packed all of my stuff at the end of my fall semester and said my goodbyes. My friends thought I was crazy, because I didn't have the official word and didn't get the 4.0.

After Christmas, I went to discuss my situation with the admission counselor. She made me wait all day, just to see how determined I was to attend Spelman. Then she came out at the end of the day and extended her hand and stated "Welcome to Spelman"

That was a miracle in my life. A miracle is an act of God, an amazing event or marvelous example. It's also a situation you know is beyond your means.

God will provide us amazing opportunity in our lives to show us it doesn't matter what the World says, it's not over until God says it's over.

So today: be willing to fight and wait for your miracle. Don't allow yourself to become discouraged when the world says no. There isn't anything too tough for God and you just have to be willing to stand on the Word of God. Wait on the Lord.

O Lord, thank you for your sins. Please forgive me for your sins. Allow me to stand on my faith and believe you will provide my miracle. Help me to have strength to ignore all of the haters, naysayers and skeptics. Lord, I trust you and I believe all things are possible.

Be the catalyst for change.☺

DAY 282: Persecution

Today is about Persecution.

During the mayoral campaign, because I decided to become a write-in candidate, I was persecuted.

Persecution isn't an easy thing to experience. Persecution is harassment, bullying and maltreatment. You will feel like you're alone in the world.

We are all different and unique people. We all see the world in different ways due to our life experiences.

So we all have the ability to judge people based upon what we believe is correct. Most of the time, our decisions and actions are based completely on personal biases.

There are times in life when you'll suffer, be treated different, or feel slighted. This can be part of your refining process.

When a diamond is found it must be refined in order for the diamond to be ready to be placed on a ring. We, as the people of God, are similar to diamonds. We must be refined, cut and shaped into the image of God. While the process might be painful, it's essential to truly live our your destiny.

So today: embrace the persecution. Know that better days are coming and this is a part of the process for you to get to the next level.

O Lord, thank you for this day. Please forgive me for my sins. Allow me to endure this persecution so I may become stronger in life and have enough stamina to run the race of life for the Glory of God.

Be the catalyst for change.☺

DAY 283: Purity

Today is about becoming pure.

Growing up, I always tried to be a little a worse than I actually was. Especially the last two years of college all the way into college. Being a preacher's kid came with a reputation of being a handful, so I try to keep it up. I would go to a club and be out all Saturday night, yet still be at church bright and early on Sunday morning.

Pure isn't something we seek in today's society. We seek to be as dirty as possible. Dirty seems to be interesting and sexy.

However, that isn't aligned with God's will. We all have been the victim of peer pressure in today's society. We all have done something and heightened our personality a bit to seem cool. Unfortunately trying to look cool isn't something that leaves you at high school. It stays forever. ☺

Purity is about being free from contamination, clear, untainted and wholesome. The purer you are, the better you can hear God. When you lack purity, this is separation between you and God. When you're separated from God, you can't hear from God and spend a lot of time in a holding pattern.

What separates you from sin? Continuous and repeated sin. God will touch your heart and let you know when you're outside of His will. If you continue to ignore it, that's when the separation occurs.

So today: become pure. Allow yourself to be open to hear from God when He tells you your actions are outside of His will. Ask for forgiveness and stop the behavior. When you do this, not only does it open the windows of heaven for blessing but it helps to increase your connection with God.

O Lord, thank you for this day. Please forgive me for my sins. Allow me to become pure and connected to you. Help me to stop repeated sins so I can hear from you continually.

Be the catalyst for change.☺

DAY 284: Reconciliation

Today is about Reconciliation.

When my parents go divorced, I was totally obsessed with my parents getting back together. I would give both of my parents tips and even cry when my dad left because I thought my mom was being mean but not sticking it out. I definitely acted out. My parents attempted to reconcile off and on when I was between four to eleven years old until my mother got remarried. I believe my mother attempted to work it out for me more than anything and told me as an adult she felt guilty about not sticking it out. My mother now regrets not fighting hard enough for the great love of her life.

When you know you've met the one, it will hit you like a ton of bricks. Now it may take some longer than others to process their feelings. Some are cynics or just don't want to be emotionally vulnerable.

Life is filled with regrets. That's why many times we, as imperfect humans, will step back and attempt to make sense of the heat of the moment decisions. When we realize our decisions are not founded in reason and common sense, we will seek to reconcile.

None of us are perfect. We should set things right. It's easy to allow haters to get into your mind and allow you to become uncertain about your decisions. Misery loves company.

In my case, misery wants you to go to hang out with them and help them find a man instead of being with the one you love.

Love is for the end of time. Love withstands addictions, financial difficulty, unemployment, infidelity, and overall life issues. Love is about being willing to apologize and being quick to forgive. Love is about pushing that person to be the best they can be.

However, love must be reciprocal as well. You can't continually take love from another without giving any in return. Everyone deserves to be loved at the same intensity and time.

All we have in life is love. You must be courageous to express and live it. Life is too short not to fight for love.

So today: seek reconciliation. None of us are perfect. We will, at times, disappoint and hurt one another. However, as long as you're willing to try to make amends, there is always hope. Throw caution to the wind and be willing to be your passionate and romantic self. Allow love to take over and watch your life change forever.

O Lord, thank you for this day. Please forgive me for my sins. Please allow me to be strong enough not only to feel love but receive it as well. Help me to remove all insecurities making me feel uncomfortable about receiving and giving love.

Be the catalyst for change.☺

DAY 285: Daddy's Girl

Today is about being Daddy's Girl.

At the ripe age of thirty-one, I'm still a daddy's girl. I love my daddy beyond comprehension. My dad taught me so much about myself and helped set my spiritual foundation. My daddy's love just as much as well. When he talks about me, people assumed I'm was ten until they ask and find out I'm thirty-one. ☺ When you call my dad's cell phone, it's my voice you hear. Very funny. ☺

My daddy and I have always had an open relationship where we discussed relationships, sex and life. He was the biggest advocate of my celibacy to ensure that on my path. He has been honest and foresight on the mistakes in his life so I wouldn't repeat them.

I enjoy being a daddy's girl. That means, until I get married, the most important man in my life is my father. He is my support system until God sends me a mate.

Now there are many who are not lucky enough to have a positive relationship with their father. I implore you all to seek and give homage to all men in your life who support you like a father. It should be your uncle, a cousin, your pastor or even postman. However, attempt to give light to the males in your life who are trying to be positive role models to others. While they all may not be perfect, allow them to grow just as we grow as well.

So today: become a daddy's girl to some man in your life. Thank God for all positive influences you have in your life. Allow yourself to believe there is good in everyone.

O Lord, thank you for this day. Please forgive me for my sins. Thank you for the positive male role model in my life. Help me to understand and forgive while we are all in this race called life.

Be the catalyst for change.☺

DAY 286: Redemption

Today is about Redemption.

After the mayoral campaign, I was filled with a lot of disgust, resentment and frustration. It actually froze my heart for a while and I was completely numb emotionally. I was still also very angry at a lot of people because they didn't come through with the support I needed. However, it was slowly going away.

Then, one day at my church, Cascade United Methodist, Pastor Moss, preached a sermon that touched my heart and changed me as a person. He spoke about forgiveness and I realized the one person I never forgave in the process was myself.

I was angry at myself for letting everyone down and not being able to produce results. However, in that moment during that sermon, my heart became thawed and I was redeemed.

Redemption is the improved state of somebody or something saved from apparently irreversible decline.

God is constantly redeeming us with his spirit and will. We all make mistakes and not ever fully recover from them. We mark that time in our life, we never really move past and constantly wonder what could have been.

You must believe in yourself. If God didn't intervene on an opportunity for you, then He must have something better in the works. You must believe your best days are in front of you, not behind you. Allow yourself to move on past disappointment and sorrow.

So today: allow God to redeem yourself. God can help you recover and liberate you from all setbacks, disappointment and struggles in your life. He will never leave you or forsake you. You must continue to believe.

O Lord, thank you for this day. Help me to allow your redemptive spirit to wash over me. Help remove me out of 'pause position' and allow me to get life back on track.

Be the catalyst for change.☺

DAY 287: Sanctified

Today is about being sanctified.

I can remember going to church and hearing people talk about being sanctified and filled with the Holy Ghost. My sister and I questioned what that meant.

Growing certain words and phrases were considered church speak and held no relevance to us. For example, being blessed and highly favored, the devil is a lie; I'm sanctified and filled with the Holy Ghost. These were just sayings.

I know why we felt that way. It was because we were not mature in our faith. We lacked a certain amount of spiritual experience to truly understand those quotes. They were not sayings but rather a statement of being.

When we make something or somebody sanctified, you make it holy, you bless it, purify or approve it.

God can make you whole and holy after the refinement process. He will make you a whole new being in Jesus. When you become a whole new being in Jesus, you become a completely different person. You will talk differently, act differently. Things that once felt comfortable, no longer feel comfortable again.

This can be a weird place to exist. You don't feel comfortable with your old life but still definitely shaky with your new life as well. However, rely on God and He will settle your life in no time.

So today: allow God to sanctify you. He will change your mind, heart and spirit. While becoming a new creature in God will be slightly disconcerting but it will settle quickly.

O Lord, thank you for this day. Please forgive me my sins. Allow me to become a new creature in Christ and become sanctified and filled with the Holy Spirit. Allow my life to be forever changed.

Be the catalyst for change.☺

DAY 288: Suffering

Today is about suffering.

I probably have the best relationship and prayer life with God when I'm sick. When you're sick and you feel bad, it doesn't take anything for you to call on the name of Jesus. You will talk to God all night with the promises of what you will do when the suffering ends. It also gives you a sense of perspective. Things that seemed to be devastating before, no longer seem to be that way at all. Now they seem like disagreement. Suffering has a way of making us decrease the size of problems in our lives. It really gives you a sense of perspective.

Suffering is a part of life. It's unavoidable. It can't be chosen, scheduled or bribed. Suffering is something we as Christians have no control over.

Suffering is anguish, misery and agony. Suffering is a set of experiences that bring nothing but pain.

Most things in life are going to require a bit of sacrifice and suffering. Suffering allows you to appreciate things in your life more because it becomes clear your life could change in an instant if it's not for God's Grace and Mercy.

Suffering helps to become a thank you for all we have in our lives. While things may be bad, they could also be worse.

So today: allow yourself to be thankful for the suffering in your life. Suffering brings us closer to God and in direct relationship with God.

O Lord, thank you for this day. I also thank you for the suffering experience. It allowed me to see the tiny blessings in my life but also increase my furor of trying to seek you.

Be the catalyst for change.☺

DAY 289: The Power of a Testimony

Today is about the power of a testimony.

My experiences in my life have enabled me to have a powerful testimony. Testimony is proof, demonstration and statement of God's power.

We all have a testimony. However, the million-dollar question is: will you share your story with others so they can become an example of God's work?

I never really thought I was the testimony type. Sure I believe God was good but I thought I'd see God's work in my life by the way I lived my life.

However, sometimes it's not enough. God will put an urging in your spirit to share your experience. People can learn so much through the power of storytelling. That's essentially what sharing your testimony is. You're showing others you have been exactly where they are but yet you were able to make it over.

This is what helps people, Testimonies are great tools for day-to-day living. When we talk about God in the abstract, people can connect but not the way they can when you put your personal perspective on it.

So today: Share your testimony with others, Don't be ashamed to share your struggles in life. Sharing your human struggles gives others strength to endure this race called life.

O Lord, thank you for this day. Please forgive me for my sins. Help me to have courage to share my testimony with others.

Be the catalyst for change.☺

DAY 290: Wisdom

Today is about wisdom.

My father and uncle have an impressive amount of wisdom. They also have a tremendous amount of insightfulness that goes beyond their years. They are excellent in having a discerning spirit and can pick up on what is going on with you without you having to say a word.

I always go to them both when I'm attempting to make critical decisions. I know, no matter what, they have my best interest at heart.

Wisdom is accumulated learning, perception or knowledge or a bit of spiritual intelligence. It's good to have someone in your life to provide wisdom and feed your soul.

God will place angels in your life as guides. These guides will provide powerful insight in crucial junctures of your life.

No one can make it in life on their own. You need to have someone to confide in, to discuss or flesh ideas out with. It's difficult to keep yourself on track without the expert knowledge of others.

Also, don't be afraid to share your wisdom as well. Wisdom has nothing to do with age but rather it's about experience.

So today: seek wisdom. God wants you to step into your destiny but you must be willing to seek others in order to get to the next level.

O Lord, thank you for this day. Please forgive me for my sins. Please send angels into my life that can provide wisdom so I may step into my destiny.

Be the catalyst for change.☺

DAY 291: Broken in Spirit

Today is about being broken in spirit.

There have been times in my life when I have been broken in spirit. When broken in spirit is beyond disappointed, it's shattered and defeated.

Most of the time, you take disappointment in stride. You might feel it in your heart but mostly your ego is affected. There is a small part of us that believes we are above failure. That if you work hard enough, it won't happen to you.

That's simply not the case. Obstacles are a part of life. However, when you allow obstacles and setbacks to seep into your spirit and it catches you off guard, that's when you become broken in spirit.

When you're broken in spirit you don't have plan b, you were working hard for your passion. When so far into an endeavor, a person or venture and it doesn't go well, there will be some brokenness in the process.

God can heal our wounds including the ones in our spirit. God will give you peace and mercy to weather the storms of life. While it may be difficult to understand and comprehend, allow God to lead on this journey. Every journey or phase in your life has purpose. Trust God and allow yourself to be emotionally present.

So today: ask God for mercy to relieve our brokenness in spirit. God has plans for all of our lives. We must allow ourselves to trust and believe there's purpose in every moment in our lives including to the bad ones.

O Lord, thank for this day. Please forgive me for my sins. Help give me peace and mercy when I'm broken. Allow me to have enough faith in me to stand on your word.

Be the catalyst for change.☺

DAY 292: God Isn't a VISA Check Card

Today is about God isn't a VISA Check Card.

We often treat God like a Visa Check Card. We make hundreds of blessing requests similar to the way we spend with a check card. We do it without thinking.

Until we start to get overdraft fees (i.e. unanswered prayer). Then we become angry and want to talk to someone. Similarly, when we get an influx of unanswered prayers, we attempt to pray to find out why God hasn't answered our prayers.

God doesn't have to answer to us. However we do have to answer to Him. God wants to ensure we understanding the process. When prayers go up, blessings come down within reason, similar to a check card. We must pay attention to not only prayer for blessing but also give praise and be thankful as well. God gives us way more than we deserve in life even in the hard times. If we allow ourselves to stay focused on intake of blessings we will miss the major part of our relationship with God. Our relationship with God isn't about what He can do for us but rather the thankfulness for what He has already done.

So today: don't treat God like a Visa Check Card. God does bless us. Take a little time to praise and thank Him as well.

O Lord, thank you for this day. Please forgive me for my sins. Help me see God is more than a blessing machine; He does more than that. Allow me to spend time thanking Him for what He has already done. Allow God to have mercy on me despite the mistakes I have made.

Be the catalyst for change.☺

DAY 293: Born Again

Today about being born again.

While I'm now United Methodist, after my father took a sabbatical, I was able to go to church anywhere. I went to a lot of Baptist and non-denominational churches. They spoke a lot of being born again.

When you become born again, you become a new creature in Christ. Your whole life is left behind. You must be strong enough let go of your previous self-destructive habits.

When God enters your heart and you're born again, you've made the decision to make God the center of your life. You life will forever be changed due to decisions in a new and positive way.

God will make all things you used to do no longer fun. The places you used to love to go, you won't want to go anymore.

You'll be brought into existence with a whole new frame of mind, body and spirit.

However, that doesn't mean there won't be bumps along the way. There may be times the new lifestyle will be overwhelming and you may be tempted to slip back into old habits. Don't. Evil will attempt to make you feel like you have given up too much to be born again.

Don't think about it so hard. Just give God your hand and allow Him to enter your heart. Your life will be fulfilled and never be the same.

So today: become born again. Confess that Jesus Christ is your savior. Change your life and become a part of the body of Christ.

O Lord, thank you for this day. Thank you for your sins. Allow yourself to be born again and created in the likeness of God.

Be the catalyst for change.☺

DAY 294: Anything is Attainable

Today is about anything is attainable.

Growing up, I have always been an aggressive person. I believed 'No' meant, 'Not yet' or 'A little later.'

I have been successful in my life not because I'm smart, but rather because I'm determined. I'm willing to do what it takes to produce results.

I was taught I can do anything I set my mind to. Nothing is life is unattainable. The only things that stop us from greatness are our own insecurities.

I believe that's why I can get knocked down so many time but still keep coming forward. Once I set my mind on something, watch out.

God wants us to be courageous, driven and ambitious. You must strive for the unattainable or you will settle for mediocrity.

Allow yourself to believe in yourself and your abilities. While all of the situations in life may not be ideal and you may have challenges to overcome, you can overcome; you can succeed.

Just focus on having a place to help get you to your dreams and destiny. God will provide guidance but you do need an administrative-like plan so you will know what to do on a day-to-day basis.

So today: anything is attainable. All things are possible, achievable and feasible if you believe. Don't allow your fear of the unknown, frustration and just basic fear to get in your way.

O Lord, thank you for this day. Please forgive me for my sins. Allow me to push myself past any discomfort so I can achieve anything.

Be the catalyst for change.☺

DAY 295: Sometimes It's in His Name

Today is sometimes it's in His name.

There have been many times I have been in trouble and didn't know what to do. Whether it is real physical danger or just emotional, you're overcoming with rushing of everything coming at you at once. You keep trying to think of different ways to do things and nothing seems to pan out.

Then, I just say Jesus, and something just clicks in my mind. It gives me an ability to figure out what I need to do.

For instance, I was sitting on the bed watching the news around 9 pm in March 2008. I noticed the reporter I was watching had been talking about a storm coming into Atlanta and suddenly she lost all sense of professionalism. Then, I noticed it stopped raining, it looked very eerie outside. Then I noticed the cloud moving. However, it was dark; it wasn't a cloud but a tornado coming toward me. I jumped up and started grabbing stuff.

I backed away from my window and said Jesus and I noticed the storm moved to the left. I immediately went downstairs in the basement of my condo community for safety.

There is a tremendous amount of power in God's name. Many things in our life could be solved with the pure calling of His name.

He is the only One in our lives who can settle our spirit and bless us at the same time. We must allow ourselves to release anxiety from excessive worrying and trust God will take care of us.

So today: call His name. When life gets you down and you're feeling a little stressed, call out the name of Jesus. Not only will He come in an instant, it will make you relaxed in the process.

O Lord, thank you for this day. Please forgive me for my sins. Help me to rely on your strength and understand the purpose in calling your name.

Be the catalyst for change.☺

DAY 296: Showing Up

Today is about showing up.

My sister was a part of student government in high school and I decided to follow in her footsteps. So the second day of school, I went by the student government office to sign up to run for freshman representative.

Then a week later in homeroom, I was called up by a teacher who told me I was being transferred to student government for homeroom. She gave me my attendance card.

I walked into the student government room and they all greeted me. I asked, how I won. By default of course. Since I was a freshman, most of the freshman class didn't even know student government existed so I ran unopposed and won.

I was shocked because I hadn't run for office since fourth grade and was a little uncertain about being unopposed.

That's how my student government career began. Sometimes, all you have to do is show up.

Sometimes in life, God has something ordained for you. You don't have to worry about anything; you just have to show up. You'll feel uncertainty and maybe at times that you shouldn't go through with it.

We say God's in control but the first sign of trouble we run away like scared children. God will speak to you and let you know that you haven't anything to worry about. We must learn to trust Him and follow orders. If He tells you to just show up, then do it and don't give it a second thought.

So today: be willing to show up. God has blessings He wants to showers on us if you can just believe and follow instructions.

O Lord, thank you for this day. Please forgive me for my sins. Help me to trust you and be willing to just show up.

Be the catalyst for change.☺

DAY 297: Sentiment

Today is about Sentiment.

I was working on a group project in graduate school. We had our part but this one girl was flaky from the beginning. She offered to do things and she'd never complete them. We eventually stopped counting on her to do things after a while. Then she decided she would turn in our last project. The class was online so we would be able to see if she did or not. Unfortunately, we agreed. The project was due by Sunday at midnight. Around 11:40, I noticed the project wasn't uploaded. So I send a message to my group members telling them I had bad feeling and I was going to go ahead and load the project. They responded immediately with agreement. I loaded and we made the deadline.

We found out the other girl actually had dropped to class and forgotten her duties. If we hadn't checked behind her, we would have lost over 40% of our grade.

I'm happy we shared the same sentiment. Sentiment is a deep feeling, emotion or response. A sentiment can happen to you or a group of people together.

We believed she wasn't going to come through, so we made alternative arrangements. It works to our benefit.

God will also give you a sentiment that you may need to make alternative arrangements. It can be various areas in your life. Don't question, just follow God's instructions.

So today: listen for God's sentiments and don't doubt them. God knows what's best and will work hard to ensure you're protected.

O Lord, thank you for this day. Please forgive me for my sins. Help me to listen to your sentiments you send to me daily. They can provide me guidance on this journey called life.

Be the catalyst for change.☺

DAY 298: Not Part of the Club

Today is not part of the club.

While I'm a preachers' kid, I have also been a member of churches where I have family members in leadership. Church is a very different place.

Without guidance of a family member, I'm not part of the exclusive club and I have to start from scratch.

Unfortunately, church is supposed to be a haven, a relief from the outside aka secular world. However, it can also become your own hellish nightmare if you're not careful.

Churches are often very cliquey and difficult to infiltrate as a new person in Christ. It's treated more like the club and less like the hospital it is. We are all struggling and are coming to church to get fixed.

Yet, there are some in the body of Christ who are more concerned about appearances, status, wealth and other silliness instead of getting their soul right.

Where you sit in the church has nothing to do with your spiritual walk. So sitting close to front on Sunday but being a horrible person during the week isn't going to land you any closer to heaven; in fact it may fast track you to hell.

So today: for those of you who feel like a outsider, keep going and don't give up. While it may take you some time to find a church and group of friends you feel comfortable with, don't throw in the towel just yet. God wants to keep you on the path to your destiny and it's important for you to have a church home in this process. Trust Him, His word is more important than some crazy look from 'church' lady when you come in a little late to church.

O Lord, thank you for this day. Please forgive me for my sins. Allow me to continue on the path to greatness even when I don't fit in the exclusive club.

Be the catalyst for change.☺

DAY 299: Accountability

Today is about Accountability.

Accountability is about structure and clarity in your life. We must be held accountable for our behavior in life. Accountability is essential for me. I need boundaries in my life or I will run amok in the world.

It also helps to provide me with direction for where I'm going and where I don't need to go.

I realized when you live in a condo community, there are some people who will take the concept of accountability too far. They will act like a parole officer and your home will feel like a jail. I realized I liked spiritual accountability but I'm now sure if I need accountability in my home environment.

Accountability is a strange things. You might like it in some areas but not in every aspect of your life.

God wants us to be responsible for our actions but it's hard to distinguish being responsible and being overwhelmed with rules and regulations.

So today: take accountability with a grain of salt. God wants to have structure in our lives but He also doesn't want to become overwhelmed. Stick to God's spiritual guidance He will never steer you wrong or off track.

O Lord, thank you for this day. Please forgive me for my sins. Allow me to stay focused and wait for You to provide guidance so I may be made accountable for my behavior.

Be the catalyst for change.☺

DAY 300: Becoming Dynamic

Today is about becoming dynamic.

Growing up and even now on certain level, I absolutely adore Sean 'Diddy' Combs. I admire him because of shrewd business sense. He completely changed the game. He made evolution cool for rappers and producers. For the longest time, people thought artists should only focus on that. However, he became a change agent. He showed the best way to have independent wealth is to have various businesses. Becoming a mogul isn't an exclusive club, rather one we can all join if we are willing to work for it. Diddy is dynamic.

Being dynamic is characterized by vigorous activity and producing or undergoing change and development. A dynamic person is energetic, vibrant, and self-motivated.

A dynamic person never gives up, just takes breaks. A dynamic person just takes tactics in order to achieve their goals. A person who may get disappointment but doesn't allow the disappointment to stop them in their tracks.

A person who's God fearing and Holy spirit led, may not always have the answer but are willing admit their mistakes.

I believe we all possess those qualities you just have to ignite them. God wants us to reach our goals but it takes a strong belief in yourself to get there.

The road may not be easy. You may hit a couple of testing periods that seem like they never end. There might be times when you become broken and disillusioned. You may not have all of the answers but God will provide you with the guidance needed to continue to run in this race called life.

So today: becoming dynamic. Allow yourself to become energized and immersed in change and development of your life and the community in which you live. Don't allow fear to take you out of the game. Push through and make your dreams a reality.

O Lord, thank for this day. Please forgive me for my sins. Allow me to become more dynamic and focused so I may become a change agent and allow myself to live my destiny.

Be the catalyst for change.☺

DAY 301: Orchestrating Your own Advancement

Today is about orchestrating your own advancement.

Every couple of years, I create a game plan aka vision place for the next two to three years. I plan out what I want to achieve and break the tasks down into timelines on a weekly basis.

Now, I may not be able to keep up with my ambitious plan. Most of the time, they have to be retooled and adjusted based upon life's occurrences you can't predict.

You must take responsibility for your own advancement. In order to move your career from the minor leagues to the majors, you must create a place for yourself.

God will provide guidance in your life. To receive some career blessings in your life, it's up to you individually to stay focused on putting effort and organization into your life.

Life can be tough and it can be easy to get caught in the waves and waves descending upon us each day. However, we hold our head about a sea of contempt and use God as a lifeline to the shore of peace.

So today: don't be afraid to orchestrate your own advancement. No one will care as much about your life and career as you. You must be willing to set up a plan for your life instead of life leading you wherever. Because when life leads you, it usually ends up nowhere.

O Lord, thank you for my sins. Help me to work through these trying times.

Be the catalyst for change.☺

MONTH 11

DAY 302: Controversial

Today is about being controversial.

Being a Believer is always controversial. Simply because, being a Believer, you live your life by a different standard that the world. That alone will set you apart from most.

I have always been a slightly controversial figure. I have never been afraid to say how I feel and what I think. Usually, it's things that the general public may be thinking but may not want to admit. I always make sure I stay true to myself and am a transparent individual, for better or worse.

If you want to truly be an innovator, you will be controversial as well. You can't bring fresh and eclectic idea into this world and think everyone will agree with them.

There will always be jealous and haters who are disappointed in themselves that they were unable to think as creatively as you.

However, you can't worry about them, or work to keep them off track. You will always keep them off track but you can't be duplicated because you're creative. The only way you're duplicated when you're creative is because you have been telling too many people your plans.

You should guard your dreams with your life. Your dream is your vision for your life. This will allow you to live out your destiny. So be careful with those you share your vision with; it can literally derail your dreams in a big way.

So today: don't be afraid to be controversial and a little innovative. In order to live out your destiny: you will stand out from the crowd. Allow yourself to walk in your destiny and be forever changed.

O Lord, thank you for this day. Help me to stay centered and focused on you. Allow me not to become dissuaded by things in my life to keep from being close to you. Help me not to be afraid to being different.

Be the catalyst for change.☺

DAY 303: Unquenchable Thirst

Today is about Unquenchable thirst.

When you run, you will begin to have an unquenchable thirst. You need more than water, a coke, orange juice. You need a mixture of all three.

I believe life is similar. We constantly run through life attempting to find something to quench our thirst. We try to fill it with career, love, food and nothing works.

When you have a thirst that doesn't seem to be quenched, try God. Sometimes, a thirst we have is the search for something more to life than what we see around us. A belief in a higher calling and understanding there's someone to run to in the face of adversity.

It's difficult to try to make it on your own in this world. It can be a lonely and strange place. You can easily place faith and importance on items in your life that may not be good to your overall development. Then your thirst will increase.

Don't fret. God can provide you with spiritual nourishment that will help you to have the stamina in this race called life.

We all need something to believe in and to count on. Life can be devastating and overwhelming at times. You must push through and allow yourself to believe you can continue in this race called life.

So today: allow God to quench your spiritual thirst. God can provide the spiritual nourishment that's good for the soul.

O Lord, thank you for this day. Please forgive me for my sins. Allow me to look to you for advice and strength. Help cure my unquenchable thirst for salvation and knowledge.

Be the catalyst for change.☺

DAY 304: Insatiable Appetite

Today about insatiable appetite.

Despite being a slim girl, I love to eat. I enjoy tastes and smells of diverse groups of food. I will pretty much eat anything and anywhere.

I will cook but that isn't really my thing. I will cook so I can eat but not so people can eat my food. I love eating so much I will buy food pretty much anywhere… the dirtier the better. I will even buy BBQ off the side of the road when I see it.

However, I do know how to exercise restraint in order to keep my figure in check. While exercise is important, you must watch what you eat in order to keep yourself healthy.

However, when I'm in a zone to eat: usually on the weekend or a big holiday, it's on.

Some of us have an insatiable appetite in life.

We have big ideas and dreams. We like everything fast and in excess. There's never any thought of the future or thought about the possibility of slowing down.

We can enjoy life on a shallow level for a little while but unfortunately real life issues will start to creep in: unemployment, underemployed, financial troubles, personal life issues, etcetera, will hit like a freight train.

You won't know how to handle or resolve these new and perplexing problems in your life.

Allow God to tame that insatiable appetite. He can provide with the nourishment you need without all of the silliness that exists in your life.

So today: allow God to curb your insatiable appetite. He only wants you to take the correct things into your spirit so when there are challenges, you have something to carry you through.

O Lord, thank you for this day. Please forgive me for my sins. Help me to stay focused on and let go of my insatiable appetite for excess in life.

Be the catalyst for change.☺

DAY 305: The Depth of Your Commitment

Today is about the Depth of your commitment.

When I commit to something, I'm totally in. I have a really extreme personality. Either I'm completely in or out. There is no in between for me.

So I have been training for the Peachtree Road Race for six months and I'm totally committed. I have run in rain, sleet, snow and heat. I have run when I'm frustrated, exhausted, angry and broken. I learned to treat this training the way I treat my businesses. It's a priority.

There hasn't been a time I have skipped running except when my grandmother died and we were in Gulfport, Mississippi and there was too much going on. However, then I was running seven days a week, so my body probably needed to rest.

We must all take a similar stance on our relationship with God,

We all would be nothing without God's grace and mercy. All we have received in life is because of Him.

We must seek to deepen our commitment to God. We must work to live our lives as close to being Christ-like as possible.

We must have work to follow rules for life God established but also be a beacon of light to others. Being light for those in darkness is the best way to show God to others.

So today: deepen your commitment to God. Go beyond the lukewarm connection. Help to show others the path of righteousness so we can all walk into our destiny.

O Lord, thank you for this day. Please forgive me for my sins. Allow me to be the light in the darkness of life. Help me to see the good in others and help them attain the contagious energy of kindness.

Be the catalyst for change.☺

DAY 306: Disqualifying Ourselves

Today is about disqualifying ourselves.

When I was younger, I was a sore loser. I didn't like to lose. (I still don't ☺), but I'm better at hiding it. I can remember playing in a mini-Uno card game tournament with friends and family. I would snitch on the other teams who were cheating in hopes of getting back into games. Did it work? Negative. Because no one likes a snitch.

There are many things we do on this Christian walk that could possible disqualify ourselves from the best life we could have: our own sins. God will forgive us for our misgiving but it takes time to recover and get back on track.

However, we must work hard not to disqualify ourselves from the glory of God. God wants to shower us with blessings but you must be in a correct relationship with God in order receive it.

An active prayer life is necessary, in order to have a correct relationship. You must be able to have direct communication with God. Prayer will help you to endure the uncertain times, so don't do something unnecessary and silly that can totally change the course of your life.

So today: don't allow yourself to be disqualified from God's grace. Try to stay on the path of righteous and in line with God through Prayer.

O Lord, thank you for this day. Please forgive me for my sins. Help me not to disqualify myself from your glory by being trapped in sin. Allow me to lean heavily on my prayer life so I can get through these tough times.

Be the catalyst for change.☺

DAY 307: Opportunistic

Today is about being opportunistic.

I can't stand people who are opportunistic. People who are opportunistic are those looking for and taking opportunity often in a way that's unfair or harms someone else.

I believe you can succeed in life if you focus on creating your own opportunities instead of taking them from someone else.

However, there are many in the body of Christ who are opportunistic. They aren't bold enough to create their own opportunities so they steal from others. Or they lack loyalty and focus. They will do anything for a dollar.

Your integrity is worth more than any amount of money you can imagine. Don't allow your life to be shaped by greed; it isn't good luck.

So today: allow yourself not to be dissuaded by all glitz and glamour. Don't become opportunistic. Wait for God to send you the right opportunity at the right time. He knows what's best for you.

O Lord, thank you for this day. Please forgive me for my sins. Allow me to become a stronger person in Christ. Help me stay focused on you and no one else.

Be the catalyst for change.☺

DAY 308: Contributing

Today is about contributing.

When you go out to eat with friends, it's customary to split to check. Everybody will pay for what they order except that one person. That person always orders the most but yet will request everyone to split the check based on the number of people.

Is it fair for you to pay $10 and you only ordered a salad? This person isn't contributing even a little trifle.

There are many of us like this in the body of Christ.

We are going to church, prayer daily and living a just life. However, there is one problem: we are not sharing our testimony with others and bringing them to Christ.

This isn't what God wants us to do. God gave us a testimony to share with others. Your blessing can be directly tied into your ability to share your testimony and life with others.

If you're unclear about whether you want to share your testimony, you can share it by giving your time at your church. Join a ministry such as the choir, finance, or even ushering. By giving up your time to God and helping to touch others when they come into the House of the Lord is a testimony in itself.

So today: contribute more to the body of Christ. Give your time or share your life story of how you made it over with other believers. Help to encourage others and God will encourage you. Allow God to enter your life and watch your life be changed for the better.

O Lord, thank you for this day. Please forgive me for my sins. Allow me to have the courage to contribute more to the body of Christ by joining a ministry or sharing my story. Help me encourage others to trust God and believe.

Be the catalyst for change.☺

DAY 309: It's Worthwhile

Today it is about worthwhile.

During these tough economic times, this question is the question we all ask ourselves before doing anything. Go to work, work out, go on vacation, visit a friend, pay for dinner, even going to church etcetera. We are now establishing worth on pretty much everything.

When you're determining worth, you're establishing meaning, usefulness and value. Most of the worth is a subjective not objective perspective.

We must curb the inclination to do this. They are some things we do they can't easily determined by worth but it makes us happy as people.

Don't allow your present circumstances to change your mind set. God wants us to be able to enjoy ourselves and life despite chaos around us.

While this can be difficult to do, it's essential in life. You must be able to function despite the challenges you're attacked by. You can't falter or hesitate. You must stand and endure the pain in order to move up to the next level.

So today: don't worry about whether or not something is worthwhile. Do what makes you happy and help to keep you focused on this Christian walk. While it may be difficult to endure, ultimately this will refine you and allow you to see what is really important.

O Lord, thank you for this day. Please forgive me for my sins. Allow me to focus on what makes me happy and not what isn't necessary. Help me to remain driven toward living a Christian life.

Be the catalyst for change.☺

DAY 310: Your own Agenda

Today is about continuing your own agenda

I have always been proficient in having my own agenda and following it. It's very difficult to get me off track from my own agenda because I'm a stickler for it. I don't make excuses for my agenda also. I act like it doesn't exist. I always try to be transparent so everyone knows my priority is to complete the goal I have created for myself.

It's important for all of us to have an agenda. An agenda is a plan, outline, schedule or list of items that must be completed. Each task is critical for you to reach your destiny.

No one will help you complete your agenda but they have their own agenda to complete. It's for you and only you to stay focused on your agenda. The agenda must be followed and items completed.

God will provide you with a helping hand but you must be wary of Evil because it will send you tasks to keep from completing your agenda. The items sent by Evil are always competing, serious and deadlines suspicious close to your agenda.

You must put your foot down with family, friends and loved ones. You won't be any help to them if you don't follow your agenda and aren't able to live your destiny. So ask for the understanding and give it in return.

So today: be selfish and stick to your agenda. While it might cause anger and frustration with loved ones and it will put you one step closer to your destiny.

O Lord, thank you for this day. Please forgive me for my sins. Allow me to stay focused on my agenda and not distracted on the trials of life.

Be the catalyst for change.☺

DAY 311: Defeat

Today is about defeat.

We all have experienced defeat in some point in our lives. It's a painful part of life.

However, defeat should not be seen as a *diss* to your skills but rather feedback about areas where you need work.

This is an opportunity for comeback if you get past the blow to your ego and listen to what God has for you.

God will also do something to defeat us, not just because He is trying to hurt us but rather to strengthen us on this journey called life. The defeat also helps us to work on certain areas in our lives that need work.

God wants you to become powerful and conquer the world but you must be ready for all that it brings. In order to conquer, you must ensure you have an active prayer life and confidence in yourself.

An active prayer life helps you to receive direction from God. Prayer does not change God but it helps to change how you deal with challenging situations in your life.

Finally, you need a huge dose of confidence in yourself. Through God's help you must believe you're able to do anything. Confidence isn't something that someone can give you; it comes from within.

So today: take defeat in stride. Remember that's part of life. Let the blow to your ego heal and then take feedback for what it's worth. Then allow yourself to get back in the race of life and conquer the world.

O Lord, thank you for this day. Please forgive me for my sins. Please let me take defeat as feedback and not allow it to crush me. Help to keep my prayer life active and keep my confidence in myself so I can achieve anything.

Be the catalyst for change.☺

DAY 312: Stop Running

Today is about stop running.

We all have a habit of racing around and attempting to juggle all of the various things in our lives.

We all quietly resent those who really don't help or respect us. We push through the knowledge that we are alone as each one of our so-called friends drifts off.

These are times when you must keep stop running and face what God is trying to show you.

When every time you attempt to gravitate toward anybody and they disappear suddenly, there is something God wants you to get out of this process. Don't get angry or frustrated. Embrace the process.

God is trying to show you something about your life and the life you want. He will give you a back stage pass to the life of a legend without you realizing it.

He will show you the dark side first before showing you the good side.

He is grooming you for something big and He has to allow you to hit rock bottom to ensure you will not allow anything or anybody to get the glory except Him.

So today: stop running and turn around. Take God by the hand and follow Him. Allow Him to show you what is holding you back from your destiny. Trust and believe there is purpose in all God does.

O Lord, thank you for this day. Please forgive me my sins. Allow me to stop running and see what you're trying to teach me. Open my eyes to areas in my life that need to be fixed.

Be the catalyst for change.☺

DAY 313: Becoming Wiser

Today is about becoming wiser.

From the age of five to twenty-five, getting older rocks. Then as you continually get older, not so much.

I look really young but it's still a complete downer when someone says wow, I can't believe thirty-one, I didn't realize you were so old. Or they think you older than you are because of your maturity.

I guess it's a compliment…sort of.

It's difficult, particularly when you're single with no children in your thirties. You never thought you would be where right now. This is the American dream we are all dealing with in some area of our lives.

Life comes with various twists and turns in our lives. It becomes difficult to get past when you're in a turn that isn't quite so good.

However, there are benefits to becoming wiser. You're able to make sensible decisions and judgment on the basis of personal knowledge and experience.

When you see situations reminding you of things in the past, you pickup on patterns immediately and then work hard to remove yourself from those situations.

God will give you a vision for your life and help guide your life until you see it. Once you see it, you will make it your life's work to achieve. Regardless of the trade offs in the process.

So today: embrace your wiser self. Thank you for allowing yourself to live long enough to share some of your experiences and you still can pursue your destiny.

O Lord, thank you for this day. Please forgive me for my sins. Thank you for allowing me to become wiser and to learn from my experiences. Help me to realize the vision you have for my life and allow me to become focused on achieving it.

Be the catalyst for change.☺

DAY 314: Apprehension

Today is about apprehension.

I'm from a family of professional worriers. We have worrying down to an art. I try not to allow it to overtake me but I do indulge from time to time. However, my situation is slightly different. I'm more of an apprehension kinda girl.

Apprehension is a part of life. Apprehension is a feeling of anxiety or fear that something bad or unpleasant will happen.

Apprehension doesn't mean anything has happened yet but you're overly concerned that something will. It can be caused from previous bad experiences or just plain old living vicariously through others.

No matter what happens to you in your life, you're able to live to fight another day. You keep a positive and fresh outlook on life. While it may be difficult to ascertain at times, it's important to keep yourself in a good and positive place.

Allow God to lead you path and trust Him. You can't get through life on your own accord and decisions. That's how we all mess our lives up by making our own decisions instead of seeking God.

So today: remove all apprehension from your mind, body and spirit. Allow yourself to wholly trust and allow Him to lead you through life. While life may not be perfect, He won't steer off course.

O Lord, thank you for this day. Please forgive me for my sins. Allow me to remove all apprehension from my mind, body and spirit.

Be the catalyst for change.☺

DAY 315: Assurance From God

Today is about needing a little assurance from God.

Sometimes when life throws you a curve ball, it's difficult to get back on track. We need a bit of assurance from God. Assurance is a promise or making something certain.

God's word actually means something; He's probably one of the few. Others can give you assurance but it can also always be beyond their ream of understanding,

God knows how our story will end. His assurances are based on fact. So if God says, don't worry, then don't. He knows what's going to happen so allow yourself to trust in His word.

God is patient and understands when we need a bit of assurance from Him. Sometimes, we just want to know we're doing the right thing or going in the right direction.

He understands we're not questioning His authority but rather attempting to grasp how we're going to endure in this race called life.

So today: if you need a little assurance from God, go ahead and ask for it. God knows our worries and concerns. Don't allow your faith to be shaken by what's going on around you.

O Lord, thank you for this day. Help me to trust your assurances. Allow me to rest on my faith in you and your previous work that it will all work out within Your divine will.

Be the catalyst for change.☺

DAY 316: Confessing

Today is about confessing.

I don't really like to confess. It's about admitting you've done something wrong. Even though I do, I don't necessarily like to admit it all the time.

However, alas, it's necessary.

Confession isn't about making you feel bad about yourself. However, rather about helping you to see the areas in your life where you need work.

We all struggle with something in our lives but how we can handle it is the defining factor. Confession is about humbling yourself, putting your ego aside and saying to God I'm sorry and I need help.

Confession can feel like you have a weight lifted off of your shoulders. You're freeing yourself from the guilt of your actions. You can stop repressing your feeling and actions. When you fess up to God and make up your mind to stop certain behaviors, you feel lightly and able to think clearer. You will be able to open your mind so you can be more creative as well.

Today: take a deep breath and confess your sins to God. Allow yourself to let go of all heavy baggage sins are causing. Once you let go and confess, watch God give you a happiness along with a new testimony that you have never had.

O Lord, thank you for this day. Please forgive me for my sins. Allow it to be easier for me to confess my sins in my life to you. Help me to create a stronger relationship with you.

Be the catalyst for change.☺

DAY 317: Approval

Today is about getting approval.

I have never been one to seek approval even when I needed it career-wise. I would usually jump that step even without thinking.

I thought the higher ups would understand once the project was completed. Not always.

Even now as an entrepreneur, I'm held accountable to someone whether it be my customers or corporate sponsors. There will always be a need to seek approval. You must get used to it.

I believe One we should constantly seek approval from is God. God wants you to seek Him when you're unsure so He can give us direction. His direction is divine and will lead us on the path to our destiny.

While it may be difficult to humble yourself to seek His approval, it can possible change the course of your own life.

Allow yourself to remove your ego, which could be hurting your relationship with God. There's no need for egos and arrogance with God. You'll never win; He knows more—period.

So today: allow yourself to seek God and get His approval on various things in life. Allow Him to shape and mold your life into what He has for your destiny.

O Lord, thank you for this day. Please forgive me for my sins. Allow me to seek you in all aspects in my life. Help to let go of my ego and arrogance in the process so I can have a better relationship with you.

Be the catalyst for change.☺

DAY 318: Desire

Today is about desire.

My desire for my life is to be happy. I would like to be happy in my business and personal life. I'm not there yet but I would like to make an effort to get there. If I can't get happy, I would at least like to be content in both.

Desire is to wish and to want something very strongly.

We all have desires in our life. The question is how do we get them?

We first have to make sure our desires are aligned with God. It's easy to develop desires for inappropriate things. However, we must be able to temper these desires.

Once you have determined your desires are aligned with God's will, then you must work hard to get them, just like anything else. Ask God to open a window of blessings in order to get your desire.

God wants us all to be happy. However, we must be willing to work to reach the desires of our hearts. We work to receive our desires by attempting to live a Christian life.

So today: go after what you desire. Allow yourself to make an effort to get what you want in your life. You must be willing to work for your desires. If you work hard enough, God will create a shower of blessings for you.

O Lord, thank you for this day. Please forgive me for my sins. Please help me to get the desires of my heart. Help me not become discouraged as I continue on the path of life.

Be the catalyst for change.☺

DAY 319: Depression

Today is about depression.

Depression is a part of life. At some point, we all become overwhelmed and resentful of what's happening in our lives.

However, you can learn to be a functionally depressed person. You will do what is only necessary and then go back to sleep.

There have been many times when I have been depressed and retreated into a world of sleep when I couldn't deal with what was going on around me.

However, in the Christian world, depression is taboo. No one likes to discuss it because it's seen as a lack of belief if you allow yourself to become depressed.

Nothing can be further from the truth. Depression is a state of unhappiness and hopelessness. If you stay in a testing period for longer than six months, which I have experienced, you will become depressed.

You can get through this. You can make it. Hold on. While things are bad right now, they can change in an instant with God's help.

So today: it's ok to be depressed. It's part of life. However, if it lasts longer than a couple of weeks, seek help. It can be a secret between you and God. However, it's ok to feel blue and not be a bad Christian. Life gets tough, so it's ok to feel burned from it.

O Lord, thank you for this day. Allow me to become more focused on you. Help lift me from this depression I feel. Allow me to know with you all things are possible.

Be the catalyst for change.☺

DAY 320: Restraint

Today is about restraint.

When I get angry, I have a problem exercising restraint. I'm usually good about not allowing myself to get to a level where I can't control myself. However, unfortunately there are times I can't handle it.

Restraint can be difficult to have, especially when you've reached the point of no return. Restraint is the act or the quality of holding back, limiting or controlling something. However, restraint is necessary when attempting to reach your destiny.

There will be many times in life you will be provoked and you must resist action. Evil knows your areas of weaknesses and will send things deliberately to annoy you in order to get your mind off God and onto some silly situation.

If you do find yourself without any restraint, immediately ask for forgiveness. We are all human and are prone to anger at times. None of us are perfect. However, the key on this spiritual walk is to bounce back every time. The quicker you can bounce back, the quicker you can reach your destiny.

So today, allow yourself to practice restraint but if you fail, bounce back. We all make mistakes. Allow yourself to become tougher and be able to take the hits of life.

O Lord, thank you for this day. Please forgive me for my sins. Allow me to exercise restraint when provoked. Allow me to exhibit patience even when I don't feel like it.

Be the catalyst for change.☺

DAY 321: Support

Today is about providing support.

Support is to keep something or somebody upright or in place, prevent something or somebody from failing.

I remember I was attending a church where I was extremely active and I was starting to feel burn out and underappreciated. I was spending almost every day at church and paying for a lot of things out of pocket. I never asked for anything in return.

When it came time to ask for support while running for Mayor, the church power brokers became indifferent. I felt like it was a complete slap in the face of all the hard work I had put in.

Then I had money stolen from my purse while ushering. Instead of them attempting to make it right, I was told maybe I had misplaced my money and left it at home. @#$%~

I was beginning to lose it under the pressure. I remember, I tried to reach out during revival to my ushers board class and I was rebuffed. A couple of the ushers told me to develop tougher skin at church.

I didn't believe I needed tougher skin; I needed to be around people who loved, appreciated and supported me. I called my dad crying. He told me it was time to move on to a church home that would support me.

I did and I've never looked back since. Sure there are times I have flashbacks and someone is attempting to get over but I realize they are not and we all are working hard for the glory of God.

I understand what it feels like to work and work and have no success. Don't allow yourself to be used and belittled by those who don't respect.

So today: go find solace somewhere that will support, love and nurture the way you need to continue in this race of life.

Lord, thank you for this day. Please forgive me for my sins. Allow me to find support with you but also lead me to human support as well. Help me to lean on someone who gives me strength to stand in the race called life.

Be the catalyst for change.☺

DAY 322: Prayers of Positive Energy

Today: prayers of positive energy.

O Lord, allow only positive energy to seep into my spirit. I know I can manifest all of my dreams and aspirations with strong belief in myself. While you may knock me down, I'm not beaten. I will weather the storm. I will continue to believe.

O Lord, continue to protect me from all enemies aka haters. Allow me to reach my full potential and step in the destiny right now. Allow my heart to continue to stay open to others and not darken with negative thoughts. Help me to understand the only protection I need right now is you, Lord.

Transform me, Lord, into the person I'm destined to be. Allow me to be shaped by words of wisdom in every aspect of Your life. Help me to have a discerning spirit to hear Your words as closely as possible. Allow my actions to be aligned with Your will.

Allow me to stay focused on you, Lord, while I'm grindin'. Allow exhaustion and frustration not to get the better of me. Help me understand You have my best interests at heart. Help me to step into my destiny without fear.

Allow me to understand the purpose of silence. Help me to keep my most important dreams and goals close to my chest. Protect my dreams and goals before they are produced in my mind. Help me not fear progress but embrace it.

I embrace the favor you have given me, Lord. Not because I was so good or deserving, but out of clear mercy on my soul. I thank all of those who prayed for me when I couldn't or wouldn't pray for myself. I will also pray for others. Continue to allow the favor to rain down on my life and allow my life to forever be changed.

Allow me to weather to storms to life. I feel myself become stronger and more resilient. No one can stop me. When you Lord, are with me, then who can be against me? Allow me to believe in myself and fulfill my dreams. I will never stop trying to achieve my goals and one day they will be fulfilled. They will be fulfilled because it's my destiny.

Be the catalyst for change.☺

DAY 323: Prayers for Guidance and Direction

Today: various prayers for guidance and directions.

Lord, remove all of my stubborn tendencies in my being. Help me allow You to steer the course of my Life. I must trust You and have faith that You will take care of me. While I don't understand all of your actions or non-actions, you truly have my best interest at heart.

Lord, help me to develop my mind, body and spirit. I know now all must be centered in order to be truly fulfilled. Allow me to give my will to You so You may lead my life that's aligned with Your Will. Give me a sense of purpose and clarity in my life to live my life in a just way.

Lord, shape the direction of my life. Please keep me on the positive path. Allow me to resist all temptations that might come my way. Help to understand it's nothing more than a test of faith. Allow me to continue to look for continuous direction for the course of my life.

Lord, provide instruction to me. Help me to know the next stage of my life. I can't do this without you. Help me to trust You despite all of the chaos I see around me. I know you have and will to continue to protect my life. Allow me to be in a fiery furnace but don't allow me to be burned.

Lord, guide my life. I need guidance to stay on the positive path. Help me not allow jealousy or resentment to build my heart. Allow me to be present in my emotions, good and bad. Allow me to be used as a vessel for your Will. Take command of mind, body and spirit. Make sure that's always aligned with your ideals and word.

Thank you, Lord, for my Faith. When I was filled with sadness, you were there. When I was filled with happiness, you were there. No matter what occurs in my life, I know you will be with me. Take control of my life and allow me to be on the path of righteousness.

Allow me to use my faith with intelligence. However, don't allow my intelligence to shape my faith. My faith should not be founded in the components of logic and reason. Your Will can Sometimes, work contrary to those components. Allow my breakthrough to come into my life in whatever will is necessary. Help me to stay focused on this journey called life.

Be the catalyst for change.☺

DAY 324: Prayers for Disappointments

Today: various prayers for disappointments.

Thank you Lord for helping me see the blessing beyond my disappointment. While I'm disappointed, lift my spirits so I may not allow Evil to enter my thoughts and change my actions. Allow me to stay centered on you and understand you will take care of the rest.

Forgive my selfish motives and out of control ambitions. Allow me to be a testimony for you. Help me to seek you to ensure my heart is in the right place and I have the best intentions. While I may not be where I want to be, thank you, I'm not what I used to be.

Help me to trust you Lord. I'm frustrated and ready to give up. Help to me meditate on your will; allow your serenity to permeate my spirit. Help me to continue to fight on the journey called life. Allow me to shake off the discouragement and focus on all of the beauty in this world.

Allow me to become more optimistic. Help me to see all of the beauty instead of the Evil in the world. There is something positive in all things if you look hard enough. Any test of your faith allows me to become closer to God and become more reliant on Him.

Thank you; bring my ego down a notch. My ego was not allowing me to hear you clearly because I was too confident without you. There is no one like you. I can do all things with your help but nothing without you. Help me to continually understand I'm a vessel for you and your will.

Thank you for allowing me to mature, Lord. Help me to have faith beyond my years. Allow me to walk into the face of danger and know God has my back. Regardless of what hate comes my way, I know you will use my haters and enemies to bestow blessings onto me. I might stumble, but won't fall. God has my back and that's all I will ever need.

Be the catalyst for change.☺

DAY 325: Prayers for Love

Today: various prayers for love.

Lord help me to be open to love. Help to let go all of the failures in my life and open to new love that's ordinate in your will. I'm important enough to be loved and love will find me. I will attract powerfully positive and healthy people into my life.

Lord, teach me how to love. Please help me to let go of all of my fears. Lord, allow me to trust you to believe you will protect me for all hurts. I bathe in the unconditional love of my Creator and God. Help me to express love freely.

Lord, allow me to express and receive affection. I'm deserving of all of the good things in my life. I feel basically worthy as a person. I follow God's example of True Love. "I'm worthy of great love and I deserve to be loved fully and completely

Allow me to be understanding to those I love. The more I love, the more love is returned to me. I'm treating those I love the most with love and respect. I pray love will fill the hearts of those around me.

Help me to be patient with those I love. In life, I always get what I give out and I always give out love. I love everyone, even though I don't always love what they do. I'm a positive person filled with love.

Lord, give me a serene spirit. I love myself and I'm in charge of my own happiness. Everywhere I go, I find love. Life is joyous. The more I love the more I will be loved. Love comes from within me at all times.

Lord, help attract love to me. Love is attracted to me and I'm attracted to love. I'm ready to love again and I welcome love with open arms. I see everything with loving eyes and I love everything I see. I love myself unconditionally.

Be the catalyst for change.☺

DAY 326: Prayers for Peace

Today: various prayers for peace.

Lord, give me peace in my life. I choose to have a peaceful and calm spirit. Help me take time for spiritual connection in meditation or prayer. Releasing any anxious thoughts, I peacefully rest securely in God. Inner peace is my true nature. It's available to me whenever I join with God in prayer.

Lord, give me a tranquil spirit. I release my past and live with calm and serenity. I choose serenity now, as I allow myself to go within and to connect with the comforting silence of my soul.

Provide harmony in my life, Lord. As I close my eyes and take a deep breath, I inhale uplifting feelings of peace and calm. I exhale and release any tension or stress. Allow me to treat each day as a new beginning.

Lord, help me to stay positive. I have a peaceful and calming heart and soul. I express anger in appropriate ways so peace and harmony are balanced at all times. Allow me express my issues and not harbor hostility. Please allow me grow spiritually each day.

Allow me to stay calm in the midst in the storm. My environment is a garden of peace. No matter what events occur during my day, I remain calm and centered. I trust my inner being to lead me in the right path.

I let go of worry. I enjoy the natural flow of this day, whatever it may bring. I'm always connected with the Divine Love of God. God's presence within me is my source of perfect inner peace. I'm calm and certain, sharing my inner peace with others wherever I go, knowing that God is with me always.

I deserve to relax. As I stop and relax I refresh my mind, my body and my spirit. God is my constant source of inner peace and strength, because I'm part of God and God is part of me.

Be the catalyst for change.☺

DAY 327: Prayers for Enduring

Today: various prayers for enduring.

The greater the resistance I meet, the STRONGER I become. The Lord will always provide the support I need. The path ahead of me is clear. All I need is to continue to stay focused on the Lord.

I give myself permission to run my own race of life with you, Lord. I can do this. I can weather the storm and get through this testing period. Help me to stay focused on you.

I'm grateful for this day. Accepting change as a spiritual adventure, I move through all my experiences as a divine being. I give myself permission to behave boldly and map my inward journey with love. No one can stop me or hinder my progress. I'm ready to live the moment and step into my destiny.

Today, I maintain my center in the midst of the events around me. I meet negativity with love, turmoil with peace, and confusion with clarity. I take life spiritually, not personally. I understand this process of testing is refining me, not punishing me. Help me to open to the total experience without judgment or resentment.

In this moment, I let go of anything that may be holding me back from full joy and creativity. I look into my life with eager anticipation for newness and change. I hold on to what is of value in my thoughts, emotions, and experiences. I lovingly release the rest. Lord, help me to becoming increasing reliant on You each and every day.

I allow my consciousness of my unity with all life to lead my way. I praise what is working, adjust what isn't, and move in positive ways to contribute to the good around me.

Today, I let my highest values and ideals guide my decisions. I have a clear intention to live my best life. I trust the Spirit to bring about all that's in alignment with my vision and intentions. Build my endurance so I can have spiritual pace to run in the race of life.

Be the catalyst for change.☺

DAY 328: Prayers of Clarity

Today: various prayers of clarity.

O Lord, give clarity to all situations. Help me to see only things that align with Your will and away from things that don't. Give me peace in order to stay aligned with Your will.

Help me be a better communicator. Help me not to only express my emotions but my related actions. Allow me to express myself fully and accurately

Help me to strive for deeper connections. Please help me to stay away from living a shallow existence without any emotional connection. Allow me to have connections that push me to be a better person under your will.

Help me to work on spending time with you Lord. You're the most important in my life and can provide solutions to all of my problems. Help me with to clearness of mind, body and spirit.

Allow me to become transparent. Allow me to express myself and allow other to express themselves as well. Help me to understand my expression is vital to my spiritual development.

Thank you Lord for providing me constant feedback. Help me to be open to feedback as a necessary part of my spiritual growth. Allow this feedback to strengthen my relationship with You. Allow me to be comfortable being enveloped in your will.

Thank you Lord for this day. Help me to strive to become a better person and forgive me for all of my mistakes both known and unknown. Allow me to build trust in our relationship with you.

Be the catalyst for change.☺

DAY 329: An Affirmation of Love

Today: affirmation about love.

I'm tired of being alone. Help me to release all worry, arrogance, judgmental spirit and any other negative emotion keeping me from finding and keeping love.

Allow my heart to heal from all negative past experiences and to learn from them. Once my heart as healed, open my heart to the positive love in my world.

Remove all game changers, haters and suckers who only take, or diminish love but not encourage it. Allow me to think systematically about retaining love in my life instead with passion.

Help me to endure these lonely nights alone. Help not to allow my present day-to-day life to lead to long-term distance that ultimately leads to heartbreak. Allow me to be strong enough to run away from drama but not toward it.

Send me a positive love role model to look up to. Show me positive healthy and loving relationship to reach toward. Help me not become broken through past relationship and critical.

I believe in true love. I believe true love is out here is this world for me. All I have to do is be patient and believe.

True Love will then come to me.

Be the catalyst for change.☺

DAY 330: Encouragement

Today: affirmations of encouragement.

It seems nothing is going right. I take two steps forward and nine steps back.

Please provide me with encouragement in this race called life. Help me to see that all in my life isn't bad. Allow me to savor the good in my life even if it's my health.

Allow me to only see the positive and forget the negative. I will continue to look forward and stop looking back and trying to figure out where I went wrong in my life.

I understand all mishap and obstacles in my life was placed there by you Lord to strengthen me.

Help me to see my life will change as long as I continue to believe. Help me when I feel pessimistic, and frustrated.

Allow me to stay inspired on a day-to-day basis so I can walk into my destiny. Allow my inspiration to give a boost to my confidence.

Send me the support I need on my Christian walk. I realize now I can't do this alone. When I stumble, help me to get up and continue on the righteous path.

Help me stand in the race called life, even when I don't understand the storms of life.

Allow me to stay focused on you and your will. Allow me to stay encouraged and lifted in prayer.

Be the catalyst for change.☺

DAY 331: Removing Disappointment

Today: affirmations of removing disappointment.

I have been let down in life and in love. I don't believe I will ever be good enough to be happy.

I worry my expectations in life and love are too high and no one will ever meet them.

Help me to remove all doubt and regret from my mind. I understand disappointment it a part of life. Help me learn how to cope.

I will push through the pain and discomfort I feel today in order to reach my destiny tomorrow.

I will reach all of my hopes and dreams. Past disappointment doesn't determine my future.

I will only surround myself with upbeat and positive people. I will not became disenchanted with those who only want to bring me down.

When it feels like it's becoming too much, I will go to You in prayer. I will focus on working hard on my goals instead of worry about others who don't care about me.

I will remove those people from my life who don't have my best interest at heart without hesitation.

I'm more conqueror, I'm fighter. I might stumble under the burdens of life but I won't fall.

I will continue to keep harder, keep striving even if I have to go at it all alone.

Be the catalyst for change.☺

MONTH 12

DAY 332: Peace

Today: affirmations of peace

There is so much chaos going on in my life become of white noise and it's difficult to make sound decision.

However, I will go to you in prayer for peace. I will not allow the Devil to get into my mind and attempt to distract me from what is important.

I will spent time coming up with a game plan for my life instead of allowing life to pass me by.

If I don't have anything positive or helpful to say, I will go silent. Silence is better than negativity.

I won't allow others looking for a quick fix to shape my mind and ability to dream.

I understand my ability to dream is my ticket to my destiny and peace. A dream isn't anything more than ordained vision God has given me. Allow it to take shape in my life.

Allow me to seek tranquil serenity in my life instead of chaos. While chaos may be exciting at times but caused unnecessary anxiety.

I will not bring drama to others and not allow others to bring it to me. I will end disagreements and not become embroiled into arguments.

I will make an attempt to remove all silliness from life to ensure harmony and peace persists in my life.

Be the catalyst for change.☺

DAY 333: Endurance

Today: affirmations of endurance

I'm struggling with the weight of the world on my shoulders. It seems everyone is having the time of their lives and I'm at the bottom of the well trying to get out.

Lord, help me to increase my endurance through the holy spirit. I will be able to bear long hardship without complaint or struggle.

I will focus on just getting myself ready for the breakthrough: mind, body and spirit.

I will tolerate struggles while continuing my day-to-day life. I will be persistence over this testing period and not allow myself to become weary in the process.

I will develop a pace of living. I will work to ensure I have staying power and stamina to get through this journey called life.

I understand this process is taking place to refine me and to prepare me for my breakthrough. While it may not be pleasant, it's necessary for where you're taking me.

The bigger the test, the bigger the blessing.

Help me to stay focused on you on my bad days. Allow me to keep my eyes on the skies in waiting for you to shower me with blessings.

Be the catalyst for change.☺

DAY 334: Temptations

Today: affirmations of temptations.

I will resist temptation that creep into my life. I know the temptations are based on my fear buried deep inside.

Help me to be strong enough to withstand the temptation that enters my life. I know I must be focused on other things in my life to get past the temptations being thrown at me.

Help me not give in to my own selfish desires and mask them as a need. Allow this craving to b e removed from my mind, body and spirit.

I know temptations are used to wreak havoc on my life. I know they are things I want to do but something holds me back.

Help me to figure out my triggers in life so I stop yearning for these temptations.

Don't allow my thirst for action and to make my dreams come true to cross over into an obsession and make me lose my sense of perspective.

Help me not allow the pressure of life's struggle to get to me or allow it to influence me into making bad decisions.

I know you're with me until the end of time. I must be patient and endure.

Be the catalyst for change.☺

DAY 335: Affirmations Against Becoming Vengeful

Today: affirmations against becoming vengeful.

I know I'm angry, hurt and disappointed. Things that have been done to me I would have never done to others. Help me to not become vengeful.

You know my every thought and you know I'm struggling in not striking back at those who've hurt me.

Help me to forgive so I can move on with my life. Please remove the desire for revenge in mind, body and spirit.

Don't allow the bitterness that's building my heart to result in some sort of action.

I'm not the one to hand out punishment, that's Your job. Help me not to attempt to conduct your duties.

Getting even only makes you feel good for a second but forgiveness can be felt for a lifetime.

Don't allow me to become a vindictive and spiteful spirit delighting in the discomfort of others.

Being bitter and nasty becomes a bad reflection of me and not of those who hurt me.

Don't allow these situations to shape my personality and actions for years to come. Thaw my heart so I can let go of the disappointment and frustration that has become revenge.

Be the catalyst for change.☺

DAY 336: Faith

Today: affirmations of faith.

I must keep the faith during the storms of life. I will trust You that You protect me from all danger and You will allow me to step into my destiny.

I'm in total devotion to you. You've provided for all of my wants and needs before and will continue to do so.

I will stay loyal to You and Your word. I will not allow despair to damage my faith and erode my relationship with You

I will believe in You and Your abilities without proof or a sign. I will believe because of who you are and nothing else.

I will live my life based upon confidence, assurance and devotion to You.

I will share my admiration for You with everyone to encourage lost souls.

I will work on making my dreams come true based upon the vision You gave to me. I will continue to work despite the circumstances around me. I will expect a breakthrough and will continue to believe until the end of time.

You will always have the last word in my life.

I will trust no one more than God. He is my sister, brother, wife, aunt, uncle, friend and husband. He's all things to me.

Be the catalyst for change.☺

DAY 337: Forgiveness

Today: affirmations of forgiveness.

Help me to become more forgiving. I know I'm not perfect. Allow me to let go of disappointments so I can have a better relationship with you.

Allow me to develop a tendency to let things go. Allow me also not to hold a grudge.

When I don't forgive, it doesn't hurt the other party; it hurts me, because I become unable to move on with my life.

I'm thankful for all the blessings you have given me even when I didn't deserve it. Help me to mirror you, Lord and provide forgiveness in the same way You would.

You give us mercy on the many mistakes we make each day. Help me apply that same mercy you bestow on us.

Allow me to see the world with a compassionate heart. Allow me to become kind to others even when they have hurt me. As I become more powerful, allow me to let go of small misgivings of others. Allow me to pray for them instead of seeking revenge.

When I seek revenge, all it does is allow the malice to build in my heart, which doesn't solve anything.

Give me a clean heart so I can let go of all grudges and begin life again with a fresh perspective.

Be the catalyst for change.☺

DAY 338: Courage

Today: affirmations of courage.

I'm a warrior; I'm a soldier in this journey called life. I've faced adversity and obstacles in my life. It's allowed me to become brave but help me to become courageous.

I believe I can do all things through God. He will protect and keep me.

I will have the ability to face danger or uncertainty without fear or apprehension that could ultimately lead to a different course of action.

I will be bold in the face of overwhelming circumstances. I will allow myself to be a testimony to others so they can see God truly does answer prayers.

I will not run from the storms in my life but rather face them. I will continue my spiritual life even when I'm broken and discouraged.

I will increase my endurance so I will not buckle under the weight of the world.

I will take risks in my life in order to achieve my goals. I recognize in order to step into my destiny, I must be willing to take risks and be courageous.

I will take God at His word. I will question Him but believe He knows what is best.

I thank you for providing me an example of courageous. I will step forward and be a beacon of life to those in darkness. I will show Your ways by my actions and not by judgment.

Be the catalyst for change.☺

DAY 339: Discipline

Today: affirmations of discipline.

I will exhibit calm controlled behavior. I will not allow myself to lose my focus on what's important to me.

Allow my discipline to be fuel in my spiritual tank to future my ambition. I will set goals for myself and then work to achieve them. I will not allow resentment, frustration and irritation to keep me from destiny.

Help me to see the value of hard work and persevering spirit. Allow me to hold on until my breakthrough occurs.

Push me further than I have ever gone before. Help me to stay focused in this race called life and not allow myself to become discouraged.

Allow me to continue despite the obstacles and problems in my life. Each day, make me stronger and more driven than the last.

I will restraint my desires and wants that don't align with Your Will. I will make sure I'm obedient to Your will.

Please allow me to have mental self-control so I can work on living a Christian life. Please give me the strength to endure all chaos in my life. The chaos in my life builds my character and ensures I will stay with You on the chosen path.

Be the catalyst for change.☺

DAY 340: Determination

Today: affirmations of determination.

I'm focused and driven. I'm aggressive in pursuing my goals.

I will have firmness of purpose and strength of mind. I have grit in me to survive regardless of my circumstances. I can make it; I can strive for the stars because God is on my side. I will figure out a way to make my dreams happen.

Anoint me with your touch and knowledge. Give me favor so I can weather the storms of life. Help me to believe despite the chaos around me.

Help me to resolve my issues. Help me to let go and allow you to make a way.

Remove all doubt from my mind. Give me confidence in myself and ability. Allow me to see myself the way you see me.

Allow me to have the confidence in myself to achieve my goals. With my determination, I can achieve the impossible.

As long as there's breath in my lungs, I would continue to believe and attempt to achieve my goals.

Open my hidden cove of determination deep within my soul. Allow me to use this hidden reservoir of strength so I can make it.

Be the catalyst for change.☺

DAY 341: Goals

Today: affirmations of goals.

I have been grindin' day and night for my goals. I have pushed myself further than I have ever before. Goals are the roadmap to my future; with them, my future never looked so bright.

While I don't understand this testing period in my life, I believe you have my best interests at heart.

Help me to continue to aim for what I want to achieve. I know my goals will be realized but I must remain patient and focused.

Allow my patience to renew my strength so I will have stamina to receive the blessing I have been waiting on.

Make me distinct with my professionalism, focus and driven. While everyone may not like me, they will respect me. Allow me to become powerful so I can know how and be a self-starter in order to achieve my goals.

Help me to move forward and not backward. Allow me to see my dreams come true. Allow my goals to inspire and not make my day-to-day living quite so difficult.

Allow me to stretch myself to become the best I can be. Through this stretching, allow me to advance in this world.

Be the catalyst for change.☺

DAY 342: Happiness

Today: affirmations of happiness.

I want happiness to enter my life. I'm tired of being unhappy. I understand happiness is a state of mind and not a place of status.

My life will get better. I'm willing to create a mental space for myself to believe I can do anything with Your help.

I want to be content in my life regardless of the circumstances around me. Thank you for all you have given me thus far. I know you will continue to bless me in the future.

I'm willing to help create my own happiness. I'm inclined to use my spiritual gifts to ensure my own happiness and help to facilitate others' happiness as well.

I will not let haters hold me because they are jealous. They see my destiny and want to keep me from it. Allow me to not become distracted by these issues. Allow me to stay focused on my destiny and to know God will handle everything that's too big for me.

Help me to hold on so God can shower me with raindrops of blessings. Allow me to be able to handle the amazing blessings coming my way.

Be the catalyst for change.☺

DAY 343: Worship

Today: affirmations of worship

Thank you for this day. I will worship you all the days of my life. I'm so thankful for you keeping me from danger that I didn't know was behind every corner.

You kept me when I'm at my best. You also kept me when I was at my worst. You were with me when I didn't know myself. You stayed with me with I was arrogance and full of myself.

You touched me when you knew I needed it. You walked with me when everyone left.

When I cried out for mercy, You gave me mercy and peace. When life broke me, You strengthened me.

I respect You for all You have done for me and will continue to do. My relationship with You is because I have realized I'm nothing without You.

I can't stay focused without You and I need You in my life. I love you Lord.

I know there is such tremendous power in your name and I understand when I call on your name things will start to happen.

Help me see the power in worship and praise so I will have the strength to stay on this journey called life.

Be the catalyst for change.☺

DAY 344: Weariness

Today: affirmations of weariness.

Lord, I'm so tired. I keep trying to do everything myself. I can't and I'm exhausted. Every option I had and every backup plan has failed.

I don't know what to do or who to turn to. Give me comfort in my time of need. I'm standing in the need of prayer.

I'm so alone and can't see my way out of this situation. I need a miracle.

You've helped me live through things I didn't think I could. You've carried me when I ran out of strength, patience, and endurance.

Please don't allow fatigue to set in. Help me to stay in this race called life. Allow me to have peace in my spirit so I retain my energy to continue to fight to make my destiny come true.

Allow me not to become disillusioned by the obstacles and testing in my life. Allow me to have enough stamina to receive my blessing and become lost in the test.

I'm strong, I'm determined, I'm a warrior. I can make it.

Give me creative energy so I may be able and open to hearing from You.

I may be down but not out. I can push myself and let go of uneasiness to fight my dreams.

Be the catalyst for change.☺

DAY 345: Salvation

Today: affirmations of salvation.

Thank you Lord from delivering me from sin. I was blind and I refused to see. Now I see you have been with me the whole time.

You saved me from myself and my selfish desires. You rescued me from the drudge of the world. I will overcome; I will become stronger in my faith.

Allow me to grow in my faith so I'm not shaken by every obstacle coming my way.

Help me to believe, if I continue to work hard, even in the face of adversity, it will pay off.

Life will get better. The obstacles will lessen and occur less often. I will be able to stay focused on my goals despite the chaos.

Life will not always be difficult but I must endure the hard times in order to get to the next level.

I'm strong, I can endure. I can make it through because I believe.

Be the catalyst for change.☺

DAY 346: Discernment

Today: affirmations of discernment.

People are not always what they seem. There are some who seem good when they're not and vice versa.

Help me have the ability to make good judgments. Allow me to discriminate about what I expose myself to.

Speak to me and alert me when something or someone isn't good for me. Allow me to trust You that You're here to protect me.

I haven't always been able to trust You. Please forgive me for that.

Allow me discern what is good for me. I know that you want what is best for me.

Give me a discerning spirit so my life is guided by God and not my own thoughts and desires.

I know I can't always anticipate the true nature of others but You can help keep me from any harm or danger.

Help me see my spiritual gifts and to know how to use them to help others and my community.

Allow me to be able to sense Your urging in my spirit, so I may be able to walk into my destiny.

Be the catalyst for change.☺

DAY 347: Repentance

Today: affirmations of repentance.

Please forgive me for my sins. Thank you for all of the blessings you have bestowed on me. Help to change my ways that are not positive for me. Keep urging me in my spirit to make the necessary changes.

While I've been wrong in the past, there isn't anything God can't handle. Help me to stay on the path of the righteous.

Help me to forgive myself for all of the ugly, hateful, mean things I have done. Let the shame of my less than perfect actions wash off for me.

Allow me to also not become judgmental of others who make the same mistakes I did.

Let me let go of all regrets in my life and anew. I can't change the past but I can learn from mistakes; so I can have a brighter and more secure future.

I will not allow my frustration over life's struggle to cause me to backslide into ugly behaviors.

You didn't say life would be easy but You promised You will forgive me even when I can't forgive myself.

I know You have made me stronger, so I may be able to be a testimony for others about the imperfect nature of Christians.

None of us are perfect but what makes us special is we stay in this race called life with faltering.

Be the catalyst for change.☺

DAY 348: Prophecy

Today: affirmations of Prophecy.

God, you know what is best for me. Thank you for all You have done for me.

Give me the gift of prophecy over my life. Help me to be able to have divine prediction. Allow me to be able to see what is coming in my life so I may prepare.

Allow me to have insight into various areas of my life needing improvement. Thank you for protecting me against all danger and snares to occur in my life.

I know I'm not always perfect but yet you still love me. You protect me when I don't deserve it and allow me not to become affected by life's troubles. I may feel the heat from life's obstacle but I don't feel the true burn.

Bless me with divine knowledge so I can have a good life. Combine this with a discerning spirit and I will know there isn't anything I won't be able to handle.

I'm strong; I can climb mountains of defeat and despair only because of the strength you have given me.

Give me the sheer will power to leap bounds and overthrown any kind of pressure coming my way.

Be the catalyst for change.☺

DAY 349: Prayer

Today: affirmations of prayer.

Thank You for talking to me. I thank You for giving me a prayer life even though I don't talk to You as much as I should.

Increase my communication with You. Help me to pray even when I get no answers or it seems You're not listening. I know You're there, yet it feels like you're not. I know You will never leave me or forsake me.

Help me become more intimate with You. Allow me to tell how I feel instead of using prayer as time to ask for blessing. You're not a check card or ATM of the Bank of God's blessings. I must work harder to have a relationship with You that's open and transparent.

Allow my prayers to wash over my spirit like mountain dew. Help my prayer change me inside and let it reflect on the outside.

My prayers will help to change how I deal with conflict in my life. My prayer will make me a stronger person who can whether the storms of life.

My prayer will help me to triumph over Evil and deal with defeat when it does occur.

My prayers will help to overcome all obstacles in my life and every step in my destiny. My prayer will allow me to have higher expectations of God and His works.

My prayer increases my faith in myself and belief that all things are possible.

Be the catalyst for change.☺

DAY 350: Miracles

Today: affirmations of miracles.

I believe in miracles. I believe God is in the blessing business and there isn't anything in life God can't handle.

Miracles are an act that's contrary to all laws of nature and is believed to be an act of God.

Thank you for all the miracles that occurred in my life thus far. I feel I'm in line for a miracle right now.

I feel myself become stronger as I near the cliff of doubt. Help me to have strength to jump off and land into the sea of belief.

God's actions go beyond intelligence, nature, and probability. The more impossible and unattainable the goal, the easier it will be for God to make it happen.

God will allow the miracle I need to occur. I must have the belief and faith to wait on my breakthrough.

Help me to hold on while I'm waiting. Keep me grounded in the word while I wait. The wait's when Evil steps in and allow me to become disorientated.

I'm sick of being stuck going nowhere; I'm ready for the radical change a miracle can bring.

Help my unbelief when I become discouraged in this race called life. Be the catalyst for change.☺

DAY 351: Healing

Today: affirmations of healing.

Thank you for all of my blessings you have bestowed on me.

Please heal me mind, body and spirit. Repair my soul from all the wear and tear in this race called life.

Help me recover spiritually or emotionally for all of the testing in my life.

You will heal my body. Please keep all diseases and affiliates from growing in my body.

You will heal my mind. Please keep all of my negative thoughts and perceptions out of my mind. Help me to weather the storms of life without causing damage to my psyche.

You will heal my spirit. Please keep my spirit from becoming broken and disillusioned and losing hope in everything. Help me hold on so I can reach my breakthrough

You will heal me from all that may hurt me. You will cure me from what ails me. You will provide restoration to my life so I can get back on track.

You specialize in mending souls and you will repair mine. Help me to hold on while I wait for you heal to me.

While it may be difficult to hold on and wait on my healing, it's worth the wait.

Be the catalyst for change.☺

DAY 352: Hope

Today: affirmations of hope.

Give me hope for the future.

Help me to get better days. Today may be rough but all days won't be like this. Allow me to focus on the good days so I can weather the storm of the bad days.

I want love in my life. Help me bring love in my life by having positive thinking.

I want more wealth in my life. Help to bring my lucrative opportunity into my professional life by allowing myself to believe it will occur.

Help me become more confident in my beliefs that something is coming. It will be good and not bad. Allow me not to believe just because I have a testing period recently doesn't mean my whole life is a test with no positive effects.

Increase my likelihood of success by standing positively and removing negativity from mind, body and spirit.

The source of success is my belief in myself and my abilities.

Help me to trust you will provide all blessings to me right on time. I will have expectations that my blessing are coming and that you provide everything I need and more in my life.

Allow my anticipation to rise each day as my faith and belief increase.

Be the catalyst for change.☺

DAY 353: Grace

Today: affirmations of grace.

Thank you for all of the blessing you have given me so far. Lord give me grace. Allow me to transform my life and become free from sin. Allow me to become favored by you. Shower me with blessings. Be kind to me. Please provide me with grace so I may be able to share it with others.

Bless me and enlarge my territory. Allow all of my dreams to come through. Help me to stay focus in this race called life and living a Christian life.

When I fail, please forgive me. Help me to pick myself up and get back on track. Thank for giving me grace even when I don't deserve it. You allow me to be blessed on Your words and not on my actions. I thank You for that. I thank You for grace because it's based upon me just existing and not related to any actions at all.

Thank you for giving me power through grace. With grace, I can achieve all things and there isn't anything I can't handle.

All I need to do is trust and believe my breakthrough is coming.

Be the catalyst for change.☺

DAY 354: Forgiveness

Today: affirmations of forgiveness.

Thank you for forgiving my sins. I'm not perfect but I'm striving to be better than what I used to be. I want to work on bestowing Your ability to forgive my family and friends.

When I forgive, it allows me to be closer to you. All I need to do to be forgiven is believe. Allow your will and character to show in my actions.

I will stop the tendency not to forgive small offensives.

I will stop not forgiving myself for all wrongdoings.

I will stop allowing myself not to admit when I'm hurting.

I will stop repressing my emotions and will begin to let them out.

I will not keep myself from having mercy on those who've wronged me.

I will stop playing the victim and admit to myself the part I play in the problems in my life.

I have love in my heart, so I will forgive. The biggest example of love is to forgive. When I forgive, I will receive unspeakable peace and love in return.

Help me to forgive my enemies because You will allow me to move on with my life. Without forgiveness, I won't be able to move on and will stay resentful and bitter.

Be the catalyst for change.☺

DAY 355: Blessings

Today: affirmations of blessings.

I'm strong; I can withstand the storms of life in order to receive my blessings.

I'm worthy of blessing from you. You know my heart's desire and I believe that you can provide to me.

I believe that you will bless me. I believe that my breakthrough is coming. I believe that all the heartache and pain I'm enduring has a purpose.

I must continue to fight the battle to survive on the dealing basis. Yes, I will get weary but I will not give up the fight.

I will not allow negative forces to get into my mind and allow me give up before I even reach my destination.

Help me whether the storms of life while attempting to reach my destiny.

Help to stop seeking the approval of the world and only seek your will.

While I'm waiting of my blessing from you, help me to experience the power of being a blessing to someone else.

There is no great power than to help someone else on the spiritual journey. Help me to look beyond myself and see that others are hurting as well.

Be the catalyst for change.☺

DAY 356: Obedience

Today: affirmations of obedience.

Help me to see that being obedience to your word is essential in order live out my destiny.

I will submit to your authority to my life.

I know that you're the only one that knows how my story will end. I will trust you and know that you have my best interest at heart. I know that you love me and will help during this race called life.

I will respect your wisdom and ability to see my success that I'm now only dreaming about.

I will be obedient to your will and aligned myself your rules for daily living.

I will find a church home. I will attend church regularly.

I will ignite my prayer life. I will walk by faith and not be sight.

I will not allow myself to become emotionally invested in events I can't control. I will give up control and allow you to guide my life.

Be the catalyst for change.☺

DAY 357: Evolution

Today: affirmations of evolution.

Thank you lord for allowing me to evolve. I'm transforming and growing as a part of the Body of Christ.

I want to better person, to become the person I'm destined to be. Help me to be patient with myself as I grow.

I'm not where I want to be but thank you that I'm not what I used to be.

I understand that my transformation is developmental process that will take time and is gradual. I know that I want to process to be gradual so I will be able to maintain the necessary changes.

As I progress and begin to walk into my destiny. Allow me my tree of life to bear fruit from all my personal hard work.

I will push myself to growth spiritually. I will make sure I keep an active and consistent prayer life.

I will allow myself to focus on the future instead of being despondent in the past. I now know that I can't change the past but I understand the past help me to the person that I'm today.

You make no mistakes. While I may not understand the purpose of the pain and suffering in my lives if I just rely on my faith, You will reveal everything in due time.

Help me to remain focused on you until my breakthrough comes.

Be the catalyst for change.☺

DAY 358: Abandonment

Today: affirmations of abandonment.

I will leave my old unsaved life behind. I'm not a new creature in Christ.

I will leave those people behind in my life who choose not to respect to new person that I have become. I will not waste time trying to convinced them of my transformation. I will allow time to speak for me.

I will surrender control of my life to you. You've my best interests at heart.

I will not halt my spiritual transformation in progress just because it has become too difficult or dangerous.

I will give in to emotion of thankfulness to you for keeping me when I was spiritually lost. You were there for when I had complete lack of self-restraint in the things of this world.

Thank you for giving me the strength to discard all the people and past behavior that is not good for me. Help me become protective over my mind, body and soul.

I will live leave behind all hating, jealousy, resentfulness, gossip and etc. I will let go my ugly behaviors and try to live my Christian life.

Be the catalyst for change.☺

DAY 359: Acceptance

Today: affirmations of acceptance.

Thank you accepting me just as I am, flaws and all.

I have a willingness in my spirit to believe that all things are possible for me.

Thank you for allowing me to come to terms with all failures and obstacles in my life.

I realize now that even in the bad times you were with me, guiding and keeping out of more trouble. I thank you for being there for me even when I didn't know it.

There were times where I was so confused that I didn't know myself. However, yet you still kept me.

You gave me recognition by allowing my evolve and change step by step as I spiritually matured.

I will continue to seek your approval for the rest of my life. I will look to you when I need help.

I will believe that I can step into my destiny if I just believe that all things are possible. I will stop allow myself to become discouraged after the small setbacks. I will continue to man up.

If I want to get the next level, they I must become stronger and more resilient in the process.

Be the catalyst for change.☺

DAY 360: Abstinence

Today: affirmations of abstinence

Thank you for all you have done for me.

I will abstain from all things that take me away from God and does not promote healthy living.

I will show restraint from indulging in excessive alcohol, drug use and sexual promiscuity.

My body is my temple and I will respect my body.

I know that you have big plans for my life and I must train my mind, body and spirit to be aligned in order to get the next level.

I will not allow myself to get out of control and miss my opportunity with destiny.

Help me to self-discipline to one of the keys to success. If I can't show you that I can regulate my own behavior then why should you trust me additional responsibilities?

Help me to get it together and become a legend in my own right.

I know that I will reach my destiny and I will continue to enjoyed and even some of its excesses but in moderation.

Nothing will control me and I will be able to regulate my own behavior so I'm always aligned with God's will.

Be the catalyst for change.☺

DAY 361: Awakening

Today: affirmations of awakening

I'm now spiritually awake. I see the world for what it's, a place should not be in and but not of.

I'm beginning to grow in my faith. Allow this to continue and become stronger,

I have a renewed attention to my faith and my spiritual walk. I realize that I'm role model to the secular world. They view me based upon my actions and words. Help me to grow as a person so I will not crack under the tremendous of pressure.

I thank you for the sudden realization of what are blessing is in the be a part of your kingdom.

I now know that you have loved me even before I loved you. You've walked with me when I thought I was utterly alone.

You allow me to stay sane when the chaos and pressure was so serious that I thought I would lose my mind. However, then you gave me peace.

You allow me to walk through the valley of death and through fire and brimstone but yet be unharmed. I feel the heat of experience but never burned.

You've truly shown me what love truly is and I thank you for that. You've awakened my very being and soul.

Be the catalyst for change.☺

DAY 362: Belief

Today: affirmations of belief.

Thank you for coming into heart and changing it. I'm now a believer.

I'm certain that I do all things with you by my side.

I have confidence that my life will be amazing but I chose to walk with you.

I believe that you change lives in a instant and even in pits of a struggle there is purpose in it. You don't allow us to be hurt for no reason.

You seek to be a protector over our soul.

I will believe when I'm happy, when I angry, depressed and frustrated. I know that you have best interests at heart despite it all.

I will unbreakable faith in face of adversity.

I will not allow myself to stop being when life isn't going my way. I will stay in the race and fight the good fight.

I will increase my spiritual stamina so I may endure these tests of faith. I know that after the tests of faith you will pour down blessings that I have been waiting a lifetime for.

Be the catalyst for change.☺

DAY 363: Betrayal

Today: affirmations relief of betrayal.

Thank you for allowing me to see another day.

Thank you for showing me who my real friends and family are. Thank you for allowing me to see who I can count on and who I can't.

Help me not become angry with those who don't have stamina to walk with me on my spiritual journey.

Allow me to thank them that they opted out before they could do real damage.

I will surrender to you when I'm overwhelmed by feeling hatred and red-hot rage. Kept me from doing or saying something that I will regret.

I will keep myself from showing my vengeful side and allow you to handle them.

Let the haters and naysayers that you're coming for them.

Allow me not be disloyal to you because of a rocked by betrayal from others.

You're the only one to trust and I will keep myself focused on you when things in life happen I don't understand.

Be the catalyst for change.☺

DAY 364: Boundaries

Today: affirmations of boundaries.

Help me to implement boundaries in my life.

I will not allow anyone infringe on my personal space.

I will not allow anyone to dump their problems on me and allow me to become overwhelmed with them

I will provide limits to my interactions with those who I'm unsure whether they have best interests.

I will remove those from my life that I'm uncertain whether they have my best interest at heart.

I will not allow anyone to steal my joy of life.

I will impose limitations on myself to ensure that I'm focused and driven to reach my destiny.

Allow me not be shaken easily, or thrown off course. I'm warrior, a conquer and nothing will stand in my way to reaching my destiny.

Be the catalyst for change.☺

DAY 365: Breakthroughs

Today: affirmations of breakthroughs.

Thank you for allowing having breakthroughs in my life.

You brought me my blessing just in time. The time that I thought all was lost and I was about to give up.

I thought that I couldn't take anymore heartbreak, and stress. I knew that no help was coming and all was lost. In that instant, my breakthrough came just in time.

You removed all barriers to my progress. You may success stream into my life. You will allow me to receive public recognition for all my hard work.

You will allow my innovation to start of revolution of believers to hold on and stay on the path of righteousness.

I will not allow my life struggles to destroy. I will walk against the rain and become stronger and wiser.

I will come through this experience armed with tremendous knowledge that I didn't know I even needed.

I will push myself not to become so emotional invested in those who don't care about me.

I will train myself to weather the storms of life and learn how to patiently wait on you

Be the catalyst for change.☺

Index

DAY 1: Unstoppable, 11

DAY 2: Having Direction, 13

DAY 3: Blessings in the Midst of Disappointments, 14

DAY 4: Taking care of yourself, 16

DAY 5: Peace, 18

DAY 6: Endurance, 19

DAY 7: Sharing Feelings, 20

DAY 8: Motivation, 21

DAY 9: Answering the Call, 22

DAY 10: Motivators, 24

DAY 11: Unique Blessings, 26

DAY 12: Pushing Through, 27

DAY 13: The End is near, 29

DAY 14: Temptation, 30

DAY 15: Too Busy, 32

DAY 16: Letting go, 33

DAY 17: Passed Over for a Blessing, 35

DAY 18: Fight for Your Success, 37

DAY 19: Waiting for a Sign From God, 39

DAY 20: You're Covered, 40

DAY 21: Giving it all to God, 41

DAY 22: Navigating the waters, 43

DAY 23: Refusing to Settle, 44

DAY 24: Constructive Criticism, 46

DAY 25: New Beginnings, 47

DAY 26: Establishing a Covenant with God, 48

DAY 27: Staying Focused and Being Positive, 50

DAY 28: Why Believe, 51

DAY 29: Having a Revelation, 52

DAY 30: Encouraging Yourself, 53

DAY 31: Waiting on God, 54

DAY 32: Keep the Faith, 59

DAY 33: Panic, 60

DAY 34: Drive and an Ambitious Spirit, 61

DAY 35: Going to Battle, 63

DAY 36: Prayers of Progress, 65

DAY 37: The Beyond the Scenes Story, 66

DAY 38: Having Your Guard Up, 67

DAY 39: It's all Just an Illusion, 68

DAY 40: God's Promise, 69

DAY 41: Looking Around, 71

DAY 42: Don't let Anyone Steal Your Joy, 72

DAY 43: How to Pray, 73

DAY 44: Mercy, 75

DAY 45: Change, 77

DAY 46: Confirmation, 79

DAY 47: Judgment, 80

DAY 48: In our own Little World, 81

DAY 49: Making it Through Difficult Times, 82

DAY 50: Maintaining Hope, 84

DAY 51: Learning to Love, 85

DAY 52: Fighting for Happiness, 86

DAY 53: Love and Being Single, 87

DAY 54: Dream Killers, 88

DAY 55: Finding the Perfect Mate, 89

DAY 56: Toxic Friends and Stress, 91

DAY 57: Relying on God, 93

DAY 58: Repeating our Parents' Mistakes in Relationships, 94

DAY 59: Becoming a Visionary, 96

DAY 60: Knowing where you stand, 97

DAY 61: Maintenance, 98

DAY 62: Protection, 101

DAY 63: How to Handle the Journey, 102

DAY 64: Soul Connection with God, 104

DAY 65: Getting the Basics, 106

DAY 66: How to Deal With Silence From God, 107

DAY 67: Call Me When You're Ready, 108

DAY 68: Knowing it All, 110

DAY 69: Getting Salvation, 111

DAY 70: How to Forgive, 113

DAY 71: Inspiration, 115

DAY 72: Learn to Discern, 116

DAY 73: Don't Worry, 118

DAY 74: The Last One Standing, 119

DAY 75: Confusion, 120

DAY 76: Enabling, 121

DAY 77: Creating Your Destiny, 122

DAY 78: Feeling Whole, 123

DAY 79: Getting Caught Up, 124

DAY 80: Courageous, 125

DAY 81: Quiet, 126

DAY 82: Deciding to Wait, 127

DAY 83: Transformation, 128

DAY 84: Letting go of Pride, 129

DAY 85: The Importance of Worship, 130

DAY 86: Obedience, 131

DAY 87: How to Listen to God, 132

DAY 88: Powerful, 133

DAY 89: Focused, 134

DAY 90: God's Will, 135

DAY 91: Light Versus Darkness, 136

DAY 92: Praying for Others, 139

DAY 93: Joy, 140

DAY 94: Grindin', 142

DAY 95: Favor, 143

DAY 96: Becoming Resilient, 144

DAY 97: Instructions, 145

DAY 98: Real Love, 146

DAY 99: Relaxation, 147

DAY 100: Showing God to Others, 148
DAY 101: Getting Lost in the Moment, 149
DAY 102: When God is Silent, 150
DAY 103: Taking the Joy out of Everything, 152
DAY 104: Too Good to be True, 153
DAY 105: The Unexpected, 155
DAY 106: Grief, 157
DAY 107: Curiosity, 159
DAY 108: Going Home Again, 160
DAY 109: Shock, 161
DAY 110: Expectation, 163
DAY 111: Annoyed, 164
DAY 112: Confidence, 165
DAY 113: Choosing, 167
DAY 114: Being Knocked Down, 168
DAY 115: Indulging Yourself, 170
DAY 116: Isolation, 171
DAY 117: Flipping Out, 172
DAY 118: Distancing Yourself, 173
DAY 119: Living a Different World, 174
DAY 120: Counting to Ten, 175
DAY 121: Fantasy, 176
DAY 122: Spiritual Growth, 179
DAY 123: Progress, 180
DAY 124: Discouraged, 182
DAY 125: The Wrong Idea, 183
DAY 126: It's Your Time, 184
DAY 127: Shock, 185
DAY 128: Life Changing Events, 186
DAY 129: Needing a Do Over, 187
DAY 130: Living in the Moment, 189
DAY 131: Going for It, 190
DAY 132: Lack of Focus, 192
DAY 133: Hustler, 193
DAY 134: Wasting Time, 194

DAY 135: Addiction, 195
DAY 136: Jumping Into the Deep, 197
DAY 137: Being Free, 199
DAY 138: In Control, 200
DAY 139: Survival, 201
DAY 140: Knowing What is Best, 202
DAY 141: Expect the Unexpected, 203
DAY 142: Mean, 205
DAY 143: Being Prepared, 206
DAY 144: Paying the Price, 207
DAY 145: Overwhelmed, 208
DAY 146: Feeling the Aftershocks, 209
DAY 147: Staying Connected, 210
DAY 148: Getting the Job Done, 211
DAY 149: Being Yourself, 212
DAY 150: A Taste of Home, 213
DAY 151: You Never Know, 214
DAY 152: A Stress Reliever, 217
DAY 153: Loyalty, 218
DAY 154: The Future, 219
DAY 155: The Life of a Believer, 220
DAY 156: Revenge, 221
DAY 157: Being Creative, 222
DAY 158: Glory, 223
DAY 159: Deceit, 224
DAY 160: Feeling Burdened, 225
DAY 161: Being Trapped in Captivity, 226
DAY 162: Comfort, 227
DAY 163: Making a Commitment, 228
DAY 164: Confirmation, 229
DAY 165: A Contender, 230
DAY 166: Coveting, 231
DAY 167: Digging Deep, 232
DAY 168: Distractions, 233
DAY 169: Distressed, 234

DAY 170: It's Done, 235
DAY 171: When in Doubt, 236
DAY 172: Early, 237
DAY 173: Empty, 238
DAY 174: Excuses, 239
DAY 175: Express Yourself, 240
DAY 176: Don't Faint, 241
DAY 177: Farewell, 242
DAY 178: Fear, 243
DAY 179: Fellowship, 244
DAY 180: Stop Fighting, 245
DAY 181: Filth, 246
DAY 182: Fleeting, 249
DAY 183: Follow Me, 250
DAY 184: Foolish, 252
DAY 185: Forgetful, 253
DAY 186: Fulfilled, 254
DAY 187: Giving, 255
DAY 188: Appearances, 256
DAY 189: Too Busy for God, 257
DAY 190: Being out of Order, 258
DAY 191: Watching Your Motives, 260
DAY 192: Keeping Secrets, 261
DAY 193: Habits, 262
DAY 194: Bringing it to a Halt, 263
DAY 195: Headstrong, 264
DAY 196: Bringing the Heat, 266
DAY 197: Help, 267
DAY 198: Humiliation, 268
DAY 199: Idleness, 269
DAY 200: Doing the Impossible, 270
DAY 201: Don't' let the World Define You, 271
DAY 202: Slow Down, 272
DAY 203: Pushing Through the Pain, 273
DAY 204: Going the Wrong Way, 275

DAY 205: Indignant, 277
DAY 206: Inheritance, 278
DAY 207: Making Inquiry, 280
DAY 208: In an Instant, 281
DAY 209: Feeling Invisible, 282
DAY 210: Taking a Journey, 283
DAY 211: Justification, 284
DAY 212: Making up for What's Lacking, 287
DAY 213: Letting go of the Drama, 288
DAY 214: Meditation, 290
DAY 215: Think it Over, 291
DAY 216: In for the Long Haul, 293
DAY 217: Turning a Blind Eye, 294
DAY 218: Willingness to Deliberate, 295
DAY 219: Regrets, 296
DAY 220: Underestimated, 297
DAY 221: Not a Good Fit, 298
DAY 222: Leave me to my own Thoughts, 299
DAY 223: Some Experiences are Priceless, 300
DAY 224: Don't Become Detached, 301
DAY 225: Being up Front, 302
DAY 226: What about Your Intentions?, 303
DAY 227: Staying Away From the Victim, 304
DAY 228: Empowering Yourself, 305
DAY 229: Mistakes, 306
DAY 230: Lifting Yourself Up, 307
DAY 231: Being Selfish, 309
DAY 232: Evolving, 310
DAY 233: When Desperation Sets In, 311
DAY 234: Time for Spring Cleaning, 312
DAY 235: Surviving a Spiritual Avalanche, 313
DAY 236: Chaos of the Mind, 314
DAY 237: Throwing out the Trash, 315
DAY 238: Holding On, 316
DAY 239: Burying the Dead, 317

DAY 240: Breaking the Cycle, 318

DAY 241: The Power of Fasting, 319

DAY 242: Spiritual Awakening, 323

DAY 243: A Person of Character, 324

DAY 244: God's Love, 325

DAY 245: Released, 326

DAY 246: Building a Strong Infrastructure, 327

DAY 247: Hitting a Brick Wall, 328

DAY 248: Becoming Weary, 330

DAY 249: People who Just Don't get It, 331

DAY 250: Saving Yourself, 332

DAY 251: Vulnerable, 333

DAY 252: Pretending to Agree, 334

DAY 253: Helping me to See, 335

DAY 254: Tolerance, 336

DAY 255: Sidestepping Trouble, 337

DAY 256: Pettiness, 339

DAY 257: Keeping Your eye on the Prize, 340

DAY 258: Prospering, 341

DAY 259: Enhancing, 342

DAY 260: Learning to Thrive, 343

DAY 261: Don't Lose Sight of Where You're Going, 344

DAY 262: Making the Right Decisions, 345

DAY 263: Building a Team, 346

DAY 264: What's Limiting you Right Now?, 347

DAY 265: Losing Hope, 348

DAY 266: The Pitfalls of Getting Your Way, 349

DAY 267: Vengeful, 351

DAY 268: Taken Advantage of, 352

DAY 269: Elevating Yourself, 353

DAY 270: Finding Your Identity, 354

DAY 271: I Told You So, 355

DAY 272: Painful to Accept, 359

DAY 273: Life Changes, 360

DAY 274: Startling, 361

DAY 275: Having an Imagination, 362
DAY 276: A Legacy, 363
DAY 277: A Sense of Accomplishment, 364
DAY 278: Needing a Helping Hand, 365
DAY 279: Be Careful What You Wish For, 366
DAY 280: Atonement, 367
DAY 281: Miracles, 368
DAY 282: Persecution, 369
DAY 283: Purity, 370
DAY 284: Reconciliation, 372
DAY 285: Daddy's Girl, 374
DAY 286: Redemption, 375
DAY 287: Sanctified, 377
DAY 288: Suffering, 378
DAY 289: The Power of a Testimony, 379
DAY 290: Wisdom, 380
DAY 291: Broken in Spirit, 381
DAY 292: God Isn't a VISA Check Card, 382
DAY 293: Born Again, 383
DAY 294: Anything is Attainable, 384
DAY 295: Sometimes It's in His Name, 385
DAY 296: Showing Up, 386
DAY 297: Sentiment, 387
DAY 298: Not Part of the Club, 388
DAY 299: Accountability, 390
DAY 300: Becoming Dynamic, 391
DAY 301: Orchestrating Your own Advancement, 393
DAY 302: Controversial, 397
DAY 303: Unquenchable Thirst, 398
DAY 304: Insatiable Appetite, 399
DAY 305: The Depth of Your Commitment, 400
DAY 306: Disqualifying Ourselves, 401
DAY 307: Opportunistic, 402
DAY 308: Contributing, 403
DAY 309: It's Worthwhile, 404

DAY 310: Your own Agenda, 405

DAY 311: Defeat, 406

DAY 312: Stop Running, 407

DAY 313: Becoming Wiser, 408

DAY 314: Apprehension, 409

DAY 315: Assurance From God, 410

DAY 316: Confessing, 411

DAY 317: Approval, 412

DAY 318: Desire, 413

DAY 319: Depression, 414

DAY 320: Restraint, 415

DAY 321: Support, 416

DAY 322: Prayers of Positive Energy, 418

DAY 323: Prayers for Guidance and Direction, 420

DAY 324: Prayers for Disappointments, 422

DAY 325: Prayers for Love, 423

DAY 326: Prayers for Peace, 424

DAY 327: Prayers for Enduring, 425

DAY 328: Prayers of Clarity, 427

DAY 329: An Affirmation of Love, 428

DAY 330: Encouragement, 429

DAY 331: Removing Disappointment, 430

DAY 332: Peace, 433

DAY 333: Endurance, 434

DAY 334: Temptations, 435

DAY 335: Affirmations Against Becoming Vengeful, 436

DAY 336: Faith, 437

DAY 337: Forgiveness, 438

DAY 338: Courage, 439

DAY 339: Discipline, 440

DAY 340: Determination, 441

DAY 341: Goals, 442

DAY 342: Happiness, 443

DAY 343: Worship, 444

DAY 344: Weariness, 445

DAY 345: Salvation, 446

DAY 346: Discernment, 447

DAY 347: Repentance, 448

DAY 348: Prophecy, 449

DAY 349: Prayer, 450

DAY 350: Miracles, 451

DAY 351: Healing, 452

DAY 352: Hope, 453

DAY 353: Grace, 454

DAY 354: Forgiveness, 455

DAY 355: Blessings, 456

DAY 356: Obedience, 457

DAY 357: Evolution, 458

DAY 358: Abandonment, 459

DAY 359: Acceptance, 460

DAY 360: Abstinence, 461

DAY 361: Awakening, 462

DAY 362: Belief, 463

DAY 363: Betrayal, 464

DAY 364: Boundaries, 465

DAY 365: Breakthroughs, 466

CPSIA information can be obtained at www.ICGtesting.com
Printed in the USA
239824LV00002B/70/P